"*Rediscovering Humility* is a mi
of a Christian grace that is as im
some of the Christian church's v
ing, Chris Hutchinson reminds t ...y is to Christian
piety. Most importantly, Hutchins... shows us how that piety is rooted
in the teaching of Scripture. I warmly recommend this book."
  Guy Prentiss Waters, James M. Baird, Jr. Professor of New Testament, Reformed Theological Seminary, Jackson, MS

"Humility is a crucial and tricky topic about which to write. An author is expected to be an expert in his field but humility eschews expertise. Only an author who recognizes his deep need for humility is qualified to write on humility. And for that reason I'm grateful for this book by Chris Hutchinson, a desperately needed study written by an eminently humble man."
  Joe Holland, Pastor, Christ Covenant Presbyterian Church, Culpeper, VA; Assistant Editor, *Tabletalk* magazine

"How do you properly recommend a book on humility when blurbs seem consciously designed to hype and pander? How best to commend its author for a job well done? Perhaps with Farmer Hoggett's words to Babe after the pig carefully and confidently accomplished an equally unlikely feat and made it seem easy: 'That'll do'"
  Joel White, Lecturer in New Testament, Giessen School of Theology, Germany

"As a woman in a church, I worry sometimes that the voices of the lowly are too often dismissed without a good listen. It takes a robust humility for leaders to not merely tend to the needs, but also attend to the thoughts of those on the margins. Chris Hutchinson's intelligent, often funny, and truly accessible treatise on the central virtue of humility ought to be required reading for all of us."
  Paige Britton, Curator of the Grass Roots Theological Library

"Humility? We know we should desire this Christian virtue, but it comes at a steep cost—to self-love, self-fulfillment, self-promotion. Informed by much wisdom from the church's past and fueled by careful interaction with Scripture, in this helpful book Chris Hutchinson reminds us that pride is idolatry. Humility, by contrast, is essential to the gospel, for it accompanies God's grace shown to us in Christ. If you are Christian, you need this book. Take up and read."
  Shawn D. Wright, Author; Professor of Church History, Southern Baptist Theological Seminary; Pastor of Leadership Development, Clifton Baptist Church, Louisville, KY

"In his timely new book, Hutchinson not only helps readers understand humility from a biblical perspective, he shows us our urgent need for it. In particular, he demonstrates why, in this culture that so cavalierly rejects truth, we need humility to discover it, embrace it, and then graciously declare it."

> **Richard Doster,** Author; editor of *byFaith*, the magazine of the Presbyterian Church in America

"My first thought in reading this book is that I haven't read much like it for a long time. I've come to value books on the Christian life based on how much they're immersed in the Scriptures. As it's filled with biblical wisdom, this book delivers. It's also steeped in the practical theology of earlier generations who gave great credence to the value of corporate humility in the life of the church. We would do well to heed the same counsel today, and this book is a good start."

> **David V. Silvernail, Jr.,** Senior Pastor, Potomac Hills Presbyterian Church, Leesburg, VA

"I had the amazing privilege of sitting under Pastor Hutchinson's faithful and humble preaching in college. *Rediscovering Humility* is a uniquely thorough and challenging appeal on the nature of corporate humility as God's people. With each page, I found myself saying, 'we need this.' In reading *Rediscovering Humility* may we remember that in Christ the way up is down and the beautiful joy that comes with bold self-forgetfulness."

> **SharDavia Walker,** Author; Regional Women's Director, Campus Outreach Lynchburg, VA

"Humility is the bedrock of Christian maturity. It is not a spiritual gift, though it is a mark of the presence of the Holy Spirit in life. Instead it is the product of gratitude. Here this truth is both endorsed and explored. With careful exegesis allied to practical understanding our minds are expanded and our hearts challenged. In this slender volume humility is restored to the place reserved for it by Jesus."

> **Robert M. Norris,** Teaching Pastor 4th Presbyterian Church, Bethesda, MD

"Chris Hutchinson offers a compelling case that humility is the chief of all virtues and at the center of God's plan of redemption. Basing his expositions on Scripture and guided by some of the great expositors of the past, he provides rewarding practical expositions of what it means to make this often neglected ideal the central paradigm of the Christian life."

> **George M. Marsden,** Author; Francis A. McAnaney Professor of History Emeritus, University of Notre Dame

"How could someone write a book on humility without becoming puffed up and self-congratulatory? You would write it as Chris Hutchinson has done by not pointing to yourself and your achievements, but by pointing and submitting to the precepts and exhortations in Scripture. We know the drill: If you want to be great in the kingdom of God you must become a servant of all; you must go the end of the line; you must wash the feet of others. The words come easily enough, but in actual practice true humility lags way behind. We readily see the application for others, but we fail to see it for ourselves. So admit the reality of your pride and humbly read *Rediscovering Humility*. You will be challenged to desire what Paul, the once proud Pharisee, deeply desired: 'God forbid that I should boast except in the cross of our Lord Jesus Christ' (Galatians 6:14)."

Dominic Aquila, President, New Geneva Theological Seminary, Colorado Springs, CO

"Christopher Hutchinson's *Rediscovering Humility* fixes our eyes on Christ and the cross, arguing that, as we drink more deeply of Christ and Him alone, humility becomes our defining feature. Like the gospel itself, this seems at first almost too simple and unadorned to be true, but as Hutchinson ponders humility's beauty and logic, its ethics and witness, our eyes indeed turn from ourselves and toward God's glory. I pray this would be so, for all who pick up this book and for their churches."

Thomas Gardner, Author; Alumni Distinguished Professor of English, Virginia Tech, Blacksburg, VA

"In the chest-thumping, opposition-shaming, attention-grabbing ethos of today's popular culture, poverty of spirit is despised, meekness is confused with weakness, and humility is associated with losers. Chris Hutchinson's detailed study of humility is just what the church needs if Christians are to avoid 'losing our virtue,' borrowing David Wells' phrase, in the tsunamis of self-promotion that is our contemporary world."

Terry L. Johnson, Author; Senior Minister, Independent Presbyterian Church, Savannah, GA

"I need all the help I can get in cultivating humility. I am, therefore, glad for this book that helps me better understand it, want it, and apply it. Chris Hutchinson has mined Scripture, church history, and his own soul to find nuggets to share with proud, struggling Christians in the twenty-first century. 'It takes one to know one,' and because he knows himself well, he helps us a lot."

David A. Bowen, Assistant Minister, Second Presbyterian Church, Memphis, TN; founding pastor, The Church of the Good Shepherd, Durham, NC

"Having worked in pastoral ministry with Chris Hutchinson for seven years, I observed in his life much of what he has written in this book. Pride and self-exaltation grow naturally out of man's fallen condition. Genuine humility is the by-product of grace. Chris has done us a great service by reminding us that God is opposed to the proud, but gives grace to the humble."

Roland S. Barnes, Senior Pastor, Trinity Presbyterian Church, Statesboro, GA

"My brother has been working on this book for close to thirty years, and I have seen the beauty and impact its truths and themes have had on Chris' family, friends, congregations, and I hope myself, for decades now. This book helps us to see that where there is humility there is kindness, courage, and integrity. And laughter. Lots of joy and laughter, even in suffering."

Jeffrey D. Hutchinson, Coordinator of Church Planting, Mission Anabaino; Assistant Minister, Christ Presbyterian Church, New Haven, CT

"In *Rediscovering Humility*, Chris Hutchinson serves as a gentle pastor, weaving together biblical truth, personal experience, and insights from poets and philosophers throughout history. This book will bless and challenge your soul. As you read, your love for Christ will grow—your love for his sacrifice to atone for your pride and for his enabling power to display true humility."

Stephen T. Estock, Coordinator, PCA Discipleship Ministries

"In this engaging book, pastor Chris Hutchinson invites us to a rediscovery of a revolutionary, uniquely Christian virtue–humility. A masterful teacher, Chris shows how humility is at the center of the person and work of Jesus Christ and therefore at the core of the Christian life. Though humility may not come naturally to us (what Christian virtue does?), and though humility may be (in our North American context) radically subversive and countercultural, Chris adeptly shows how humility is evidence of the sanctifying work of Christ in our lives. My humble opinion(!) is that you will be challenged and inspired by Chris Hutchinson's rediscovery of humility."

Will Willimon, Author; United Methodist bishop, retired; Professor of the Practice of Christian Ministry, Duke Divinity School, Durham, NC

"In stating his case that humility has become a lost virtue in the Christian life, Chris Hutchinson winsomely restores humility to its proper place as the highest of Christian virtues. If you want a book on humility with ten steps to achieve it, skip *Rediscovering Humility*; however, if you want a book on humility that targets the heart itself, look no further."

J. R. Foster, Southeast Area Coordinator, Reformed University Fellowship

REDISCOVERING HUMILITY

. . . .

WHY THE WAY UP IS DOWN

. . . .

CHRISTOPHER A. HUTCHINSON

New
Growth
Press

WWW.NEWGROWTHPRESS.COM

New Growth Press, Greensboro, NC 27404
www.newgrowthpress.com
Copyright © 2018 by Christopher A. Hutchinson

Unless otherwise indicated, Scripture quotations are taken from *The Holy Bible, English Standard Version.*® Copyright © 2000; 2001 by Crossway Bibles, a division of Good News Publishers. Used by permission. All rights reserved.

Scripture quotations marked NIV are taken from THE HOLY BIBLE, NEW INTERNATIONAL VERSION®, NIV® Copyright © 1973, 1978, 1984, 2011 by Biblica, Inc.® Used by permission. All rights reserved worldwide.

Scripture verses marked KJV are taken from the King James Version of the Bible.

Scripture verses marked NASB are taken from the New American Standard Bible®, Copyright © 1960, 1962, 1963, 1968, 1971, 1972, 1973, 1975, 1977, 1995 by The Lockman Foundation. Used by permission.

Cover Design: Faceout Books, faceoutstudio.com
Interior Typesetting and eBook: Lisa Parnell, lparnell.com

ISBN: 978-1-945270-96-3 (Print)
ISBN: 978-1-945270-97-0 (eBook)

Library of Congress Cataloging-in-Publication Data on file

Printed in the United States of America

25 24 23 22 21 20 19 18   1 2 3 4 5

To all the unknown saints

CONTENTS

. . . .

FOREWORD

The point about Christian faith is that those who are in Christ should actually become godly people. They are the ones who should be God-centered in their minds, God-fearing in their hearts, and God-honoring in all that they do. This God-centeredness should produce a preoccupation with living out the biblical virtues. How could it not? If Christians center their whole being on the triune God, then they are centered on one whose character is pure, joyous, holy love. If this God is in the center of their world, then in all that Christians think and do, they will want to reflect Him.

God's character of holy love, of course, is the fount of all virtue in life and the standard of all that is eternally right; it frames the Christian's whole perspective. The church's great preachers, in fact, were never very far from this thought—preachers like Chrysostom and Augustine, Martin Luther and John Calvin, John Owen and Richard Sibbes, George Whitefield and Jonathan Edwards, Martyn Lloyd-Jones, and John Stott. Why, then, are pointed and penetrating expositions of the Christian virtues so rare today?

I am inclined to think that the answer to this question lies in two main considerations. First, throughout the West today, people have migrated out of the older moral world in their minds and have drifted into a newer psychological world. When people inhabit a moral world, they think of things as being either right or wrong, good or bad. In a psychological world, few ethical judgments are ever made. In an earlier time a person would have said, "I can't do that because it is wrong." Now a person is more likely to say, "I don't want to do that because I am not comfortable with it." People like this do not live in a world of ultimates but only one of choices—and those choices are made in the moment. The old moral order that once was fixed and objective has vanished. As the older moral world disappears, the practice of the virtues goes with it. Without a moral world, there is no virtue. Christian faith then becomes only a therapy, a way of helping people to feel better about themselves.

This leads to the second consideration: When Christians become indifferent to those truths that are ultimate, they lose all of their conviction. Believers lose their sense that some things are true, and others are not, that some things are right, and others are wrong. Whatever Christians then see or hear is then framed by nonchalance and indifference. This has passed into language as, "whatever . . ." and is usually accompanied by a shrug. Without conviction about what is ultimately true and right, Christians are simply unable to resist the tides of worldly thinking that roll in over them from television and movies, the workplace and its ethos, the taken-for-granted assumptions about life that meet them in every conversation. As conviction fades, Christian faith is diminished and soon it becomes just a thing that is small and very much of this world.

The reality, though, is quite different. Christian faith does not arise from people's own nature, experience, or world. It is first and foremost from above because it is first and foremost from the eternal God who is other. It is about Christ whom the Father sent into the world from above. It is about an age that is breaking into today's world as an antithesis. Today's age is sinful. The age that Christ ushers is pure. Today's age is passing. Christ's is eternal. Christian faith, then, is about being given a spirituality that people do not have and will never have until they are in Christ.

It is in this other age from whence humility arises. In today's age, pride is the coin of the realm. Today's age is a world where people think much about the self and much of the self. In this world, self-promotion, self-absorption, and the pursuit of self-esteem all seem quite natural. They are, in fact, natural but they are natural in the same way that all sin is natural. These preoccupations have no place in the kingdom of God. They are discordant, jarring, and ugly notes. Nothing is more beautiful, by contrast, nothing more enduring, than the alternative. The alternative to pride is humility—forgetfulness about the self. Humility is the least self-aware and least self-conscious of all the virtues. Humility comes from another place. It comes from the place that is always illumined by the grace, goodness, and glory of God. Humility comes from eternity.

Humility is the theme of this book, and I warmly welcome the contribution it makes to the Christian good. The book's descriptions and prescriptions are thoroughly biblical. Were believers to take to heart its plea for humility, the church would be mightily strengthened in both its life and witness. It would, in fact, become more godly.

David F. Wells
Distinguished Research Professor
Gordon-Conwell Theological Seminary

．．．．

ACKNOWLEDGMENTS

I want to thank all those who have contributed in various ways to the writing of this book. I want to thank the members of churches where I both taught and was taught humility: the Orthodox Congregational Church of Lanesville, Massachusetts; Grace Church in Roanoke, Virginia; the students of the Reformed University Fellowship chapters in South Carolina; various campus ministries here at Virginia Tech in Blacksburg, Virginia; Trinity Presbyterian of Statesboro, Georgia, where I served as associate pastor; and finally, Grace Covenant Presbyterian Church in Blacksburg, Virginia, where I currently pastor, and which graciously granted me a sabbatical to finish this book. I believe that theology is always done best when formulated together in the community of friends that make up a church, and so I thank each of my fellow members for their input.

For years, many friends and teachers have taught me humility by precept and example. Some of their stories have found their way into these pages, while others perhaps more worthy have been forgotten or neglected. I want to thank all of the pastors I have had the privilege of sitting under and those who have contributed to this book in unique ways. I would boast of them by name, but they do not need it. They know who they are.

I am blessed to serve in a church with an incredible assembly of godly and humble leaders who set an example for me. The same can be said of the faithful leaders and friends in our sister churches around town and in our presbytery.

I must not overlook those who have been my adversaries from time to time. The crucibles they provided have forced me to see my own lacks and ever-present need of humility, and so I thank them.

I wish to acknowledge and thank those that read the manuscript and provided valuable corrections and insights. Paige Britton, Thomas Gardner, and Duncan Rankin were selfless in giving their time, energy, and vital encouragement to this project. I heartily thank Mike and Vicki Powell for the use of their beautiful farmhouse, which provided a setting for days of serene writing. I thank the coffee shop baristas who sustained me with their caffeine and cheerful service. In many ways, all of these people embodied this book before reading a page.

I wish to thank all the good folks and editors at New Growth Press for their kindness and hard work and for taking a risk on me. There are too many to mention, but I want to give special thanks to John Walt and to my patient and insightful editors, Beth Hart and Irene Stoops.

My greatest thanks go to my family. My parents, siblings, relatives, wife, and daughters are all precious in my sight, and this book is, among other things, a tribute to them. It was especially my devoted wife, Kirstan, who saw me through this work by her endless encouragement and enthusiasm, carrying me through many long days of writing and editing. She has embodied a life of humble, selfless service that I can only write about at best. She lives it and awaits a heavenly reward for all the ways she has served and loved me, and so many others, through the years.

. . . .

Preface

Right off, let us get this little bit over with: the following work on humility is one of which I am exceptionally proud. Obviously I jest, but only to illustrate two important truths. First, pride is all-pervasive. It is capable of turning any old thing into a curse, especially those things that are otherwise praiseworthy. Pride so easily masquerades as godliness that even the attempt to quell pride may just as easily feed it. Secondly, people are often reluctant to speak pointedly on the subject of humility because it so often eludes the very ones advocating it. And so a rather proud and otherwise ordinary person has undertaken this task—to write about humility. And yet I write in the confidence that wherever I fail my subject, I am forgiven. For to put confidence in my own humility would undercut the central thrust of the book itself.

Early after my conversion to the Christian faith, I became convinced of humility's centrality to the new life set before me. In addition to personal experiences and the wonders of Scripture, I was immensely impressed with the beauty of humility found in C. S. Lewis's writings. A couple of years later, I discovered the logic of humility in Jonathan Edwards's theology, and things started to fall together.

After that, I found myself suddenly deployed with the U.S. Army to a foreign and distant desert for several months. I had to limit my library to roughly the size of half a rucksack, and no work provided me greater stimulation than Andrew Murray's classic, *Humility*. Many years later I was given Richard Sibbes's *The Bruised Reed*—a work on

Christian sanctification with humility at its heart. In addition to these four authors, I have benefited from many other helpful thinkers from disparate sources, for no one tradition has a corner on humility.

I have also observed the church of our day, and have become convinced that the time has come for a fresh application of humility. Modern Christians have not basked deeply in humility's beauty, nor studied much its logic, nor practiced well its ethics. Humility has often been an afterthought, something perhaps to be included if kept in its place. This book is an explicit call to return to the ancient path of humility as the one pilgrimage most necessary for Christian faith. Its path must once again be blazed down the middle of churches, well-marked and well-trodden.

As such, this work focuses on what corporate humility should look like. Meekness should characterize not only individual believers but the whole body of Christ. I propose that a healthy church is first and foremost a humble church. I have not seen this corporate aspect of humility much considered, and I believe this neglect is palpable in the pride that permeates through today's church.

Yet I want to offer far more than a critique of today's Christian culture, for negative critique rarely helps anyone grow in humility. I hope to build a positive case for the centrality of humility to the Christian life and in the church. I want humility to show itself forth in all its truth, beauty, and goodness—something to be pursued even if never fully found before heaven. I have tried to build a positive, scriptural argument in each chapter. Suggestions for Christians today to better practice and promote humility are interspersed. When building a house on rocky ground, some demolition may be needed along the way, but hopefully when all is done, what remains is the house, not the smoke.

This book has come together like a big jigsaw puzzle of jumbled pieces—experiences, church history, and Scripture that have been collecting in my mind for years. As is fitting to the subject, I am far from confident that I have entirely succeeded; instead it feels like that unsatisfactory puzzle with several missing pieces. Yet, it is the picture God ordained for me to complete, and I pray it is helpful to some as they assemble their own puzzles.

Thoughtful readers will soon discover that I have not said all that I could on the subject. There are doubtless blind spots in my observations, as well as skewed or overstated points. Addition and correction is welcome; that is the point. My main hope is that this little work may jump-start a dialogue on what humility should look like in today's church. This side of the grave Christians will always have room to grow lower. And in heaven itself, I expect that the study of humility will be never ending, always leading us to new places of joy and wonder.

Humility Introduced

*You adulterous people! Do you not know that friendship
with the world is enmity with God? Therefore whoever
wishes to be a friend of the world makes himself an enemy
of God. Or do you suppose it is to no purpose that the
Scripture says, "He yearns jealously over the spirit that he
has made to dwell in us"? But he gives more grace. Therefore
it says, "God opposes the proud, but gives grace to the
humble." Submit yourselves therefore to God. Resist the
devil, and he will flee from you. Draw near to God, and he
will draw near to you. Cleanse your hands, you sinners, and
purify your hearts, you double-minded. Be wretched and
mourn and weep. Let your laughter be turned to mourning
and your joy to gloom. Humble yourselves before the Lord,
and he will exalt you.*

—JAMES 4:4–10

CHAPTER ONE

. . . .

WHATEVER HAPPENED
TO HUMILITY?

Seek the LORD, all you humble of the land,
who do his just commands; seek righteousness; seek humility;
perhaps you may be hidden on the day of the anger of the LORD.
—**Zephaniah 2:3**

When a certain rhetorician was asked what was the chief rule
in eloquence, he replied, "Delivery;" what was the second rule,
"Delivery;" what was the third rule, "Delivery;" so if you ask me
concerning the precepts of the Christian religion,
first, second, third and always, I would answer, "Humility."
—**Augustine**[1]

Most people seem to agree that humility is a helpful quality to throw into their personality mix, at least in theory. After all, humility wins friends and influences people. Humility is an admirable trait, something that polishes all one's other assets. No one really dislikes humility—especially in someone else.

But that is not what I wish to say about humility. I do not wish to advance it as one more virtue to remember, one more pursuit to add to the calendar app. Humility is not something that can be picked up at the store on the way home and placed neatly in the cupboard, to be brought out when necessary. This book is not another attempt at self-improvement, one more feat to add to the to-do list.

I wish instead to advance humility as the central paradigm of the Christian life. I believe humility to be at the very heart of Christian faith and even to be the best paradigm of all proper thought regarding God, oneself, and others. Humility is the greatest prerequisite to faith in Christ and its most telling result. It is the alpha and omega of the gospel at work in God's people. Humility ought to be the most prominent centerpiece of any Christian worldview.

I believe that the final authority in religious matters is the Bible alone, and certainly, humility toward God, oneself, and others must be considered a religious matter. Therefore, I will not define humility from Merriam-Webster's dictionary, for as fine a definition as it might provide, it would not be authoritative.[2] Moreover, it is my belief that Scripture is as deep and rich as it is clear. The Bible is a collection of stories, poetry, and letters, and within these inspired collections, a subject like humility is dealt with in manifold ways. Humility's meaning and application is thus rich and complex. Hence, I have avoided a simple definition of humility, opting instead to provide one by the whole of this book. Insofar as it turns out to be biblical, it is a true definition.

Humility always promotes what is good, true, and beautiful, while pride only destroys the same—usually by subtle sabotage. If humility is not the king of all virtues, then at the least it is the ever-present jester, keeping the king in his place.

The Dethroning of Humility

> *That religion I got in them way-back days is still with me.*
> *And it ain't this pie-crust religion,*
> *such as the folks are getting these days.*
> *The old-time religion has some filling between the crusts.*
> **—Prince Bee**[3]

Humility is not, in my experience, a subject much emphasized, discussed, or displayed within mainstream or evangelical Christianity.

When it is, humility is often only a tertiary or peripheral subject, something not to forget rather than something emphasized. Christians have instead more often clothed themselves with pride, though they may dress it up differently in various Christian traditions, sometimes even disguising it as humility itself. On the theological left, pride has frequently displaced humility in the name of progress, tolerance, and self-esteem. Those on the right, meanwhile, glory in their numbers or, eluding that, in their ability to remain pure while they watch others succeed. High churches tend to pride themselves in the wealth of their architecture and liturgy, while low churches exult precisely in their eschewal of the same. Humility has lost a central place in today's church and, therefore, in the average Christian's life. The general Christian culture, the public images of individual churches, and the realm of personal piety are all plagued with pride.

Christian Culture

Few evangelicals have grappled with the toll
that this cultural accommodation takes on the message of the gospel.
They have all but jettisoned such key themes as suffering, humility,
meekness, courage, and truth from their thought.
—**Rick Lints**[4]

What topics circulate most around the general Christian culture? What subjects generate conferences and book publications? I have seen hundreds of conferences advertised and have attended a few, but I cannot recall a single major conference where Christian humility was a main topic. Christian conferences abound on all sorts of other good things: evangelistic methods, world missions, biblical financial principles, healthy marriages, and more. Rarely, in my observation, has a conference been centered on Christian humility. If humility is central to the Christian faith and if Christian conferences address topics important to the Christian faith, then why is humility rarely, if ever, explicitly addressed?

The exact same question can be asked of Christian publishing. One only need to visit the local bookstore or do a Google search to see that few works on the topic are available or well known other than Andrew Murray's little book, written a century ago.[5] Humility may still have a prominent place in other popular Christian books, but this does not appear to be the case according to a simple review of chapter titles and indexes.[6] For instance, in an appendix to *Nine Marks of a Healthy Church*, Mark Dever lists twenty books written in the 1990s that either set forth various trends in contemporary church life or offer their own list of the values possessed by growing and/or healthy churches. Not once is humility explicitly mentioned as a goal or value to be sought by today's Christian churches.[7] I doubt that things have improved much in the past fifteen years.[8]

I realize that this may sound like anyone harping on their pet subject, some singular detail of the Christian faith. I have heard similar complaints about the lack of books on a Christian view of recycling or a biblical perspective on spanking. But if my thesis is correct—that humility is not just a mere detail but is at the very heart of Christian faith—then this neglect is baneful.

There is a general absence of meekness as any sort of guiding principle at all. Conferences and books are almost always promoted in ways that conflict with scriptural injunctions against self-glorying and self-heralding. Large, glossy pictures, boasts about numbers, incredible claims and promises, and key endorsements from celebrity theologians are the prevailing method of advancing an event or movement in today's Christian culture. In both the ends and the means of Christian publishing and conferences, humility is frequently sidelined.

The problem is not just that Christians do not talk about humility, but it rarely crosses the Christian mind that believers should be meek at all. In short, the humble mind-set no longer exists in Christian culture. While individuals in the limelight may themselves be humble, they have usually been unsuccessful in transferring that meekness to the way their causes are advanced. The marketing machine has silenced humility, rather than itself being muzzled by Christian meekness. Yet, people are not helpless conformists to any cultural machine; they conform by choice. Christian conformity to vainglorious marketing methods demonstrates that the humble mind-set no longer exists in the general Christian culture—or at least that part which advertises itself.

Church Public Images

These hands have greeted over 600,000 converts.
—Caption under a picture of an evangelist's hands[9]

Another way to test the assertion that humility has lost its rightful place is to look at the public images of individual churches, that is, the things churches typically address, the way they advertise, and their stated goals and mottos. Is humility ever mentioned? Perhaps so, but I have yet to run across it.[10] Most church advertisements tend to focus on their perceived strengths or uniqueness—why they ought to be considered over other churches. Pictures, interesting claims, and ministry lists abound. Often, the bigger the church, the bigger the advertisement, though they would seem to need it least. As in the world of business, success breeds success. The resulting portrait is of a crowded hodgepodge of competing churches where, in the interests of effective marketing, humility finds itself treated like the short, homely cousin left in back, perhaps blocked out of the family photo altogether.

Church vision statements are typically catchy, alliterated three-point cadence calls (e.g., exalt, equip, evangelize) meant to focus the congregation and staff on the same goal. If church leaders listen to the consultants, these slogans are most effective when they are hailed often and plastered everywhere. There are even churches where the unique church logo—not the cross—is found on the pulpit and in every corner. All is done in the name of marketing their particular brand in order to build their own congregation and reputation.

This type of overt, self-referential reductionism is quite new in the church, and it seems to have been borrowed more from modern industrial culture than from the depths of Scripture. If folks such as Neil Postman are right, that the forms of communication effect content itself, is it even possible to convey Christian humility through the use of boardrooms, branding, PowerPoint, and Twitter?[11] Is it possible to adapt the corporate methods of successful worldly ventures without also imitating their worldly pride? If the question is not asked in the first place, then the subject of Christian humility has once again been left out of the church's public image. Christians may not have distinctly disowned humility, but they have forgotten somehow to call it up from the basement when company arrives.

Humility is not much dwelt upon in today's church culture, if the various venues of public display are any indicator. For instance, when Christians need to find a new church, how do they evaluate different places of worship? How do these churches want to be evaluated? Do Christians even look for humility or think it worth finding in a church? More often than not, Christians choose instead to go where the excitement is—the place with the most specialized ministries; the place with the upbeat, professional worship; and especially the place that is already growing (with the right kinds of people).

Success breeds success; humility breeds humility. Now certainly, success and humility are not mutually exclusive in a church, but of the two, which do Christians look for first? And which do they most desire? Believers can learn something about themselves by their answer. Christians can also learn something about their churches. It is time for believers to turn from the industrial model so many churches have embraced and return to a simpler, humbler approach.

Personal Piety

Expect great things from God. Attempt great things for God.
—Popular Christian slogan, attributed to William Carey[12]

What three or four main gauges have you as a Christ follower been taught to use for diagnosing your own spiritual health? All Christians have some set of standards or norms by which they measure their success in life. Some of these standards are chosen deliberately, while others are adopted almost unconsciously, often swallowed whole from the culture. Hopefully, a Christian's diagnostics are biblically informed, focused on the spiritual and the eternal rather than the worldly and the ephemeral. Where does humility make the cut? Is it chosen right away without hesitation, or is it selected only at the end, reluctantly, like that scrawny kid at kickball? (Full disclosure: I was often that kid.)

I would venture that in one's personal assessments of spiritual health, humility often finds itself displaced by other gauges, such as the frequency of some pious activity like prayer, Bible reading, evangelism, or church attendance. Of course, in themselves, these are all very good things and highly commended by Scripture. One might even safely say that if these disciplines are not there in some regular measure, then one's spiritual health is poor indeed. But are they, of themselves, the best and surest measurement of spiritual success? I have heard them advanced that way countless times, but given Jesus's encounters with the Pharisees, who were more pious in these activities than anyone, I have my doubts.

Even simplistic and pietistic slogans should be considered with caution. For example, the quote that opened this section, "Expect great things from God. Attempt great things for God," is taken from a famous sermon preached by the English Baptist pastor, William Carey, in 1792. In context, Carey gave a stirring call for his fellow Baptists to straighten their theology and do their part in spreading the gospel to foreign lands. However, a problem arises when Christians take such slogans and turn them into a test of piety or a test of God's sanctifying work. In such cases, Christians often become self-focused, wondering whether they are doing enough for God.

In this case, one of two things may happen: Christians either become despondent at their lack of accomplishment, or worse, they become prideful about what they think they have achieved for God. The slogan is not false, but what if Christians redefined "great things for God" not only as mission work, or successful careers, or raising godly children, but also as growing in humility? What if pursuing a greater meekness is in fact attempting a great thing for God? What would that meekness look like? That question drives the rest of this book.

PRAYER

Teach us to care and not to care
Teach us to sit still
Even among these rocks
—T. S. Eliot[13]

CHAPTER TWO

. . . .

WIDE IS THE ROAD:
THE LURE OF FALSE HUMILITY

"God sees not as man sees,
for man looks at the outward appearance,
but the LORD looks at the heart."
—**1 Samuel 16:7** (NASB)

The pears were beautiful,
but it was not pears that my empty soul desired.
—**Augustine**[1]

The study of humility is not just another self-help topic but a venture into the very center of the Christian faith. It is also a journey into the state of one's own heart, and as such, this study may be dangerous and painful. Solomon summarized the journey well, "For in much wisdom is much grief: and he that increaseth knowledge increaseth sorrow" (Ecclesiastes 1:18 KJV).

In other words, a venture into humility is much more like a good old-fashioned wrestling match than a peaceful walk in the woods. A sincere study of humility means exposing one's soul to God and letting Him have His way. Thomas Adams summarized, "Humility wrestleth with God, like Jacob, and wins by yielding."[2] Any real person will resist God's perfecting impulse simply because it hurts. Many people come to God for a Band-Aid, only to find out that He intends to perform full heart surgery.[3] But those who love God are precisely those who wrestle with Him and have the faith to lose even though it hurts. This is the beginning of wisdom.

People's hearts would follow many safer detours. Many know that humility is part of the Christian faith, but they wish to avoid the pain of true spiritual growth. These detours promise fewer potholes and accidents along the way, but they end at a comfortable rest stop well short of true humility. What are these detours that masquerade as true paths to humility? They are certainly legion, but this chapter considers four warnings that need to be avoided in pursuit of true humility.

Not by Human Effort

The devilish strategy of Pride is that it attacks us,
not in our weakest points, but in our strongest.
It is preeminently the sin of the noble mind.
—Dorothy Sayers[4]

The first warning is that humility takes time. People cannot just develop it in a day or two or will it into existence. If people have generally led proud lives, it is not only unrealistic to believe that they will change overnight, but it is dangerous because they will try to become humble primarily by their own efforts. This can lead to only one of two ends: either they will utterly fail and give up the effort, or worse, they will appear to have succeeded.

Benjamin Franklin points out the danger in his autobiography. By his own account, Franklin was more a deist than a Christian. He stressed his own duty and ability to lead an upright and productive life. To that end, Franklin came up with twelve virtues that he vowed to pursue all his days. He made a weekly chart for each, in order that he might examine himself.[5] When a Quaker friend kindly informed him that people generally thought of him as proud, Franklin accordingly added a thirteenth virtue: humility. After pursuing humility for a number of years, Franklin finally admitted that he may have been better at appearing humble than actually being humble.[6] He writes,

In reality, there is, perhaps, no one of our natural passions so hard to subdue as *pride*. Disguise it, struggle with it, beat it down, stifle it, mortify it as much as one pleases, it is still alive, and will every now and then peep out and show itself; you will see it, perhaps, often in this history; for, even if I could conceive that I had completely overcome it, I should probably be proud of my humility.[7]

As wise as this is, I believe that Franklin's sagacity was limited by his theology. He says that pride is hard to subdue; I say that it is impossible apart from Christ.

Pride is the very heart of sin, the root of daily rebellions against God. Therefore, when people think they have subdued it in one area, it pops out somewhere else. Pride may even take form in the means by which people are trying to fight it. As an example, I once knew a fine Christian fellow who took his faith seriously. We attended the same church and the college-age Sunday school class together. One Sunday he noticed that he far outdressed everyone else. He wore the latest expensive fashions, and he sported a meticulously long, flowing head of hair. He decided that it was prideful for him to stand out in this way so the following Sunday he showed up in denim from head to toe with his hair completely shorn. Unfortunately, he stuck out even more in this outfit, and thus his jump-start attempt at humility was spoiled by his stark, visual announcement of the pursuit. He was vigorously pursuing humility in order to combat his vanity. I am not sure if the irony ever struck him, but he eventually settled into a more temperate pursuit of modesty.

Perhaps this is why the apostle Paul warns to avoid the kind of humility that is based upon human effort. He writes,

If with Christ you died to the elemental spirits of the world, why, as if you were still alive in the world, do you submit to regulations—"Do not handle, Do not taste, Do not touch" (referring to things that all perish as they are used)—according to human precepts and teachings? These have indeed an appearance of wisdom in promoting self-made religion and asceticism and severity to the body, but they are of no value in stopping the indulgence of the flesh. (Colossians 2:20–23)

It is noteworthy that Paul considers rules of asceticism to be worldly and opposed to the gospel. They are, as Paul says, based on human effort that is contrary to the help offered by Christ. They also concentrate on external behavior rather than the heart. Rules can only produce a false, outward humility—one whose main objective is precisely to be observed by others.

Not Demeanor or Speech Alone

> *All that is gold does not glitter.*
> **—Gandalf**[8]

The second warning is that humility is not a certain type of demeanor. While some demeanors are certainly more humble than others, these same demeanors can be mimicked by those who do not actually possess the quality they project. Politicians learn to portray a certain "Aw, shucks" personality while touting their many accomplishments. Some who present themselves as self-consciously humble may turn out to have within a hidden, dangerous pride, while others who have gruff personalities turn out to be surprisingly modest. Some are even gruff because they are aware of false modesty, and they do not wish to play that game. Things are not as simple as they sometimes appear, and a meek demeanor does not always clothe a meek heart.

Even when folks utter the actual words *humble* and *proud*, they can mean just the opposite. Often after people win an award, they state that they are humbled by the honor, even as they obviously revel in their fifteen minutes of public humility. Just because they know they should be humbled by the honor and can use the word properly in public does not mean that they are humble. God alone knows their hearts. On the other hand, many honorees indeed realize that they are unworthy of the prize, but to refuse it would be ungrateful, which is another form of pride. They have no godly choice but to endure the effusive attention with grace.

Likewise, people throw the word *proud* around in imprecise ways. Few are thinking theologically when they say that they are proud of this or that. For instance, when people comment that they are proud of a past achievement or of their military service, they could mean that they were glad to be part of a good thing. It could actually be a humble statement, expressing that they were part of something greater than themselves—like the defeat of fascism in World War II. On the other hand, if they spend hours telling about all their awards, their pride of military service could reveal a sense of self-reflected glory, a spiritually harmful pride of achievement.

Just because the words *humble* or *proud* are mentioned does not mean that the speakers are really trying to signify deep meaning. Neither demeanor nor dialogue is an infallible window on the heart.

Spiritual reality and visible reality often bear little correlation to each other. Jesus says, "many who are first will be last, and the last first" (Matthew 19:30). He does not say that all who are first will be last, or that all who are last will be first. There is likely some overlap of people we see as first and those God sees as first. But the idea is that what God values and what people value may be very different, and heaven will most certainly hold a great number of surprises. When Christians are tempted to evaluate another's spiritual accomplishments, they would be wiser to heed Paul's admonishment to "judge nothing before the appointed time; wait until the Lord comes. He will bring to light what is hidden in darkness and will expose the motives of the heart. At that time each will receive their praise from God" (1 Corinthians 4:5 NIV). God most values secret piety and holy motives—things unseen.

Those perceived as the most godly, accomplished folks may seem so only because their public relations machinery is well oiled. Pride always finds its best habitation among the virtues, mixing among them in flattery and disguise, until through time and inattention, pride and virtue become indistinguishable. The clarity that heaven will bring is such a comforting hope, for believers know that finally, they shall see things as they really are, and outward justice shall reflect the inward reality.

An Inconsistent Humility

I have only two comforts to live upon:
the one is in the perfections of Christ;
the other is in the imperfections of all Christians.
—**Nathaniel Ward**[9]

The third warning is that most people tend to be more like a micro-waved bottle of milk than one heated upon a stovetop. People are terribly inconsistent, hot in some areas while cold in others. I have seen myself hold to sincere humility in one area (as far as I could tell), while at the same time nurturing great pride in other realms. As I advance well into middle age and have seen my career advance, I have developed much of the same conceit I used to criticize in others when I was younger with less opportunity for the vanity that arises from position and age. I have seen the same in other folks—remarkable humility in some disciplines and inexplicable pride in others. For example,

- Some Christians are humble in their doctrine but proud of their deeds; conversely, other believers live quiet lives of service and yet close their hearts to greater understanding.
- Some folks submit gladly to their leaders while looking down their noses toward any who happen to be beneath their station; others are genuinely respectful of those below, but arrogantly disdainful of those above them.
- Some people are modest in victory but complain in defeat; yet others are chastened by failure but obnoxious in success.

Short of heaven, all Christians tend to be hot and cold in the same body; sanctified yet sinful; humbled yet proud. Few are vainglorious enough to be prideful about everything they do all of the time, but all people have vanities that they keep hidden, perhaps most of all from themselves. One of the chief characteristics of pride is that it blinds its possessor to its own existence, but it is quite visible to others. In fact, that is one of pride's specialties. As Lewis puts it, "There is no fault which makes a man more unpopular (than pride), and no fault which we are more unconscious of in ourselves. And the more we have it in ourselves, the more we dislike it in others."[10]

Amidst their inconsistencies, people can compare their growth in humility to those around them. Whenever people do this, they inevitably stack the deck in their own favor—placing their humble cards toward the top and their vanity cards at the bottom. I may be quick to listen while my neighbor is quick to speak, and so I think him mighty conceited and myself quite modest. But I may choose to forget the fact that our conversation took place while he was helping me get my car out of the ditch beside the road.

Not Self-Deprecation

*Thousands of humans have been brought to think
that humility means pretty women trying to believe they are ugly
and clever men trying to believe they are fools.*
—Screwtape[11]

The fourth detour to avoid is self-deprecation. True humility is not a self-belittling attitude that only laments one's worthlessness. Self-deprecation is an undervaluing of the self rather than an accurate appraisal of worth. True humility has no interest in this. Humility wants to see the self as it truly is, neither more nor less. Although Christians do not deny the stench of their own sin, neither do they deny that God chooses to use stinkers like themselves for great and eternal purposes. That is part of the glory of the gospel, the God who comes to dwell among sinners.

In many ways, self-denigration is just another well-disguised section of pride's wide road. John Piper points this out in his discussion of self-pity:

> The reason that self-pity does not look like pride is that it appears to be needy. But the need arises from a wounded ego, and the desire of the self-pitying is not really for others to see them as helpless, but as heroes. The need self-pity feels does not come from a sense of unworthiness, but from a sense of unrecognized worthiness. It is the response of unapplauded pride.[12]

Self-pity and self-deprecation are just another way for a person to be self-focused, which is the essence of pride.

The chief consequence of this self-consuming deprecation is loss of service to God and neighbor with one's legitimate gifts. In the name of humility, self-disparaging Christians think they have little to offer and thus spend more time bemoaning their deficiencies than serving with whatever abilities are in fact quite sufficient for God's purposes. God sees differently; nothing is small to Him when it is done with love and true humility. As Charles Spurgeon states, "The Enemy can use humility for his purpose as well as pride. Whether he makes us think too much or too little of our work, it is all the same to him, so long as he can get us off from it."[13] True humility takes no joy in underestimating one's worth or gifts, but rather continues to serve even in times of healthy self-doubt and reevaluation. Humility often reevaluates, but it never devaluates. C. S. Lewis describes what this humility looks like:

> Do not imagine that if you meet a really humble man he will be what most people call "humble" nowadays: he will not be a

sort of greasy, smarmy person, who is always telling you that, of course, he is nobody. Probably all you will think about him is that he seemed a cheerful, intelligent chap who took a real interest in what *you* said to *him*. If you dislike him it will be because you feel a little envious of anyone who seems to enjoy life so easily. He will not be thinking about humility: he will not be thinking about himself at all.[14]

The humble person is not thinking about himself, because he is consumed with something far more important, how best to love and serve his Lord.

The Path Is Deep and Narrow

> *How many nowadays are humbled, yet not humble?*
> *Low, but not lowly?*
> —John Trapp[15]

Having considered some of the safer—but ultimately unhelpful—imitations of humility, a picture of the real thing emerges by the process of elimination.

- If greater humility cannot be attained by human effort or regulation, then it must be accomplished by the Holy Spirit.
- If humility cannot be defined by one's demeanor or speech alone, then it must instead be an entire disposition rooted deeply in the heart.
- If humility is not consistent in anyone, then it must be something that happily purposes to overlook that same fault in others.
- If humility is not found in self-consumed devaluation, then it must instead be a trait that somehow causes people to become boldly self-forgetful.

Humility reverses pride and makes way for faith, hope, and love. All that is true, good, and beautiful is founded upon humility. As believers grow in meekness, step-by-step they begin to see more clearly the author of humility and its perfect owner. They also begin to see that this same Lord of glory dares to build His kingdom through them—not by might, not by power, but by His Spirit.

PRAYER

Thou most Beautiful of all, Creator of all,
Thou good God, my Sovereign and true Good . . .

There is a certain show of beauty in sin.
Thus pride wears the mask of loftiness of spirit,
though You alone, O God, are high over all.
Ambition seeks honor and glory,
although You alone are to be honored before all
and glorious forever . . .

Thus the soul is guilty of fornication when she turns
from You and seeks from any other source
what she will nowhere find pure and without taint
unless she returns to You.

—Augustine[16]

CHAPTER THREE

. . . .

RETURN OF THE JESTER: THE VISION OF HUMILITY BACK AT THE TABLE

Let no man deceive himself.
If any man among you seemeth to be wise in this world,
let him become a fool, that he may be wise.
—1 Corinthians 3:18 (KJV)

I have known many, many humble Christians. Most of these are quite unknown in this world, though I suspect that they will soar high in the next. By and large, I contend that these dear sisters and brothers are humble despite current Christian culture, rather than because of it. Christian culture has not learned to honor those who do not honor themselves, but instead, it propels to the front those who have visibly succeeded. The gospel, however, is always more powerful than any worldly trend, and it has produced a kingdom full of people who have been humbled by grace and show it—even if few notice.

What would happen if Christians changed the paradigm by deliberately placing humility at the top? What if they returned humility to its place as the chief of Christian virtues, the surest indicator of true faith? What if Christian culture robustly celebrated humility? What if individual churches sought humility above all else, even over the pursuit of dynamic ministries and numerical growth? What if Christians sought humility first in all of their activities, zeal, and doctrine? What would a humble Christian culture look like? Experience, church history, and most especially, Scripture give hints about the answers—stories of men and women treating each other with amazing humility that could only have been wrought by God's Spirit within them.

- Abraham, though God's first pick, surrendering his rights to the first pick of the land to his nephew, Lot (Genesis 13:9);
- Jonathan laying down his armor, sword, and crown as it were, at the feet of David, renouncing his own inheritance of the throne (1 Samuel 18:4; 20:17);
- Hannah and Mary singing praise to the God who brings redemption by bringing down the mighty and lifting up the lowly (1 Samuel 2:1–10; Luke 1:46–55);
- John the Baptist rebuking his own disciples who were jealous of Jesus, saying, "He must increase, but I must decrease!" (John 3:30);
- Peter, first among the apostles, repenting of his Judaizing ways when confronted by that new upstart apostle Paul, a former persecutor of the church (Galatians 2; Acts 15);
- Jesus Himself, very God of very God, did not consider equality with God something to be grasped but made Himself nothing, taking the form of a servant—who came not to be served but to serve and to give His life as a ransom for many (Philippians 2:6–7; Mark 10:45).

Even if one remains unconvinced that humility should have the throne all to itself, what would happen if Christians at least invited humility next to the throne as the ever-present jester? Jesters are members of the court who have no ambition of their own but whose role is critical to the health of the kingdom. By acting the fool, jesters continually remind the king, by wit and whim, of his own limits—that he puts on his royal pantaloons the same way any peasant does. The fool forces the king to laugh at life and not take his own majesty so seriously.

So whatever paradigm one pursues as the king of one's Christian life or church—whether it be numerical growth, or mountaintop experiences, or deep knowledge of doctrine—one had better have the fool of humility around to keep things in perspective or pride will surely reign in one form or another. As Christians pursue these passions and perhaps accomplish some of these goals, they must not neglect to ask what humility should look like in their lives. If there exists much disparity between the two pictures, then they are off course from true discipleship. The paradigm, however noble it may be, has become a source of petrifying pride. The king has become an idol and the only proper recourse is complete revolution. They would be better off with the fool on the throne, even if he appears less impressive to the watching world. Better to be ruled by a live jester than a stone emperor.

There is nothing wrong with zealously pursuing any biblical injunction or ideal. However, if believers seek it without humility, then they will be insidiously corrupting the very kingdom it appears they are building. On the other hand, if believers keep a Christ-focused humility at the top of their goals, then whatever other paradigm they are also pursuing is bound to help them grow in grace—even if the ideal itself is imbalanced or has inherent flaws. If believers are in Christ, whatever good He works in them He multiplies to their blessing, and whatever is flawed in them, He ultimately forgives. That is how good the gospel is. I believe that the old saying, "God draws straight lines with crooked sticks," applies not only to individuals but also to the various ideals they have embraced—but only if they are pursued with meekness.

Humility is thus the necessary gauntlet through which any paradigm, doctrine, method, or goal must pass before it can be judged useful for authentic Christian growth. Humility should help Christians navigate every decision they face. Try asking questions such as the following:

- How can I try to resolve the office conflict in such a way that best promotes humility in all parties, myself especially?
- Am I open-minded enough to realize my hard work and research may be flawed? Is looking competent more important than discovering truth?
- Will the purchase of this house or car or dress negatively affect my growth toward greater meekness? What can I do to guard against the dangers?
- Do I seek that promotion at work to better serve others with my gifts or for reasons of vanity and reputation?
- Did I receive my wife's correction with contrition? If not, why not?
- What pride in me caused me to react that way on the soccer field?
- What do I believe about justification and sanctification, and what doctrinal approach most promotes God's glory and my humility?
- What sort of church polity best supports meekness in its leaders?
- When maxed out, should the church attempt multiple services, satellite campuses, building expansion, or church planting?
- How is my driving? Do I let my pride literally put others in danger?

This list could continue infinitely. There are not always simple or right answers to these questions, and they may differ from person to person or circumstance to circumstance. That is why people need the book of Proverbs, not to mention the rest of Scripture. As Christians plot their way through these issues, they must include the cause of humility in the appraisal. As they open up life's map, they must first consult the key—humility in all things.

Christ as Central

For every look at yourself, take ten looks at Christ.
—Robert Murray M'Cheyne[1]

One of the dangers of this book is that readers will focus on becoming more humble and forget the One who alone can make them so. Christians can unintentionally reify humility to the extent that it becomes detached from its author. Believers can become so inwardly focused that they begin to think the gospel is more about what God is doing in their lives than what He did in history once for all through the Lord Jesus Christ (1 Corinthians 15:1–7). Indeed, there can be no humility without Christ and what He did upon the Cross. As Paul wrote to the Corinthians—a church that was much too fond of itself—"And I, when I came to you, brothers, did not come proclaiming to you the testimony of God with lofty speech or wisdom. For I decided to know nothing among you except Jesus Christ and him crucified" (1 Corinthians 2:1–2).

D. A. Carson explains that Paul was not anti-intellectual but that "all he does and teaches is tied to the cross. He cannot long talk about Christian joy, or Christian ethics, or Christian fellowship, or the Christian doctrine of God, or anything else, without finally tying it to the cross. Paul is gospel-centered; he is cross-centered."[2] Carson explains his concern about today's church, "I fear that the cross, without ever being disowned, is constantly in danger of being dismissed from the central place it must enjoy, by relatively peripheral insights that take on far too much weight."[3]

The surest way to a greater humility is to gaze upon Christ hanging on the cross. If believers do that in faith, they cannot help but to be laid low in gratitude for God's grace. But if anyone pursues a Christless humility, they have missed the whole point—it will do no good and is sure to make them a great deal worse. They will become insufferable in their humility as they let everyone know how hard they are pursuing it. Instead, when Christians' eyes are fixed upon Christ and upon the cross, their self-referential tongues are silenced into amazement and adoration. When believers focus on Christ and His work on their behalf, then they get both Him and humility to boot.

There are many people who may have never formally studied humility and probably could not define it if asked, but who live it. Their focus is simply upon Christ, and they are so busy loving and serving Him that they have become humble without even knowing it. As C. S. Lewis explained, truly humble people are not thinking about themselves at all. Their lives are so caught up in bringing God glory by serving others that they simply do not see how much they have grown in their own imitation of Christ. That is why the sheep of Matthew 25 are so surprised when Jesus commends them for their many good works. By the grace of God, they did not even realize they were doing good works; it was simply who they were.

The Structure: Humility Found, Embraced, and Applied

Humility is mother, and root, and nurse, and foundation,
and bond of all good things.
—John Chrysostom[4]

This work lays out a rudimentary structure, a small systematic theology of humility. Through this structure, I attempt to demonstrate my central thesis: that humility is the chief of virtues, the best paradigm of all proper Christian thought, word, and deed—the very definition of what it means to have a Christian worldview. The book is therefore arranged into three parts, based on Paul's abiding trio of faith, hope, and love (1 Corinthians 13:13):

- the humility of faith as grounded in the logic of the gospel and then accordingly, in Christian doctrine and discipleship (Humility Found);

- the humility of hope as displayed in believers' deportment toward themselves, their future, and their neighbors (Humility Embraced);
- the humility of love as shown in believers' relationships as members of the church, in its purity, unity, and evangelism (Humility Applied).

In addition to this Pauline trio, it so happens that Jesus addresses the supreme need for humility on three separate occasions, teaching about quite a different subject each time, and yet all including the same stock phrase,

"For everyone who exalts himself will be humbled, and he who humbles himself will be exalted." (Luke 14:11; 18:14; Matthew 23:12)

These three passages will serve as a central focus and organizing principle. In these three sections, my hope is to rediscover the truth, beauty, and goodness of humility and to apply it to the church in a fresh way.

PRAYER

Lord, high and holy, meek and lowly,
Thou hast brought me to the valley of vision,
where I live in the depths but see thee in the heights;
hemmed in by mountains of sin I behold thy glory.

Let me learn by paradox
that the way down is the way up,
that to be low is to be high,
that the broken heart is the healed heart,
that the contrite spirit is the rejoicing spirit,
that the repenting soul is the victorious soul,
that to have nothing is to possess all,

that to bear the cross is to wear the crown,
that to give is to receive,
that the valley is the place of vision.

Lord, in the daytime stars can be seen from deepest wells,
and the deeper the wells the brighter thy stars shine;

Let me find thy light in my darkness,
thy life in my death,
thy joy in my sorrow,
thy grace in my sin,
thy riches in my poverty,
thy glory in my valley.

—Arthur Bennett[5]

Humility Found—Faith

He also told this parable to some who trusted in themselves
that they were righteous, and treated others with contempt:

"Two men went up into the temple to pray,
one a Pharisee and the other a tax collector.

The Pharisee, standing by himself, prayed thus:
'God, I thank you that I am not like other men, extortioners, unjust,
adulterers, or even like this tax collector. I fast twice a week; I give
tithes of all that I get.'

But the tax collector, standing far off,
would not even lift up his eyes to heaven,
but beat his breast, saying, 'God, be merciful to me, a sinner!'

I tell you, this man went down to his house justified,
rather than the other.

For everyone who exalts himself will be humbled,
but the one who humbles himself will be exalted."

Now they were bringing even infants to him
that he might touch them.
And when the disciples saw it, they rebuked them.

But Jesus called them to him, saying,
"Let the children come to me,
and do not hinder them, for to such belongs the kingdom of God.

Truly, I say to you, whoever does not receive the kingdom of God
like a child shall not enter it."

—LUKE 18:9–17 (EMPHASIS ADDED)

CHAPTER FOUR

· · · ·

LEST ANYONE BOAST:
HUMILITY AND THE GOSPEL

For thus says the One who is high and lifted up,
who inhabits eternity, whose name is Holy:
"I dwell in the high and holy place,
and also with him who is of a contrite and lowly spirit,
to revive the spirit of the lowly,
and to revive the heart of the contrite."
—Isaiah 57:15

There are two things that are suited to humble the souls of men . . .
a due consideration of God, and then of ourselves.
Of God, in his greatness, glory, holiness,
power, majesty and authority;
of ourselves in our mean, abject and sinful condition.
—John Owen[1]

It is the gospel itself that demands humility. Therefore, Christian discipleship cannot be supplemented with a dash of humility for flavor, but must have humility as the main ingredient. The Bible does not mention humility as just one of many good things, but actually places humility at the center of its whole system of thought, the glue which makes redemption stick. Humility is thus the not-so-secret key to God's plan of redemption.

Theology of the Gap

Nothing pleases man more than the sort
of alluring talk that tickles the pride that itches
in his very marrow. Therefore, in nearly every age,
when anyone publicly extolled human nature
in most favorable terms, he was listened to with applause.

—**John Calvin**[2]

If humility is central to the gospel, why then is it so rarely studied in the church today? Why do Christians not more readily embrace humility as "good news"? It is because many Christians, myself included at times, have forgotten the greatness of grace—the massive height and depth and width of God's love for them in Christ Jesus. All too often poor theology has narrowed the vast moral gap that exists between God and mankind. It has turned God into a buddy, and people into His loyal, if slightly flawed, sidekicks. God the Father becomes the folksy "man upstairs"; God the Son the huckleberry friend who walks and talks with me in the garden; and the Holy Spirit my "copilot," there to ensure my life lands smoothly. But in reality, the Bible teaches that God is holy and therefore hates evil. And by their fallen natures all people possess exactly that which He hates.

One look at Isaiah 6 proves God's inscrutable goodness, where God is heralded by the angels as "holy, holy, holy." The angels thus proclaim God's absolute and unapproachable moral perfection. God is a consuming fire, a speedy chariot bringing judgment, and a storm whose unmediated presence brings instant death to any sinful being, which is to say, all people (Hebrews 12:29; Ezekiel 1; Exodus 19).

As for the utter sinfulness of fallen human nature, Jesus states it directly in the Sermon on the Mount, when He says, "If you then, being evil, know how to give good gifts to your children . . ." (Matthew 7:11 NASB). There it is, Jesus calling His listeners, average folk like you or me, evil. On another occasion, Jesus tells His disciples,

That which proceeds out of the man, that is what defiles the man. For from within, out of the heart of men, proceed the evil thoughts, fornications, thefts, murders, adulteries, deeds of coveting and wickedness, as well as deceit, sensuality, envy, slander, pride and foolishness. All these evil things proceed from within and defile the man. (Mark 7:20–23 NASB)

If people want to be followers of Christ and call themselves Christians, they would do well to believe what Jesus has to say about their nature. A small gap between God and man needs a small amount of grace, a hand up from God. But the massive gap the Bible describes requires a *great* grace, and I am saying that biblical grace is nothing if not extreme.

The greater the gap between God and people, the greater the need for God's grace to effect a reconciliation. The greater the need for grace, the greater the need for humility to receive it. If God does not really hate sin that much or if I am just a *little* bit sinful, then I need only a little forgiveness. But if my need for forgiveness is extreme and deep, then I must be altogether desperate for God's mercy and my only recourse is to cry out for a Savior with a radical humility that must leave its brand upon me forever.

I remember a conversation I had with a dear friend of mine in high school, some years before his conversion to Christ. He was a brilliant individual, proper and self-confident, with many accomplishments. I myself had been surprisingly converted only a few months before and since he was a dedicated churchman, I was questioning him about the state of his own faith. We were driving around town in his little red Datsun (in which he had installed a trucker's air horn just for fun), passing cars right and left as he puffed furiously on his cigarette. He allowed that despite his allegiance to the Christian religion, he did not possess a personal faith in Jesus as his Savior and frankly resisted Christ's Lordship over his life. When I pressed him for reasons why he resisted the gospel, he confessed an answer that I will never forget. "Because," he said, taking another draw on his cigarette, "I do not want to accept something for free without giving anything back in return!" He was too proud to accept a salvation that was by grace alone.[3] Years later, while excelling at an Ivy League college, he thankfully had no such reservations, as he saw his sin for what it was and his desperate need for a personal and saving faith in Christ.

As Isaiah 57 recounts, God dwells in two distinct places and two places only. The one is in His high and holy place, representing His transcendence, His otherness, His unapproachable perfection. Yet He also dwells with the contrite and lowly in spirit, and to them, God is immanent, present, known, near, and felt. The contrite have sinned greatly and know it. The lowly in spirit are oppressed by their personal guilt and need of a savior. These are precisely the people with whom God comes to dwell and upon whose doors He knocks.

The Pharisee and the Publican

> *The very design of the gospel is to abase us; and the work of grace*
> *is begun and carried on in humiliation. Humility is not a mere*
> *ornament of a Christian, but an essential part of the new creature.*
> *It is a contradiction in terms*
> *to be a Christian, and not be humble.*
> **—Richard Baxter[3]**

Some may be thinking, *I know all this already. I have already humbled myself and accepted Christ by faith alone as my Savior and Lord. I did so when I was young or at youth camp when I was thirteen or perhaps as a freshman in college or off in the service.* If so, consider the words of Jesus from Luke 18:9–17. These words warn believers that unless their devotion to Him is continually and primarily characterized by an ongoing humility, then they may in fact have never accepted anything about Christ except what suited them, which is to say, they have not accepted Christ.

Consider the historical context of the Pharisee and the tax collector. Many modern-day Bible readers have been taught to think of the Pharisees as pompous, hollow, upper-class hypocrites who were insincere in their religious devotion but played along because of the personal power it brought them. This may have been true of some Pharisees, but it is not an accurate portrait of the majority.

First, the Pharisees were the Jewish party which most appealed to the commoners; they were the populists. Their rival party, the Sadducees, tended to be from the upper class, those who coddled the Romans in order to maintain their privilege. In contrast to the Sadducees, the Pharisees tended to be the ones who really believed the Bible. They believed in the literal reality of angels and the resurrection of the dead (see Acts 23:8). Furthermore, they had a tremendous, sincere zeal for their religion and worked hard both to maintain rigorous moral standards and to win others to their cause. In short, typical Pharisees were Bible-believing, evangelizing, morally upright commoners. They would fit into most evangelical churches today without a second glance.

If that is a likely description of the praying Pharisee, who then was the tax collector (or publican) meant to represent? He was probably not the sort of smelly, washed-up decrepit sinner that is often portrayed. First, he was undoubtedly understood to be rich, as was Zaccheus (Luke 19). Second, by the very nature of his profession, he was a collaborator with the enemy, the Romans. Third, as a collaborator or Hellenist, he portrayed a Jew who did not take his faith seriously. The publican represented a man who obtained a worldly, self-satisfied success—the kind of man who may show up in church, but only when his golf game was cancelled because of rain.

The publican and the Pharisee offer two very different prayers, and Jesus evaluates them by saying, "For everyone who exalts himself will be humbled, but the one who humbles himself will be exalted" (Luke 18:14). In this case, the one who exalted himself (the Pharisee) was exactly the one whom most Christians would have guessed to have humbled himself. The one who humbled himself (the publican) was the one whom most Christians would see as having spent his whole life exalting himself. However, the attitude of their hearts in their prayers makes all the difference to Jesus and determines which one of them went home "justified."

The word *justification* is a critical one in Christian theology, for it means nothing less than for a person to be declared completely innocent and sinless by God Himself. Justification is to be proclaimed "just," perfectly righteous in God's sight. If one is justified, one has it all—the forgiveness of sins, friendship with God, and life eternal.

Jesus chose this word precisely to draw the strongest of all possible contrasts between the Pharisee and publican in the conditions of their hearts. The Pharisee displays a heart full of pride and therefore remains "unjustified"; the publican demonstrates a heart of humility and goes home "justified" in the sight of God. Their justification, or lack thereof, was based on the state of their hearts, not on their outward behavior. As David Wells observes:

> What separates these two families of religion is apparent right here. . . . In the one, a sense of undoing before God, of inner wretchedness because of sin. . . . In the other, there is no such sense. Instead there is the confidence that there is an ascent that can be made, a hill that can be climbed . . . for surely God is obliged to reward the effort. . . . It is from these two starting points, illustrated by these two figures, that all the other religious divergences arise. In the one conception, the movement is upwards. In the other, it has to be downwards. . . . The one, then, is all about self-assertion albeit clothed and hidden in noble religious language. The other is about grace.[4]

All approaches to God and all religions boil down to only one of two possibilities: a religion of merit that feeds pride or a religion of grace that demands self-abnegation.

As God's unmerited grace is the basis of Christian salvation, so humility must result and remain in believers or they had no grace and no salvation to begin with. Now, if this holds true for the new Christian, how much more so for one who has been a professed believer for decades! If humility before God is not an ongoing, primary aspect of personal piety, then Christians have every reason to doubt whether they have any true piety at all. Folks should then question whether they are Christians, no matter how long they have worn the label or how much they have done for church and community. At the very least, Christians should agree that spiritual growth is intimately tied to growth in humility, no matter what their lives look like on the outside. According to Jesus, humility is a nonnegotiable mark of true followers of Christ, as they rest upon Him alone for their salvation.

Humility: The Link between Grace and Glory

*The promises of God give what the commandments of God demand
and fulfill what the law prescribes
so that all things may be God's alone,
both the commandments and the fulfilling of the commandments.
He alone commands, He alone fulfills.*
—Martin Luther[5]

Paul was the premier systematic theologian in the New Testament, and he was insistent on two clear themes: that believers are saved in Christ by grace through faith alone, and that God alone receives glory for this salvation and for all good things. These were the great cries of the Protestant Reformation—*Sola gratia* and *Soli Deo gloria*. Paul makes a clear link between the two ideas: God receives all the glory for salvation precisely because salvation is by grace through faith alone. Once the first is grasped and embraced, the other quickly follows. And Paul's link between the two—between grace and glory—is humility.

The only way people can reach and share in the glory of God is by placing their faith—complete trust—in Jesus Christ. Paul says,

> But now the righteousness of God has been manifested apart
> from the law, although the Law and the Prophets bear witness
> to it—the righteousness of God through *faith* in Jesus Christ
> for all who believe. For there is no distinction: for all have
> sinned and fall short of *the glory of God*, and are justified by
> his *grace* as a gift, through the redemption that is in Christ
> Jesus. (Romans 3:21–24, emphasis added)

Paul explains that this faith, this trust, saves people because of what
Jesus has done on their behalf—dying a sacrificial death as atonement
for sin. God is both just in His holy punishment of sin, and the One
who justifies the man who has faith in Jesus (Romans 3:26).[6]

But now consider Paul's very first application of this good news,
his next statement: "Where, then, is boasting? It is excluded. Because
of what law? The law that requires works? No, because of the law that
requires faith" (Romans 3:27 NIV). The gospel, this salvation that is
entirely by grace through faith, excludes boasting about oneself. Pride
has absolutely no place in the Christian's life—none. It is excluded.
What should take its place? An undying worship and gratitude to God
with an ever-increasing humility. As the hymn writer contemplates,

> Therefore, kind Jesus, since I cannot pay Thee,
> I do adore Thee, and will ever pray Thee,
> Think on Thy pity and Thy love unswerving,
> Not my deserving.[7]

The gospel demands and cultivates a deep and abiding humility in
all who would embrace it. How can it not? Andrew Murray expands
upon this idea when he writes,

> The more abundant the experience of grace, the more intense
> the consciousness of being a sinner. It is not sin, but God's
> grace showing a man and constantly reminding him what a

sinner he was, that will keep him truly humble. . . . I am afraid there are many who have sought to humble themselves by strong expressions of self-condemnation and self-denunciation . . . [but] being occupied with self, even amid the deepest self-abhorrence, can never free us from self. . . . The law may break the heart with fear. But it is only grace that works that sweet humility which becomes a joy to the soul.[8]

The gospel humbles believers not only by showing them their great sin through the law, but even more so by lavishing upon them a greater grace completely undeserved and unmerited. Whenever believers meditate on the amazing grace of the gospel, it always works a greater humility within them. As John Piper says, "When a little, helpless child is being swept off his feet by the undercurrent on the beach, and his father catches him just in time, the little child does not boast; he hugs."[9]

The only response to salvation can only be one of love and thankfulness, with no room—or need—for pride. Faith compels humility; it must or it would not be faith. For faith achieves precisely a salvation earned by Christ alone—a salvation that is by God's grace alone.

How then should believers first apply the gospel to their lives? Many of us have heard exhortations such as "read your Bible," "discover your spiritual gifts," and "go and tell others about Jesus." These are all excellent applications and not to be neglected. These instructions have their place in Paul's letters, but they are not the first or primary applications of salvation. Closer perhaps would be instructions to "join a good church," "pray continually," or "display the fruit of the Spirit," but once again, Paul does not go there first. These things will follow in short order if the gospel has been truly planted and rooted in a person's life. But Paul's point in Romans 3 is as poignant as it is clear: humility comes before all these things, all these applications. That is why he begins by saying that, for the Christian, boasting is excluded (Romans 3:27). That is what *Sola gratia* defends and demands.

Ephesians 2

For by grace are ye saved through faith; and that not of yourselves:
it is the gift of God: Not of works, lest any man should boast.
For we are his workmanship, created in Christ Jesus unto good works,
which God hath before ordained that we should walk in them.
—**Ephesians 2:8–10** (KJV)

Paul begins Ephesians by explaining that salvation is all of God: Father, Son and Holy Spirit, each person of the Trinity accomplishing their particular part in service to the other two. The redeemed find themselves mysteriously caught up in the eternal circle of God's perfect love for Himself. Then, turning to the human state, Paul declares that "God, being rich in mercy, because of the great love with which he loved us, even when we were dead in our trespasses, made us alive together with Christ—by grace you have been saved" (Ephesians 2:4–5). And then Paul delivers this famous summary, "For by grace you have been saved through faith. And this not your own doing; it is the gift of God, not a result works" (verses 8–9a). Paul's very next statement, the first stated goal of salvation, proclaims, "so that no one may boast" (verse 9b). Paul does not stop there, continuing, "we are his workmanship, created in Christ Jesus for good works, which God prepared beforehand, that we should walk in them" (verse 10). But significantly, snuggled between Paul's explanations of salvation by grace alone and the good works which result, Paul wedges this connecting phrase, "so that no one will boast"—the reason God saves His people by grace.

In our day, why do believers say that God saved them? Oft-stated reasons are that people should have eternal life, forgiveness of sins, and a relationship with God. All of these reasons are true and scriptural and not to be overlooked. But they should also remember this reason which Paul lays out so clearly—that those saved by grace should no longer boast.

Do the sins of boasting and pride make it into Christian testimonies alongside drunkenness, violence, lust, and so forth? Do believers who were raised in Christian homes and never rebelled still see their need to repent of pride? Perhaps some unwittingly boast in their upbringing or their own conformity to that heritage, all under the guise of giving thanks.

I remember sitting in Sunday school one week as a teenager and discussing the parable of the Prodigal Son, sometimes renamed the parable of the Forgiving Father (Luke 15:11–32). The teacher asked with whom we most identified. I remember stating clearly that I was just like the older, faithful brother who had never strayed. I was not a sinner like the younger brother at all, and I had no need for forgiveness as he did. I was still confident that I had something of which to boast—my own obedience and righteousness. I did not yet know that Jesus had come precisely to destroy that confidence.

1 Corinthians 1

Let the one who boasts, boast in the Lord.
—1 Corinthians 1:31

Why is boasting excluded in the Christian worldview? Why does God want believers to cease boasting in themselves and their accomplishments? God wants people to know that the only thing in the universe worth glorying in ultimately is Himself. Consider what Yahweh says through the prophet Isaiah about Israel's judgment.

"*For my name's sake* I defer my anger, *for the sake of my praise* I restrain it for you, that I may not cut you off. Behold, I have refined you, but not as silver; I have tried you in the furnace of affliction. *For my own sake, for my own sake, I do it*, or how should my name be profaned? *My glory I will not give to another.*" (Isaiah 48:9–11, emphasis added)

God reserves all the glory for Himself, and if God alone is to be glorified, then it logically follows that there is no room for anyone else to boast. Unsurprisingly, the apostle Paul continues this same theme. Paul concludes the doctrinal half of Ephesians with the same thought as Isaiah, "Now to him who is able to do far more abundantly than all that we ask or think, according to the power at work within us, to him be glory in the church and in Christ Jesus throughout all generations, forever and ever. Amen" (Ephesians 3:20–21). All the glory of redemption belongs to God alone.

Paul communicates the same theme when he concludes eleven straight chapters of doctrine in Romans with this one verse, "For from him and through him and to him are all things. To him be glory forever. Amen" (Romans 11:36). Jonathan Edwards sees a Trinitarian structure to Romans 11:36, saying, "Thus God has given us the Redeemer, and it is by him that our good is purchased. So, God is the Redeemer and the price; and he also is the good purchased. So that all that we have is of God, and through him, and in him."[10] God the Father gives a Redeemer; God the Son is that Redeemer; and God the Holy Spirit is the instrument of the Redeemer's work. Thus, God alone receives the glory for redemption. *Soli Deo gloria.*

If grace is the beginning of humility, God's glory is its end. Humility thus serves as the essential bridge in believers' souls between *Sola gratia* and *Soli Deo gloria.* As grace humbles believers, they are further able to glory in God alone. Paul makes this link clear in 1 Corinthians:

> God chose what is foolish in the world to shame the wise; God chose what is weak in the world to shame the strong; God chose what is low and despised in the world, even things that are not, to bring to nothing things that are, so that no human being might boast in the presence of God. And because of him you are in Christ Jesus, who became to us wisdom from God,

righteousness and sanctification and redemption, so that, as it is written, "Let the one who boasts, boast in the Lord." (1:27–31)

According to Paul, most people in the church are those who are not well regarded by the world—commoners and sinners all. Paul clarifies that even those few believers who are better off or well-educated are so by the will of God alone. Paul asks, "For who makes you different from anyone else? What do you have that you did not receive? And if you did receive it, why do you boast as though you did not?" (1 Corinthians 4:7 NIV). Therefore, Christians are those who realize that they are nothing apart from the grace of God, lest they boast of their own wisdom or strength or station.

Christian humility is more than mere emptiness of self—the goal of the Christian life is not only to die to self, but to live in Christ. Believers are to "put off your old self" that they may "put on the new self" through Christ (Ephesians 4:22–24). Believers must not only repent of sin but be filled with the Spirit (Ephesians 5:18). Believers must not just resist boasting in themselves. They must go on to boast in the Lord. They must move from *Sola gratia* to *Soli Deo gloria*.

Paul says that believers must empty their hands to receive grace. He then fills their hands with God's glory. Those who have been made meek by God's grace have been brought low for a reason, which is that they might glorify God and enjoy Him forever.[11] All of redemption is of God—from, through, and to Him. How then could Christians possibly dare to boast in anything but Him?

The Gap, the Publican, and the Glory of Grace

The gospel itself places humility at the center of Christian doctrine and discipleship. The following four biblical truths stir up humility in believers:

1. The greater their grasp of the chasm that exists between God's perfect holiness and their complete sinfulness, the greater they see their need for grace.
2. A gospel-wrought meekness must indwell and characterize all true believers.
3. The doctrine of salvation by grace alone banishes all their boasting—the very first application of the gospel to the Christian life.
4. The principle of God's glory alone compels the believer to boast only in the Lord.

These principles surround Christians throughout their earthly pilgrimage. As believers truly grow in Christ, the more the gap will appear to grow between God's holiness and their sinfulness—a gap the cross always fills. There may be times when believers realize that they have become more Pharisee than publican and need to repent of an ongoing self-righteousness. It happened to Peter, who knew grace better than anyone. There may be other times when believers are so pleased with the good works God prepared for them, that they will forget the first application of the gospel—that boasting is excluded. Or Christians may begin to brag about how much "God is doing through us," drawing attention to themselves and forgetting that God reserves all the glory for Himself—that their only boast is in the cross (Galatians 6:14).

But the more believers see their need for grace and the beauty of God's glory, the more they will grow in true humility. The more Christians abase themselves and magnify God, the more they have understood and believed the gospel of Jesus Christ, "For everyone who exalts himself will be humbled, but the one who humbles himself will be exalted" (Luke 18:14).

PRAYER

O the depth of the riches of Thy wisdom and knowledge, O God!
How unsearchable are Thy judgments,
and Thy ways past finding out!
For who hath known Thy mind, O Lord?
Or who hath been Thy counselor?
Or who hath first given to Thee, that he shall be recompensed?
For of Thee, and through Thee, and to Thee, are all things:
to Thee be glory forever. Amen.

—adapted from Romans 11:33–36

CHAPTER FIVE

. . . .

HOPE FOR A FOOL:
HUMILITY AND TRUTH

Do you see a man who is wise in his own eyes?
There is more hope for a fool than for him.
—Proverbs 26:12

Dilettantism, hypothesis, speculation, a kind of amateur-search for
Truth, toying and coquetting with Truth: this is the sorest sin.
—Thomas Carlyle[1]

Years ago I gave a talk to a small gathering of people from various religious backgrounds. My topic was none other than humility. Some were appreciative; others were skeptical, including one young fellow who described himself as a convert to Buddhism. At the end of the talk, he responded, "You have asserted many things as true. I have come to the point where for me true humility means admitting that I can never know anything, that I cannot even find my own rear end in the dark."[2]

Despite its bluntness, such a statement is attractive and even puts forth an appearance of humility. This is the challenge that postmodernism poses to Christian humility as many scholars have pointed out.[3] The challenge captures well one side of humility—not wanting to be too confident about our own knowledge—but the problem is that no one really lives as if they cannot know what is true. People do not willingly put their hands into the fire with the idea that it may or may not burn them. Such an act is not humble but the very opposite. People do know what they know, or at least live that way regarding most practical matters.

But that is an example from the physical realm, and many people do not believe that truth is knowable in the spiritual realm. Commonly people may say, "That may be true for you—but don't impose your beliefs on me." Ever since the first Parliament of the World's Religions in 1893, it has become increasingly common to assert that no one religion has an exclusive claim on truth and that it is the height of arrogance to assert otherwise. This mind-set is, in part, a proper reaction to the imperialistic certainty that many religious authorities have used to control and even terrorize minorities in their midst, Christianity included. Medieval torture and military campaigns and forced baptisms of whole populations in the name of Christ are facts of history. Not to mention slavery, racism, and discrimination in the United States, also sometimes done in the name of Christ.

The problem is what this relativistic impulse has done to the concepts of truth and humility. People are afraid to assert anything with certainty for fear of being thought arrogant. I imagine that some have already thought the same of this book. This chapter addresses the relationship between humility and truth. May Christians confidently assert that Jesus is the only way of salvation and remain humble? I confidently, and humbly, assert yes.

Humility Seeks Truth

If one gives an answer before he hears,
it is his folly and shame.
—Proverbs 18:13

And so these men of Indostan
Disputed loud and long,
Each in his own opinion
Exceeding stiff and strong,

Though each was partly in the right,
And all were in the wrong!
—**John Geoffrey Saxe**[4]

When I was in college, I had the privilege of attending several lectures by the well-known Anglican priest John Stott, who addressed a gathering of Methodist ministers. Stott said many memorable and striking things in these lectures but one pithy quote has stayed with me more than any other: "The purpose of an open mind is to find something solid on which to shut it." Immediately Americans may flinch at the idea that they should shut their minds on anything. Stott's point remains that the goal of an open mind is to discover the truth about oneself and the universe. But what is the point of looking for truth if one does not think it exists?

Humility presupposes that there is truth to be found, or it is not humility. Until people arrive at the truth, it is indeed good and proper that they are cautious and self-doubting. They must insist on getting facts checked and double-checked. That is why the best scientists are humble scientists. People should not arrive at a conclusion until they have all the data. But, in the end, good scientists also arrive at conclusions when they can.

It is not arrogant to maintain that certain religious dogmas can be known and believed, even if such dogmas contradict other religions. In fact, if humility respects logic, then it must be admitted that every major religion contradicts the others on cardinal points of doctrine. Either God is Triune, or He is not. Either believers are saved by their own works, or they are not. Opposites cannot both be true at the same time. As G. K. Chesterton sardonically observed about the illogical conflation of religions, "Christianity and Buddhism are very much alike, especially Buddhism."[5]

Moreover, the assertion that *there is no such thing as absolute truth*, is in fact an absolutist claim. It has the appearance of humility, but few statements could be more arrogant. The very idea that no one religion can be the true religion is in fact a claim to know the truth. The mindset that there is no absolute truth is arrogant precisely because it asserts a truth while not wanting to arrive at the truth. It does not want to do so because the truth requires change. Truth calls people to faith and repentance. Many people would rather "find joy in the journey" but never arrive anywhere that matters.

Then why is it considered arrogant to claim that God reveals Himself most perfectly through just one religion? It might not be true, but such a claim by itself is not necessarily proud. Now, it is true that people had better be certain that God really has said what they claim He has. They dare not take the Lord's name in vain. However, if God really has spoken, and if, in good conscience, people become convinced that He has, shouldn't they, in humility, accept it? Would it not be close-minded to refuse to believe something God has actually said?

So then, the question is, has God revealed who He is through the Bible and in Jesus Christ? Christians believe He has. Believers may be arrogant, but it is not because of that claim. With all their many faults, believing God at His Word is the most humble thing Christians can do. As theologian David Wells writes, "It is not immodest, nor arrogant, to claim that we know (the truth), when what we know is what God has given us to know through his Word."[6] Christians are not claiming that they have discovered the truth themselves, but that a gracious God has revealed it to them.

The New Testament insists that people can know the truth of the gospel given to them in Christ Jesus simply because the gospel has been revealed to them by God's grace. "I write these things to you who believe in the name of the Son of God, that you may know that you have eternal life" (1 John 5:13). Christians do not trust their feelings, or their intellect, or their own church or pastors. Believers trust the facts surrounding the incarnation, crucifixion, and resurrection of Jesus Christ of Nazareth. Paul tells Timothy to "follow the pattern of the sound words" and "guard the good deposit entrusted" to him (2 Timothy 1:13–14; 1 Timothy 6:20).

Believers do not shout out like the Greeks, "Great is Jesus of the Ephesians!" in partisan fervor (cf. Acts 19:28). Rather, they proclaim grace. Only one religion offers salvation that is entirely free and received apart from human merit. Only one religion claims that the one God of the universe became a man to die and rise again for His people. If God did become a man, it is not arrogant to proclaim that this one man is Jesus Christ of Nazareth, crucified under Pontius Pilate, and that He is the Way, the Truth, and the Life. No one comes to the Father but by Him (John 14:6), because He alone provides a salvation by grace.

Humility Maintains a Healthy Distrust in Oneself

It is not good to have zeal without knowledge,
nor to be hasty and miss the way.
—Proverbs 19:2 (NIV 1984)

Many set out to find God in the conceit of their learning,
swelling their breasts instead of beating them.
—Augustine[7]

Closely connected to the idea of resting in Christ's accomplished work is the dictum of healthy self-doubt. In a related way, self-doubt is the very basis of science—not trusting one's own instincts until an experiment can be repeated and verified. Science simply puts into practice what the Scriptures says, "in an abundance of counselors there is safety" (Proverbs 11:14). Humility distrusts one's own instincts and seeks verification and advice.

I have often participated in religious or philosophical discussions with people who had made up their minds long before and without any real examination of the issues. They are sure they are right and cannot wait to tell anyone who will listen. How often people say something like, "I think God is like this or that," without any consideration that they ought not to think anything about God unless He has first told them. Wisdom reminds us, "A fool takes no pleasure in understanding, but only in expressing his opinion" (Proverbs 18:2). Fools would rather hear themselves talk than actually grow in knowledge and perhaps even change their minds. In contrast, humility is "quick to hear, slow to speak, and slow to anger" (James 1:19). I have often had to remind myself of this verse when the sound of my own voice begins to become over-pleasing, and I find myself filibustering a conversation.

Americans have a strong tradition of rugged individualism that pushes against humility. In *Self-Reliance*, Ralph Waldo Emerson says, "to believe that what is true for you in your private heart is true for all men—that is genius."[8] So what happens when my genius heart disagrees with yours? That is exactly why Scripture warns against trusting one's own heart, "The heart is deceitful above all things, and desperately sick; who can understand it?" (Jeremiah 17:9). Humility teaches people to distrust their own hearts and judgment until wisdom has grown and been proved by an abundance of counselors.

What then are believers to do? They are to distrust their own first instincts and listen to facts—the facts of the world around them, the facts of other people's thoughts and opinions, and most of all, the facts found in God's Word (cf. James 1:19, 22). They are to heed the advice found in Proverbs,

> Trust in the LORD with all your heart,
>   and do not lean on your own understanding.
> In all your ways acknowledge him,
>   and he will make straight your paths.
> Be not wise in your own eyes;
>   fear the LORD, and turn away from evil. (3:5–7)

Christians are not the Christ. Instead, they must listen to Him, distrusting their own hearts even as Jesus sanctifies them into organs of greater truth, wisdom, and humility.

Embracing Truth Requires Humility

The fear of the LORD is the beginning of knowledge.
—Proverbs 1:7

The heart has reasons which reason does not know.
—Blaise Pascal[9]

Why is it that people do not accept the truth of the gospel? After all, it is the best news in the whole world, buttressed by an overwhelming case for its truthfulness for those who care to explore it. Yet, people disbelieving the gospel in the face of the evidence is nothing new; it occurred during Jesus's ministry. Some of the Jewish leaders accused Him of doing miracles by the power of Beelzebub since they could not refute the facts (cf. Mark 3:22).

Jesus clearly teaches that facts are not enough. People need a changed heart. "If they hear not Moses and the prophets, neither will they be persuaded, though one rose from the dead," Abraham tells the rich man who wants to warn his brothers about hell (Luke 16:31 KJV). As the apostle Paul puts it, "The natural [i.e., unconverted] person does not accept the things of the Spirit of God, for they are folly to him, and he is not able to understand them because they are spiritually discerned" (1 Corinthians 2:14).

Faith comes by hearing, which means looking to things that are unseen (Romans 10:17; 2 Corinthians 4:18). Thomas believed because he saw the risen Christ, but blessed are those who have not seen, and yet believe (cf. John 20:29). In that sense, today's Christians are all more blessed than the apostles. For though we have not seen Jesus, we love Him and are filled with an inexpressible joy (1 Peter 1:8–9).

Faith and humility are required for receiving the spiritual message of the gospel. People hear the facts of the gospel with their minds, but the Holy Spirit must convince their hearts. It is, as Jonathan Edwards says, the difference between knowing that honey is sweet and tasting its sweetness.[10] The Holy Spirit must work to make the gospel sweet, which He does precisely by working faith and humility in people's hearts. As the famous Proverb says, "the fear of the LORD is the beginning of knowledge" (Proverbs 1:7). Until people have that fear—that awe, that faith—they will have no spiritual wisdom, and the facts of the gospel will do no good.

T. S. Eliot illustrates this work of the Spirit. Most know Eliot from his masterpieces, *The Waste Land* and *The Love Song of J. Alfred Prufrock*, written during his extended period of existential, atheistic angst. Later in life, Eliot famously became a Christian, and his latter writings and poetry explicitly evidence his conversion. But while still an atheist, Eliot had the honesty to write the following:

> I am moved by fancies that are curled
> Around these images, and cling:
> The notion of some infinitely gentle
> Infinitely suffering thing.

Eliot is talking about Jesus, the Son of God, who infinitely suffered upon the cross. But Eliot was not yet a believer when he wrote this poem, so he immediately responds to this fancy which has moved him:

> Wipe your hand across your mouth, and laugh;
> The worlds revolve like ancient women
> Gathering fuel in vacant lots.[11]

Even though Eliot was not yet ready to repent of his despair and atheism, he nevertheless sensed the Holy Spirit working upon his heart. He admitted frankly that the notion of a suffering God moved him and gave him a glimmer of hope in his own personal wasteland. The fear of the Lord is the beginning of wisdom.

Truth Must Be Proclaimed Humbly

> *Knowledge, a rude unprofitable mass,*
> *The mere materials with which wisdom builds,*
> *Till smoothed and squared and fitted to its place,*
> *Does but encumber whom it seems to enrich.*
> *Knowledge is proud that he has learned so much;*
> *Wisdom is humble that he knows no more.*
>
> **—William Cowper**[12]

When many people today object to the idea of epistemological certainty, I believe their true objection is that many in the church hold to their beliefs in an arrogant fashion. Christians may embrace the truth of Christ, but when they do so in a haughty manner, it undermines the gospel. Christians often forget that "when pride comes, then comes disgrace, but with the humble is wisdom" (Proverbs 11:2). Paul warned the church at Corinth, "Knowledge puffs up, but love builds up. If anyone imagines that he knows something, he does not yet know as he ought to know" (1 Corinthians 8:1–2). Christians may hold to the truth, but they must hold to it with humility, remembering that even if they are right about a matter, it is only by the grace of God (cf. Psalm 16:2; 1 Corinthians 4:7).

Think about the way Christians come across as they present the gospel to others, firmly standing upon the truth of Jesus Christ and the Bible. Is it done meekly? Peter advises, "In your hearts honor Christ the Lord as holy, always being prepared to make a defense to anyone who asks you for a reason for the hope that is in you; yet do it with gentleness and respect" (1 Peter 3:15). Notice the two qualifiers that surround the command to make a defense. First, believers are to honor Christ the Lord in their own hearts, softening it before Him. Second, Christians are to make a defense "with gentleness and respect," reflecting the character of Christ. The medium must match the message. How believers answer may be just as important as what they answer.

Christians must embrace and advance the truth humbly. Christ must be presented in a Christlike manner.[13]

One of the most brilliant men I have studied under is a well-regarded church historian who has taught at several prominent institutions. I once took his seminar on American Puritans. Week after week, this distinguished professor sat at the head of a small table surrounded by his students. One grad student was easily distracted. I even remember him flicking spitballs at me across the table right in front of our august professor as we discussed deep doctrinal matters. Halfway through the semester, all of a sudden, this student blurted out, "What is up with this predestination thing anyway? What's that all about?" That is a topic that every class on Puritanism tackles on the first day of class, not halfway through the semester. We all snickered and looked at our professor to hear whatever snarky and pithy retort awaited this hapless fellow. Instead, this gracious man simply looked at him and then took several minutes to explain what predestination was to the Puritans. No rebuke, no high-minded put-down about this student being intellectually AWOL—he gave a straight answer with gentleness and respect.[14] This illustrated to me how believers are to embrace and advance truth: meekly, aware of their own limits and sinfulness, learning and teaching by grace alone.

Humility Celebrates Mystery and Allows for Disagreement

Who is wise and understanding among you? By his good conduct let him show his works in the meekness of wisdom. . . . The wisdom from above is first pure, then peaceable, gentle, open to reason, full of mercy and good fruits, impartial and sincere.
—James 3:13, 17

Christians may assume that because they are certain about some things, they must be certain about everything. Frankly, some believers come across that way. However, a biblical certainty also embraces mystery and allows for a great deal of disagreement about many matters. Biblical certainty celebrates that, "the secret things belong to the LORD our God, but the things that are revealed belong to us and to our children forever" (Deuteronomy 29:29).

Believers are only responsible to know and obey what God has clearly told them. But regarding most things about Himself and the universe, God simply has not chosen to say much. The secret things belong to Him.

"For my thoughts are not your thoughts,
    neither are your ways my ways, declares the LORD.
For as the heavens are higher than the earth,
    so are my ways higher than your ways
    and my thoughts than your thoughts." (Isaiah 55:8–9)

Believers must be exceedingly careful when they try to speak for God, especially when it comes to interpreting His providential work in history or what He may or may not be doing today, especially in someone else's life. Christians simply do not know. They can make good guesses and suggest them as such, but believers do not know for certain what God is doing.

When Harvard University was founded as a Christian institution in 1636, it soon adopted the motto, *Veritas* (Truth), under the seal of three books: two open and one closed. Historians wonder what each book was meant to represent. Some say the two open books stood for the Old and New Testaments, with the closed book representing the truth that not will be revealed until Jesus Christ returns. Others say the two open books are God's revelation in nature and the Bible, while the closed book stood for mysteries known only to God, a symbol of humility in the midst of the intellectual. This is what historians do know: by 1847 the third book was overturned and lay open. All truth became knowable.[15]

Christians believe in truth and proclaim it as certain, but only the truth that they can know through God's Word. They gladly embrace mystery for many other things. Think about the freedom that humility brings—believers do not have to have an opinion about everything. They are allowed, even encouraged, to say about many things, "I don't know."

A close corollary to mystery is disagreement. Humility must allow room for Christians to disagree on secondary doctrinal matters. No one has the corner on truth regarding every doctrine. Some things in the Bible are crystal clear and must be believed, things such as God's Triune nature, that salvation is by grace, and that Jesus rose bodily from the dead. Other things are not as clear, such as how often leaders from different churches should meet together (cf. Acts 15), or exactly how believers are to rest on the Lord's Day. In Romans 14, 1 Corinthians 8–10, and Colossians 2, Paul admonishes believers to make room for these disagreements.

I love the way my own denomination puts it in the preliminary principles of its *Book of Church Order of the Presbyterian Church in America*.

> Godliness is founded on truth. . . . No opinion can be more pernicious or more absurd than that which brings truth and falsehood upon the same level. . . . Otherwise it would be of no consequence either to discover truth or to embrace it.
>
> While, under the conviction of the above principle . . . there are truths and forms with respect to which men of good character and principles may differ. In all these it is the duty both of private Christians and societies to exercise mutual forbearance toward each other.[16]

Even in something as staid and authoritative as a church's manual of operations, there is an appeal to mutual forbearance on secondary matters. Like Paul, believers are to be patient with other Christians, knowing that ultimately it is not their job to convince one another in every jot of doctrine.

One important caveat is that by urging patience with one another on secondary matters, I am still holding out that there are correct answers.[17] Some people define doctrinal humility as a kind of impenetrable vagueness, perhaps more influenced by American anti-intellectualism than sound, biblical thinking.[18] Jesus recognizes that some matters are more important than others (Matthew 23:23), but the less weighty matters are still relevant. Christians must each follow their own consciences as they struggle to understand what Scripture teaches.

Hope for Fools

> *But who are you, O man, to answer back to God?*
> *Will what is molded say to its molder,*
> *"Why have you made me like this?"*
> **—Romans 9:20**

When I was a young preacher, I suppose I was as arrogant as most. I was getting a seminary degree and had all sorts of things to tell God's people that they had surely never heard before. In one of my first sermons at a small church in Massachusetts, I remember praying beforehand, "Lord, if I say anything false, may it fall on deaf ears." It was a formality, a nice turn of phrase, I thought. After the service, the members greeted me at the door as they left. One dear old woman came up to me with her walker, warmly shook my hand and said, "Young man, that was a very good sermon, except that I could not hear most of it." I have since learned to pray differently before I preach.

The great irony in the matter of truth and humility is what both Proverbs and Paul teach: when people think they are wise, then they are fools. In the recognition of one's own foolishness, wisdom is found—not by emptying oneself of knowledge or despising education but rather by embracing Christ. Listen to Paul's description of believers:

For consider your calling, brothers: not many of you were wise according to worldly standards, not many were powerful, not many were of noble birth. But God chose what is foolish in the world to shame the wise; God chose what is weak in the world to shame the strong; God chose what is low and despised in the world, even things that are not, to bring to nothing things that are, so that no human being might boast in the presence of God. (1 Corinthians 1:26–29)

The church is largely made up of those who know they are not wise or powerful or privileged. Yet the gospel is available to all who know their need for grace, whether rich or poor, lettered or uneducated. The key is not one's social status, but one's spiritual state; it is not one's position in the world, but one's posture before God almighty.[19] It is remembering what Romans 9 declares—He is the potter and we are but clay.

PRAYER

Almighty God, I know that you can do all things,
and that no purpose of yours can be thwarted.
Therefore I have uttered what I did not understand,
things too wonderful for me, which I did not know.
Therefore I despise myself,
and repent in dust and ashes.
—Based on Job 42:2–6

· · · ·

CHAPTER SIX

NOT UNTO US:
DISCIPLESHIP AS HUMILITY

Not to us, O LORD, not to us, but to your name give glory,
for the sake of your steadfast love and your faithfulness!
—Psalm 115:1

When Jesus calls a man, He bids him come and die.
—Dietrich Bonhoeffer[1]

After the parable of the Pharisee and Publican concludes with Jesus saying, "everyone who exalts himself will be humbled, but the one who humbles himself will be exalted," Luke immediately follows with the famous story of Jesus blessing the little children.

> Now they were bringing even infants to him that he might touch them. And when the disciples saw it, they rebuked them. But Jesus called them to him, saying, "Let the children come to me, and do not hinder them, for to such belongs the kingdom of God. Truly, I say to you, whoever does not receive the kingdom of God like a child shall not enter it." (Luke 18:15–17)

The point could not be more obvious. Children are utterly dependent. Infants cannot live apart from the loving care of their parents or guardians. They need others. People cannot receive the kingdom of God if they refuse to see their utter dependency on God for every good thing. Believers must become like little children.[2] The parable of the Pharisee and the Publican teaches about the need for humility as sinners; Jesus welcoming the little children shows the need for humility simply as creatures.

This picture of spiritual infancy should describe a lifetime of Christian discipleship. Even as believers grow and mature in godliness, they must never outgrow their sense of spiritual infancy, as they see their need for Jesus more and more. Consider what Peter tells established believers in his letter, "Like newborn infants, long for the pure spiritual milk, that by it you may grow up into salvation—if indeed you have tasted that the Lord is good" (1 Peter 2:2–3). Peter is saying that the way for these believers to grow in grace is by continuing to sense their spiritual dependency and to long for the gospel like newborn infants crave milk. Andrew Murray explains the concept.

> We only need think for a moment what faith is. Is it not the confession of nothingness and helplessness, the surrender and the waiting to let God work? Is it not in itself the most humbling thing there can be—the acceptance of our place as dependents, who can claim or get or do nothing but what grace bestows? Humility is simply the disposition which prepares the soul for living on trust.[3]

Utter dependence may seem like a humiliating prospect for grown adults who want to be known as competent and accomplished individuals, but dependence is never discouraging for those in Christ. Rather, it is a refreshing reminder that He is the One who will provide all their needs. As mothers nurse their babies, Jesus provides for all who come to Him as little children.

King David knew such provision and delighted in it.

O Lord, my heart is not lifted up;
    my eyes are not raised too high;
I do not occupy myself with things
    too great and too marvelous for me.
But I have calmed and quieted my soul,
    like a weaned child with its mother;
    like a weaned child is my soul within me.
O Israel, hope in the Lord
    from this time forth and forevermore. (Psalm 131)

David twice describes his soul as a "weaned" child because he is no longer nursing but simply resting upon the breast of his God. David is already filled and satisfied, and his rest begins with humility. King David confesses that he should not pursue things beyond his capabilities. This is true wisdom: David is not God. David has no need to figure everything out, for he is cradled by the one who knows all things and who will lovingly protect him all his days. Humble dependence brings a sense of peace and comfort. David receives the kingdom like a little child even into old age. If great King David can do this, so must all believers.

The Way Up Is the Way Down

Not in regal robes of grandeur,
Brightly shining wreaths of gold;
Lowly-flesh his form most humble,
Veiling brilliance—his from old;
Look! The new-born King of glory,
Grace and mercy we behold!

Not a palace filled with baubles,
Throne or scepter for this child;
From the highest to the lowest
He descended to the wild;

Look! The new-born King of glory,
Mary's babe—so meek and mild!
—**Derek Thomas**[4]

Christians are on a pilgrimage of growing in their dependence upon God for all things. This means dying to self-worship and finding delight and glory in God alone. In this sense all true Christian discipleship is simply pursuing greater humility. Meekness becomes our primary goal. Of course, what concrete discipleship and humility look like on any given day is much more specific, but in all the details, the primary question remains, are believers following Christ in such a way that their pride is ever diminishing and a joyful, steadfast humility increasing? After all, Jesus Himself taught, "If any man will come after me, let him deny himself, and take up his cross daily, and follow me. For whosoever will save his life shall lose it: but whosoever will lose his life for my sake, the same shall save it" (Luke 9:23–24 KJV).

Crosses were used for only one thing in the Roman world—to torture and execute the condemned. And Jesus uses the cross to describe the daily Christian life. The cross has lost its scandal in modern times. People wear it bejeweled around their necks and set it serenely on steeples, silent and tame. But in Jesus's day, the cross was an instrument of horror and humiliation. It was as if Jesus was telling His disciples that whosoever would follow Him must sit down in their electric chair. Imagine that. What if instead of gold crosses, Christians wore earrings in the shape of tiny electric chairs? Or if a gas chamber was the image stained in glass behind the preacher each Sunday? These modern equivalents would make people ask themselves, *Do I really want to follow this Jesus? Do I really want to die to my excellent little self every day?*

Of course, this does not mean that Christ's followers should actively seek literal martyrdom. The New Testament records that the early disciples avoided danger when they could, even though they did not expect to escape persecution. The great apostle James got exactly two lines in the book of Acts, having to do with the removal of his head. Paul could barely keep track of the number of times he faced death, in the end resolutely traveling to Jerusalem where he knew arrest awaited, just as his Lord had faced. Peter, too, was faithful to the point of death, even death on a cross (John 21:18–19).

Whether Christians are martyred or not, the cross is the model for the entire Christian life. The way up is always the way down. Each day believers must die to themselves, seek humility, and serve others. This is the way of Christ. Paul repeatedly describes the earthly pilgrimage as one of daily death:[5]

> I have been crucified with Christ. It is no longer I who live, but Christ who lives in me. And the life I now live in the flesh I live by faith in the Son of God, who loved me and gave himself for me. (Galatians 2:20)

> But whatever gain I had, I counted as loss for the sake of Christ. . . . that I may know him and the power of his resurrection, and may share his sufferings, becoming like him in his death. (Philippians 3:7, 10)

> Why are we in danger every hour? I protest, brothers, by my pride in you, which I have in Christ Jesus our Lord, I die every day! What do I gain if, humanly speaking, I fought with beasts at Ephesus? (1 Corinthians 15:30–32)

> But we have this treasure in jars of clay, to show that the surpassing power belongs to God and not to us. . . . always carrying in the body the death of Jesus, so that the life of Jesus may also be manifested in our bodies. For we who live are always being given over to death for Jesus' sake. (2 Corinthians 4:7, 10–11)

Paul understood that the Christian life is cross-sculpted from head to toe. The way of growth, of sanctification, is always a godly humiliation.

Yet the story does not end with the cross. After all, Jesus teaches that whoever humbles himself will be exalted. Believers "suffer with him in order that we may also be glorified with him" (Romans 8:17). The story's finale is not abasement, but heavenly glory, life with God forever. The way up is *always* the way down. "Humble yourselves in the sight of the Lord," both James and Peter write, "and He will lift you up" (James 4:10; 1 Peter 5:6). Both Peter and James saw this pattern of humiliation and exaltation played out in their own lives.

When God invaded this world in the flesh as the long-promised greater David and second Adam, He came as a lowly infant in a country stable, and then His journey sinks even lower. If God swaddled in a manger is a picture of humility, how much more so God upon a cross, hanging naked and abandoned—all for the sake of those He loved. Rightly, the Christmas carol captures it, "Thou who wast rich beyond all splendor, All for love's sake becamest poor."[6] Jesus as the pioneer of the downward way is also captured in the early Christian "hymn" found in Philippians 2:3–11:

> Do nothing from rivalry or conceit, but in humility count others more significant than yourselves. Let each of you look not only to his own interests, but also to the interests of others.
>
> Have this mind among yourselves, which is yours in Christ Jesus, who, though he was in the form of God, did not count equality with God a thing to be grasped, but made himself nothing, taking the form of a servant, being born in the likeness of men. And being found in human form, he humbled himself by becoming obedient to the point of death, even death on a cross.
>
> Therefore God has highly exalted him and bestowed on him the name that is above every name, so that at the name

of Jesus every knee should bow, in heaven and on earth and under the earth, and every tongue confess that Jesus Christ is Lord, to the glory of God the Father.

Notice how Paul explicitly commands humility—that believers look out for the interests of others while not neglecting their own needs. Paul then gives the model of humility: Jesus's life. The way up is first down the path of self-denial, servanthood, and death. That is the Christian's path, the path of the cross. Yet, the path does not end in humiliation. Jesus was obedient to the point of death, "therefore" God highly exalted Him. In the same way Jesus was raised in glory, so shall all believers rise in Him. Believers will receive their heavenly reward, secured by grace. If they are in Christ, then they will follow Him along this downward path of dying to themselves in service to God and neighbor until their time here on earth is done. Then, as they enter glory, no matter what little good they think they did with their lives, believers will hear only words of approbation from the Savior, "Well done, good and faithful servant" (Matthew 25:21). For to live is Christ, and to die is gain (Philippians 1:21).

This downward path on earth differs from Christian to Christian, each in different stations and callings. God will ordain tests and opportunities for Christians to bear their cross and follow after Jesus in their own, particular setting. One example stands out in my memory. A successful businessman belonged to my church and grew tremendously in his faith while part of our body. He was accomplished in his career, running a factory for a major company in the area. He was given an opportunity to become the vice president of a huge, worldwide company headquartered in Texas. He took it, moving his family. But he lasted one week in the new job.

What happened? When he reported to work, his boss told him that his division was not yet scared of him, and he was expected to fire one of his managers in order to assert his authority. Which one, my friend asked? The boss said that it did not matter—pick one at a random or he would be fired instead. My friend had a choice: protect his career by ruining someone else's life or pick up his cross and follow Christ. Would he pursue the way up or take the way down, after his Lord? It is one of my greatest joys in ministry that my friend accepted the firing instead, even after moving his family halfway across the nation and being on the job just one week. My friend chose the way of the cross. God provided a new job shortly after, and his career and family are fine. Christians do not always experience such positive results after their obedience, but often God provides such exaltations as a foretaste of the greater heavenly exaltation that awaits the humble in Christ.

Imitating the Humility of Christ

Why art thou proud, O man? God, for thee, became low.
Thou wouldst perhaps be ashamed to imitate a lowly man;
at any rate, imitate the lowly God.

—Augustine[7]

Ultimately, it is not the cross but the one on the cross who is the model for Christian lives. If God were to become a man—and He did—He would be the perfect man, and the picture of true godliness. Believers know precious little about Jesus's personal preferences, traits, or quirks. Christianity is not a conformist religion, in which believers imitate the rituals and dress and daily practices of their founder. Believers retain their own little quirks and traits, but they seek to conform to Christ in His character, knowing that God is powerfully at work, "For those whom he foreknew he also predestined to be conformed to the image of his Son, in order that he might be the firstborn among many brothers" (Romans 8:29).

What we find is that this conformity to Christ's image looks like humility. Jesus said, "Take my yoke upon you, and learn from me, for I am gentle and lowly in heart" (Matthew 11:29). Jesus is gentle and humble toward believers, as they learn from Him, and He teaches them to become more like Him in His lowliness. And so we now look to find meekness is in every part of Christ's being—His Trinitarian relationship, His redemptive offices, and His overall character.

Christ's Humility within the Trinity

We have examined Jesus's humility thus far in light of His incarnation and death. Equally compelling is Jesus's submission to His heavenly Father. Christians have always understood Jesus to be equal with the Father and Spirit in the Holy Trinity—one God in three Persons. All are equally God and yet distinct from one another. Human math cannot do it justice. As the Nicene Creed puts it, Jesus, the Son of God, is "very God of very God," completely divine, even as He is fully man.

The Nicene Creed also proclaims that God the Son is "begotten of the Father before all ages." This has to do with Jesus's role within the Trinity in the great task of redemption. In some sense, God the Son willingly submits to the Father, not in His being, but in His role. Paul explains that the head of Christ is God (1 Corinthians 11:3), and "when all things are subjected to him, then the Son himself will also be subjected to him who put all things in subjection under him, that God may be all in all" (1 Corinthians 15:28). This is deep water and the purpose here is not to dive into the mysteries of Trinitarian theology.[8] However, if a willing submission is built into the character of God, it must be a very holy thing indeed. When God the Son took on flesh, He became "of the soil," *humilis*, humble.

Further, Jesus teaches that His submission to the Father is meant to be an example. Andrew Murray points out how the gospel of John reveals a bit of how Jesus's submission to the Father was the center ring of redemption:

- "The Son can do nothing of himself" (John 5:19).
- "I can of mine own self do nothing; as I hear, I judge: and my judgment is just; because I seek not mine own will" (John 5:30).

- "I came down from heaven, not to do mine own will" (John 6:38).
- "My doctrine is not mine" (John 7:16).
- "I am not come of myself" (John 7:28).
- "I do nothing of myself" (John 8:28).
- "Neither came I of myself, but he sent me" (John 8:42).
- "I seek not mine own glory" (John 8:50).
- "The words that I speak unto you I speak not of myself" (John 14:10).
- "The word which ye hear is not mine" (John 14:24).[9]

Remember, this is God the Son speaking—He who made both heaven and earth. He who formed the leviathan and makes stars to fall (Colossians 1:16; Hebrews 1:2). What cause is there for Jesus to say all these things, except that in Him, believers might see what true godliness is? Jesus displays divine humility. God perfectly submitted to God. This is the example for all Christians to follow.

Christ's Humility in His Offices

Classical Protestant theology has always understood Jesus to have three main roles, or offices, by which He fulfilled His role as Redeemer: prophet, priest, and king. All the great people who filled these offices in the Old Testament were signposts pointing to the one who would perform them perfectly. As prophet, Christ brought God's Word and is God's Word; as priest, Christ intercedes at God's right hand; and as king, Christ rules and protects His people, defeating all enemies.

When Christians reflect upon Christ as their prophet, priest, and king, they tend to focus upon the glory of His rule. That is certainly one side of the redemptive story, the full consummation that believers eagerly await (Romans 8:23). And yet, history has not yet arrived at the consummation. The model for Christian living now is Christ in His earthly state. The Westminster Larger Catechism describes Christ executing the offices of prophet, priest, and king, but then it goes on to address the "estate of His humiliation." A careful study of Christ's humiliation reveals:

- Jesus is not just Prophet; but the subject who perfectly obeys the prophetic Word of God in believers' place (Matthew 5:17).
- Jesus is not just Priest; but the very sacrifice for sin (2 Corinthians 5:21).
- Jesus is not just King; but the servant who gave His life as a ransom for many (Mark 10:45).

Jesus is the opposite of all three glorious offices in His humiliation. He is prophet, priest, and king as well as subject, sacrifice, and servant. Thus, Christ brought salvation not through the estate of His glory, which He laid aside, but through the estate of His humiliation. The question is, does that estate of humiliation of Christ continue in His followers? Jesus answers that question clearly by washing His disciples' feet on the night of His betrayal, telling them, "do just as I have done to you" (John 13:15). The model for the Christian life this side of heaven is Jesus in His humiliation, not His glory.

Christ's Humility in His Character

Think about the things most people desire in order to feel content and successful. Now think about the ways Jesus laid these all aside to accomplish redemption and for His Father's glory.

- Heritage: "Nathanael said to him, 'Can anything good come out of Nazareth?'" (John 1:46).
- Social class: "Is not this the carpenter?" (Mark 6:3).
- Education: "The Jews therefore marveled, saying, 'How is it that this man has learning, when he has never studied?'" (John 7:15).
- Appearance: "He had no form or majesty that we should look at him, and no beauty that we should desire him" (Isaiah 53:2).

- Wealth: "Foxes have holes, and birds of the air have nests, but the Son of Man has nowhere to lay his head" (Matthew 8:20).
- Reputation: "The Son of Man came eating and drinking, and they say, 'Look at him! A glutton and a drunkard, a friend of tax collectors and sinners!'" (Matthew 11:19).
- Family bonds: "For not even his brothers believed in him" (John 7:5).
- Rank: "For who is the greater, one who reclines at table or one who serves? Is it not the one who reclines at table? But I am among you as the one who serves" (Luke 22:27).
- Popularity: "He was despised and rejected by men; a man of sorrows and acquainted with grief; and as one from whom men hide their faces he was despised, and we esteemed him not" (Isaiah 53:3).
- Ability: "For he was crucified in weakness, but lives by the power of God" (2 Corinthians 13:4).
- Honorable death: "Two others, who were criminals, were led away to be put to death with him" (Luke 23:32).[10]

Christian discipleship means following and imitating Christ in His character, and Jesus's character exemplifies humility. Any authentic pursuit of discipleship means the quest for greater meekness before God and man. Jesus was humble before His Father, in His redemptive offices, and toward His fellow man. Christians are to follow Him in this lowliness—even to the point of death—remembering, "Not to us, O LORD, not to us, but to your name give glory" (Psalm 115:1).

Resting in Christ's Humility

If you lay yourself at Christ's feet, He will take you into His arms.
—**William Bridge**[11]

When Christians realize the depths to which Jesus calls them, they are helpless unless He helps them—which is exactly what He promises to do.

> "Come to me, all who labor and are heavy laden, and I will give you rest. Take my yoke upon you, and learn from me, for I am gentle and lowly in heart, and you will find rest for your souls. For my yoke is easy, and my burden is light." (Matthew 11:28–30)

Jesus is right beside believers, carrying their burdens. Following Jesus in His humility is the way to greater joy, though it stings from time to time. The Jesus who calls believers to pick up their cross is the same Jesus who came to bring them life abundantly (John 10:10). He is the same Jesus who commands them to enjoy their life's callings and all of God's good gifts (Ecclesiastes 2:24; 9:7–9; Colossians 2:8–23; 1 Timothy 4:4). Bearing the cross sustains and refreshes one's soul, even in the midst of the pain of daily self-denial.

And when believers struggle to pick up their crosses and follow Christ, they should always remember that they are already justified and cannot lessen His love by their failures. They should remember that "a bruised reed he will not break, and a smoldering wick he will not quench" (Matthew 12:20). He will treat them with the same humility and gentleness that they are struggling to imitate! He is God almighty, and His power is on their side, as He rides forth victoriously "for the cause of truth and meekness" (Psalm 45:4).

Christians do not bear their daily crosses alone. They do not grow in meekness alone. God tells them, "In returning and rest you shall be saved; in quietness and in trust shall be your strength" (Isaiah 30:15). Jesus is right there, humbly and victoriously assisting those who follow Him as they rest in His work and power. After all, is not that rest part of what it means to receive Him as a little child?

PRAYER

I greet Thee, who my sure Redeemer art,
My only trust and Savior of my heart,
Who pain didst undergo for my poor sake;
I pray Thee from our hearts all cares to take.

Thou hast the true and perfect gentleness,
No harshness hast Thou and no bitterness;
O grant to us the grace we find in Thee,
That we may dwell in perfect unity.

Our hope is in no other save in Thee;
Our faith is built upon Thy promise free;
Lord, give us peace, and make us calm and sure,
That in Thy strength we evermore endure.

—John Calvin[12]

Humility Embraced— Hope

Now he told a parable to those who were invited,
when he noticed how they chose the places of honor,
saying to them,

"When you are invited by someone to a wedding feast,
do not sit down in a place of honor, lest someone more distinguished
than you be invited by him, and he who invited you both will come
and say to you, 'Give your place to this person,' and then you will
begin with shame to take the lowest place.

But when you are invited, go and sit in the lowest place,
so that when your host comes he may say to you,
'Friend, move up higher.' Then you will be honored in the presence
of all who sit at table with you.

For everyone who exalts himself will be humbled,
and he who humbles himself will be exalted.

He said also to the man who had invited him,
"When you give a dinner or a banquet, do not invite your friends or
your brothers or your relatives or rich neighbors,
lest they also invite you in return and you be repaid.

But when you give a feast, invite the poor,
the crippled, the lame, the blind,
and you will be blessed, because they cannot repay you.
For you will be repaid at the resurrection of the just."

—LUKE 14:7–14 (EMPHASIS ADDED)

. . . .

CHAPTER SEVEN

BOLD NOBODIES:
HUMILITY REGARDING SELF

*Humble yourselves, therefore, under the mighty hand of God
so that at the proper time he may exalt you,
casting all your anxieties on him, because he cares for you.*
—1 Peter 5:6–7

*We bestride the mountains or the valleys of earthly importance
with a holy indifference, contempt, and detachment. . . .
No task is so small as to distress us,
no honor so great as to turn our heads.*
—Thomas Kelly[1]

I believe that the practice of true Christian humility will necessarily manifest itself in radical, measurable ways. If humility is once found, then it must be embraced, and once embraced, it must yet be applied. As believers grow in humility, their lives will change not only in thought, but also in word and deed. Humility has a real, visible form that manifests itself in everything from what believers title themselves to what they name their children; from how they make career decisions to how they spend their money; from the way churches worship to the way they spread the gospel. Humility, or the lack thereof, affects everything.

Bridal Tables and Inner Rings

You know how I feel about fuss and folderol.
Lord knows the job itself is reward enough.

—Barney Fife[2]

In Luke 14, Jesus gives two examples of how humility ought to direct believers—first, how to view themselves (verses 7–10), and second, how they ought to treat others (verses 12–14). Jesus wraps both examples around the same maxim of humility found in Luke 14 and 18, "For everyone who exalts himself will be humbled, and he who humbles himself will be exalted" (14:11; 18:14).

Jesus had been invited to dine at a prominent Pharisee's home on the Sabbath. The invitation was a sort of credentialing process. The Pharisees wanted to see if Jesus would break their oral traditions of Sabbath keeping. True to form, Jesus does good on the Sabbath. He heals a man suffering from dropsy, a form of painful swelling, to their apparent disapproval (Luke 14:2–4). Luke then records that Jesus told this parable, "when he noticed how they chose the places of honor" for themselves (Luke 14:7). Jesus tells them that when invited to a wedding, not to invite yourself to the head table. Do not give yourself honor.

Think about the last wedding you attended as a guest. Imagine if, as the bridal party is announced, you infiltrated into the procession and then forthwith sat yourself next to the bride and groom, even though they were just your third cousins twice removed. The acute embarrassment that would follow would prevent most people from doing such a thing. Jesus is using hyperbole here to describe the way many people do this type of thing all the time, though in more subtle ways.

At work, people strive to get face time with the boss. At family functions, people ask questions of relatives expecting them to reciprocate and give an opportunity to talk about themselves and their achievements. In church, people desperately want to be in the inner circle of those considered most spiritual. To accomplish that, they sometimes intrude into others' affairs uninvited so that they may give unsolicited advice or even public prayer—all in the interest of showing themselves as the most spiritual and caring.

These are all examples of "inviting oneself up" before it is time. People may put themselves forward rather than trusting God to promote them in His season. This kind of behavior is almost always a failure to remember the gospel. Only God's opinion really matters, and He has said that in Christ, believers are the apple of His eye. Christians cannot become more beloved than they already are. But they often forget this and look to their careers or reputations to bring them worth. They invite themselves up before it is time.

When I was a senior in college, I was preparing to be commissioned as a Second Lieutenant in the U.S. Army after four years of R.O.T.C. Somehow I got it in my head that the Army could learn a lot from me. In my vast four years as a cadet, I had seen a lot of things I disliked and was sure I could address. On the way to lunch one day, I asked a wise professor who was a retired Air Force general about it. I will never forget how gently he answered me, "First, learn to do your job as a young platoon leader as best you can. That's it. Then, maybe, after a few years, you might have something to say." I was an arrogant, twenty-two-year-old, green-behind-the-ears college kid. My professor was too kind to say it that way, but his lesson was spot-on: do not invite yourself up before it is time.

As I entered pastoral ministry, I continued to struggle with wanting to invite myself up. At conferences, I would hope to be noticed and maybe some year to speak. At presbytery (my regional assembly of elders), I wanted to be considered an influential and wise person. Despite my laziness in making any real effort, I wished to be known as a wise writer and contributor across the Internet. I wanted to invite myself up without putting in the years and tears of real pastoral work in the obscurity that properly marks the normal, successful pastor.

At the same time, I did know this parable in Luke 14 and tried to let it influence the way I advanced my career, to let God confirm in His time that He had called me to be a pastor. I determined never to invite myself to preach anywhere, nor even to let it be known that I was willing, so as not to invite myself up to the "bridal table" of my vocation, the pulpit. So when invitations did come, I was more certain it was of the Lord rather than my own ambition.

One of the most masterful treatments of these principles found in Luke 14 is C. S. Lewis's 1944 lecture, *The Inner Ring*. Lewis describes the danger of living for human acceptance, particularly by those in the "inner ring" of one's chosen field of interest. When people live for such circles, sooner or later they will start cutting ethical corners in order to be accepted. But it does not have to be that way. Lewis concludes,

> The quest of the Inner Ring will break your hearts unless you break it. But if you break it, a surprising result will follow. If in your working hours you make the work your end, you will presently find yourself all unawares inside the only circle in your profession that really matters. You will be one of the sound craftsmen, and other sound craftsmen will know it.[3]

So humble folks work not to advance themselves or weave their way into some elite group of experts. Instead they work as to the Lord and not unto men (Colossians 3:23).

Now, does all this mean that people cannot apply for new positions, or hang certificates on the wall, or put together an excellent, truthful résumé? Of course not. These are all solicited, and thus they are the opposite of inviting oneself up to the bridal table. When hiring folks, I want to know what is best about them as well as any liabilities. When I go to the doctor, I rather like to see his or her medical degree hanging prominently on the wall before they diagnose me. After all, a person cannot practice law and help others unless they first study hard and earn that degree, hopefully giving God the thanks and glory each step of the way. That is not ego; that is service. That is taking up our cross daily and following Jesus in the way of death.

Humility, thus, helps believers accomplish what is needed because God calls them to it, all to His glory—no matter how big or small the job. Christians' only ambition should be to live quietly, to mind their own affairs, and to work with their hands, just as Paul commanded (cf. 1 Thessalonians 4:11–12). Believers pursue excellence in their work simply because it is the right thing to do, regardless of whether it advances their own name or not.

The Duke of Wellington reportedly wrote to William Wilberforce, the English evangelical member of Parliament who led the fight against the British slave trade, "You have made me so entirely forget you are a great man by seeming to forget it yourself in all our intercourse."[4] Wilberforce simply had more important things to do than worry about his public image. So too, when properly focused, believers simply do what is needed; what is assigned.[5]

Reversing the Curse of Pride

We all inherit our first parents' pride and fallen natures at heart. That is what original sin is all about—sinfulness in our origin, our humanness. But why did Adam and Eve fall? There is obviously great mystery here, but we read,

> So when the woman saw that the tree was good for food, and that it was a delight to the eyes, and that the tree was to be desired to make one wise, she took of its fruit and ate, and she also gave some to her husband who was with her, and he ate. (Genesis 3:6)

So there are three recorded factors that made the tree appealing. The tree purported to feed their appetite, their vanity, and their spiritual hubris. In short, Adam and Eve fell for pride. And according to John, those same three temptations of pride are what trip us up today, "For all that is in the world, the lust of the flesh, and the lust of the eyes, and the pride of life, is not of the Father, but is of the world" (1 John 2:16 KJV). But that is not the end of the story. When God the Son came to earth as the Second Adam, He underwent the same three temptations from Satan. Yet when offered worldly remedies, Jesus did not give in, but instead trusted His Father (Matthew 4:1–11; Luke 4:1–13). That is what made Him the perfect sacrifice for the sins of the world, the Second Adam, come to make a new humanity (2 Corinthians 5:17). And as we are united to Him by faith, this curse of pride is forgiven and begins to be reversed.

How do believers cooperate with Jesus to reduce pride and grow in humility? How do believers gladly take the low seat and wait their turn? Four guidelines I hope will assist in that quest.

Discover Pride's Hidden Recesses

Forcing yourself to stop self-admiration . . . is like
fighting the hydra. . . . There seems to be no end to it.
Depth under depths of self-love and self-admiration.
—C. S. Lewis[6]

Pride does its best to masquerade as something else—some virtue or conviction—but believers must engage in introspection to root it out of the hidden recesses of their lives. Pride is that doppelganger that is only uncovered by great spiritual effort and discernment. As Lewis observed, vanity is a hydra-headed beast not slain by any sword of human forging. No, this kind comes out only by prayer and fasting.

One way to unmask pride is to discover how much it is behind all sin. Recognizing surface sins is easy enough if believers have any spiritual interest, but if they want to deepen their repentance, they will explore how all their sinful tendencies have pride at their root. When Christians confess and deal with their obvious sins, they would do well to dig deeper than just surface manifestations. Pastor Mike Sharrett provides the following examples of how pride often shows itself as believers make excuses for their own sin:

- Lying: "I don't want to tarnish my reputation if the truth be known."
- Greed: "I deserve this and should have all these things because I'm worth it."
- Lust: "I'm worthy of this pleasure that I seek beyond godly parameters."
- Gossip: "I'm important because I know secrets."
- Anger: "How dare you do that to me! How could you cross me, of all people!"
- Judgmentalism: "I'm always right and always possess the higher moral ground to find others wrong."
- Laziness: "I have a right to use time as I see fit."
- Lawlessness: "I'm a special case, an exception to the rule."
- Cheating: "No way should I risk looking like a failure or forfeiting what I want."
- Shyness: "I'm unwilling to be known by you because you might find reason to reject me."
- Impenitence: "I don't fail or make mistakes."
- Pretentiousness: "My reputation is paramount."
- Boasting: "I am so important that I need to be recognized and esteemed."
- Unapproachability: "I'm too important for you and must protect myself from you."[7]

By being aware of pride's reach, believers have hope of rooting out sin's true cause with the help of the Holy Spirit, not just the symptoms. Christians want the full regimen of sanctification, not just a humanly administered Band-Aid that covers but does not heal.

So how do believers get at the root of sin, if not by human effort alone? It is by placing faith in Christ, more and more. Again, Andrew Murray is helpful, "Pride renders faith impossible. Salvation comes through a cross and a crucified Christ. Salvation is the fellowship with the crucified Christ in the Spirit of His cross. Salvation is union with, delight and participation in, the humility of Jesus."[8] Believers tackle the problem of deep pride the same way they do all sins: faith in the Lord Jesus Christ. He will help quash their pride because He loves them.

Acknowledging All Good Things from God

You know men used to lay up
their richest wines in the lowest cellars;
so God lays up his richest treasures of his grace
in the heart of the humble and lowly.
—Ebenezer Erskine[9]

The psalmist says to Yahweh, "You are my Lord; I have no good apart from you" (Psalm 16:2). If anything is good, it is from God. Paul makes this same point to the prideful Corinthians, a church that had a rich array of spiritual gifts and knew it, "What do you have that you did not receive? If then you received it, why do you boast as if you did not receive it?" (1 Corinthians 4:7). Paul does not say that their gifts were illegitimate or boring. But they were just that—gifts given to them by God. Should a three-year-old boy boast of his new toy train he finds under the Christmas tree as if he put it together? Any good thing folks have is by God's grace. These good things may include parents, education, intelligence, health, energy, children, jobs, churches, freedoms, and virtues. We have not earned any of these, and we deserve a good deal worse.

People live and breathe each moment by sheer grace. Any good thing they have is entirely by God's prerogative and kindness. If people are in Christ, His kindness to them is guaranteed, for "we know that in all things God works for the good of those who love him, who have been called according to his purpose" (Romans 8:28 NIV). Even more, they know, "If God is for us, who can be against us? He who did not spare his own Son but gave him up for us all, how will he not also with him graciously give us all things?" (Romans 8:31–32). In short, if we need something we will have it, all by God's grace. And apart from Him, we have no good thing.

Judging Oneself

A Christian conquers, even when he is conquered.
When he is conquered by some sins, he gets victory
over others more dangerous, such as spiritual pride and security.

—**Richard Sibbes**[10]

Rooting out pride requires a way for believers to evaluate how they are doing. A number of Scriptures help Christians judge themselves. These passages summarize characteristics that should mark the believer. By the Holy Spirit's help, Christians should seek to increasingly

- depend upon God daily as reflected in the Lord's Prayer (Matthew 6:9–13).
- obey the Ten Commandments in thought and deed (Exodus 20:1–17; Matthew 5:17–48).
- embrace the Beatitudes as their own (Matthew 5:3–12).
- display the fruit of the Spirit (Galatians 5:22–23).
- seek the wisdom from above (James 3:17–18).
- be motivated by selfless love (1 Corinthians 13).

These are passages that any mature Christian ought to know and progressively embody.

Yet, there is great danger in quantifying an approach to spiritual growth. Quantifications can too easily lead to a pharisaical self-righteousness that feeds only pride, even as it takes on an appearance of godliness. Paul's solution to this danger is to apply the gospel itself, even after eleven long chapters of doctrine, "For by the grace given to me I say to everyone among you not to think of himself more highly than he ought to think, but to think with sober judgment, each according to the measure of faith that God has assigned" (Romans 12:3).

Believers are supposed to think about themselves but to do so soberly. Paul even gives a measuring stick, "each according to the measure of faith God has assigned." It seems as if Paul is saying something similar to the father who says to Jesus with tears, "I believe; help my unbelief!" (Mark 9:24). Faith in Christ is everything, and it is the chief measure of whether believers are growing in humility or not. Even the cry of this father confessing his unbelief is in fact a cry of great faith—because he knows his own weakness. He is not looking to himself for more faith but calls upon Jesus to give it to him.

Inevitably, when believers begin to judge themselves against a list of virtues, they will see how far they fall short. When this happens, excuses will not help. Instead, believers are to use "sober judgment," not thinking more highly of themselves than they ought. But then they are to ask, "Do I yet believe the gospel? Do I take the bread and wine by faith, as a needy sinner who looks to Christ alone?" If so, perhaps they are doing better than they realize.

Humility unlocks one of the great mysteries of the faith, which is put so bluntly by Thomas Watson, "Better the sin that humbles me, than that duty which makes me proud."[11] It seems counterintuitive, but if believers can grasp what Watson is saying, then they will begin to understand true growth in sanctification. They begin to understand Paul's anguished struggles with sin and faith described in Romans 7. The fight itself is the road to humility.

This does not mean that any sin is good or that believers have any excuse for it. Sin grieves the Holy Spirit and does damage to people's hearts. But God is also sovereign, and His purposes are greater and far kinder than people can yet see. When believers have been humiliated in their sin and see their need for Christ all the more, they just might grow in even more important virtues, in particular, showing mercy to others. Consider the gentleness of King David after God forgave him of adultery and murder—how kind he was to Shimei and Absalom, his sworn enemies. After having failed so spectacularly, David now knew the depths of his own sin and of his debt to God's grace. How could he then refuse mercy to fellow sinners? Instead, David cries out, "O my son Absalom, my son, my son Absalom! would God I had died for thee, O Absalom, my son, my son!" (2 Samuel 18:33 KJV).

Because believers are in Christ, their eyes are on Him, so they can declare along with Paul to the Corinthians, "But with me it is a very small thing that I should be judged by you or by any human court. In fact, I do not even judge myself" (1 Corinthians 4:3). Paul says not that he is guiltless, but that it is the Lord who judges him—and God has already acquitted Paul by grace. For there is no condemnation for those in Christ Jesus—full stop (Romans 8:1). In the end, that is the only judgment that matters.

Remembering God's Power at Work in His People

"Come to the Planetarium at the Museum of Science,
you insignificant speck in the universe."
—Billboard outside of Boston

O LORD, our LORD, how majestic is your name in all the earth!
You have set your glory above the heavens.
What is man that you are mindful of him,
and the son of man that you care for him?
Yet you have made him a little lower than the heavenly beings
and crowned him with glory and honor.
—Psalm 8:1, 4–5

Recalling God's mighty power at work in believers, even as they wrestle with ongoing sin is another tool to root out pride. Believers are now God's holy temple, a royal priesthood and holy nation (1 Peter 2:5). They have the power of the gospel at work in them. As Paul declares, "I am not ashamed of the gospel, for it is the power of God for salvation to everyone who believes, to the Jew first and also to the Greek" (Romans 1:16). Anyone who believes the gospel has this power. Do not be ashamed.

The gospel's power will often show forth most when believers feel least worthy of it. For "we have this treasure in jars of clay, to show that the surpassing power belongs to God and not to us" (2 Corinthians 4:7). When God is most growing Christians in humility, they will feel their weakest—like jars of clay.

Thus, even in humiliation, believers must obey Paul's command to the Philippians, "Finally, brothers, whatever is true, whatever is honorable, whatever is just, whatever is pure, whatever is lovely, whatever is commendable, if there is any excellence, if there is anything worthy of praise, think about these things" (Philippians 4:8).

As believers root out hidden pride and confess their faults, they are to think on those things which are true and honorable and pure and lovely. Christians can name those good things that are true about themselves, being careful to thank God for each one. Even as they grow in humility, believers must recall God's great power at work within them. For God is the most true, pure, and excellent of all things, and He has taken up residence within all who are in Christ. O LORD, our Lord, how majestic is Your name in all the earth!

Bold Nobodies

Thus says the LORD:
"Heaven is my throne, and the earth is my footstool; . . .
But this is the one to whom I will look:
he who is humble and contrite in spirit
and trembles at my word."
—Isaiah 66:1–2

Humility does not regard anyone as a true nobody. Instead, humility acknowledges that people's true purpose is to live for God's glory in service to Him and others. Despite their failures, believers are already forgiven in Christ. True humility lives in this tension and is thus bold in God's grace. Paul can tell the Ephesian elders that he lived among them, "serving the Lord with all humility with tears and trials," and at the same time, "did not shrink from declaring to you the whole counsel of God" (Acts 20:17–27). Paul's meekness made him bold, and he thus went on to serve God and others as best he could, no matter what happened to him.

The happiest people are those whose eyes are not on their own glory; who confess that they deserve nothing short of hell itself. They are Wilberforces, so consumed with helping those in need for the sake of the gospel that they have no time to consider themselves great. They would be just as happy if someone else were given their tasks and role. They want to honor their Lord, for He gave them their place. They recognize the great honor and privilege it is to serve God in any capacity. They would just as soon clean toilets as address Congress if both glorify God. They are happy to be nobodies in the sight of the world.

As a young Christian, I had no real concept of this. I thought I had a special place in God's kingdom and wanted others to see it too. One summer on a mission trip, and I was called up to be prayed over during a worship service, along with half a dozen others. Several months before the trip, I had been diagnosed with a rare blood disorder. Many prayed for my healing, and God graciously gave it—the disease went away and has never returned. But here is where I failed to be a bold nobody: just before the pastor prayed, I blurted out that I was the one who had been healed. I suppose the most charitable reading of my motives was to give God glory for His kindness and to encourage the church. However, to do so publicly, in such an unprompted way, only served to make a distinction between myself and the other missionaries, as if I was somehow more special, more deserving of the church's attention. I was not content with being a bold nobody. I wanted to be somebody different, somebody more important than those around me. I look back at that memory with embarrassment, recognizing how much pride ruled my young Christian life, and still lingers far too much.

Those who understand what it means to be bold nobodies do their work out of joy, simply in service to God. Reputation does not

matter to them, for their heavenly Father has already approved all their
works (Ecclesiastes 9:7). They eat their food with gladness and drink
their wine with joy. They do not shrink back from using their gifts to
advance the cause of Christ in the world, for it is God who calls and
equips them. And they know this bold service is always by way of the
cross. They gladly face affliction, perplexity, and persecution, bearing
in their bodies the death of Christ so that the life of Jesus may also be
revealed. They are jars of clay, humble and weak—nobodies in the eyes
of the world. Yet they are also sons and daughters of God, royal priests,
high and lifted up, crowned with honor and glory. They are bold for
Christ by the power of the gospel.

PRAYER

When I survey the wondrous cross
On which the Prince of glory died,
My richest gain I count but loss,
And pour contempt on all my pride.

Forbid it, Lord, that I should boast,
Save in the death of Christ my God!
All the vain things that charm me most,
I sacrifice them to His blood.

His dying crimson, like a robe,
Spreads o'er His body on the tree;
Then I am dead to all the globe,
And all the globe is dead to me.

—Isaac Watts[12]

CHAPTER EIGHT

. . . .

SEEKING THE CITY TO COME: HUMILITY AND ESCHATOLOGY

"Blessed are the meek, for they shall inherit the earth."
—**Matthew 5:5**

*When the corn is nearly ripe it bows the head and stoops
lower than when it was green. When the people of God are
near ripe for heaven, they grow more humble and self-denying. . . .
Paul had one foot in heaven when he called himself the chiefest
of sinners and least of the saints.*

—**John Flavel**[1]

In Luke 14, Jesus concludes His instructions on humility, saying, "For you will be repaid at the resurrection of the just" (verse 14). Thinking of promised repayment may strike people as strange, even selfish. How is focusing upon reward a reflection of Christian humility? Yet, humility is intimately connected to a proper, biblical eschatology, the doctrine of Jesus's return to make all things new (Revelation 21:5).[2]

I imagine some readers' eyes are beginning to glaze over as they contemplate a descent into the doctrinal minutiae and detailed exegesis that often characterizes the debate among various eschatological camps. My primary concern is not this debate but where believers place their hope. The practical side of eschatology, particularly as it relates to pride and humility, is focused upon hope and reward.

It was my great privilege to be the pastor to a retired missionary who lived to 105 years. He was converted to Christ on the streets of Chicago sometime during World War I, and then he spent the rest of the twentieth century serving his Lord both here and abroad, including several decades in central Africa's jungle. He retired toward the end of his earthly life, his wife and children having passed away. This brother was still doing all he could to advance Christ's kingdom—writing books, praying, and worshiping faithfully. When I visited him toward the end, his body broken and worn, he told me, "Pastor, sometimes it gets so hard and I am in so much pain, I just feel like giving in and letting go. Is it all right to want to go to heaven now?" Yes, dear brother, you can go home. To live is Christ and to die is gain. He had lived as Christ, and he could go home to his eternal rest.

But what enables believers like this to serve for so long, waiting for that great day of their true reward? In Luke 14 Jesus says to take care of those who cannot repay. Why? Believers do good deeds to help those who cannot repay because God offers a heavenly reward. Good works may still do much good for others, but if they are done for earthly, not heavenly, payment, they do not stem from faith or humility. I see this in myself because I love the praise of men. I cannot wait for others to tell me what a helpful book this is; I want to see the reality of God's promises now rather than humbly waiting until the end. I want to trust my own eyes more than God's promises.

When Christians believe that their true reward is yet unseen, then they are able to live humbly and to do good works that will last into eternity. The notoriety good deeds bring does not matter. This is why Paul exhorts believers to "not grow weary of doing good, for in due season we will reap, if we do not give up" (Galatians 6:9). The pattern for earthly lives is also the pattern for this world, as Hebrews so clearly states, "For here we have no lasting city, but we seek the city that is to come" (Hebrews 13:14). Things that are seen are temporary (2 Corinthians 4:18). The Christian's hope for their own lives or for the world itself is not in this world. They seek a city that is still to come.[3]

The failure to remember this future orientation has often caused the church to lose its way when it has too closely allied the cause of the gospel with a particular country or culture. Church history is littered with the wreckage caused by such unholy optimism and party spirit. Too often the New Jerusalem has been identified with particular lands or causes, from medieval Christendom to Puritan New England to the U.S. Confederacy, or to the modern-day state of Israel. Such a tendency comes naturally; all believers want to see God at work around them, and as patriots, of course they want to see Him most at work in their own tribe. However, earth has no lasting city—anywhere.

One man who learned this well from bitter experience was a leading English Puritan minister, Richard Baxter. Like most of his colleagues, Baxter had placed great hope in the interregnum reign of Oliver Cromwell, who despite his many shortcomings was an adamant and steadfast follower of Christ. After Charles II was restored to the throne in 1660, which led to many Puritans being executed, jailed, or exiled, Baxter wrote the following:

> I am farther than ever I was from expecting great matters of unity, splendour, or prosperity to the Church on earth, or that saints should dream of a kingdom of this world, or flatter themselves with the hopes of a golden age, or reigning over the ungodly. . . . On the contrary, I am more apprehensive that suffering must be the church's ordinary lot, and Christians indeed must be self-denying cross-bearers, even where there are none but formal, nominal Christians to be the cross-makers; and though ordinarily God would have vicissitudes of summer and winter, day and night, that the church may grow extensively in the summer of prosperity and intensively in the winter of adversity, yet usually their night is longer than their day, and that day itself hath its storms and tempests.[4]

Scripture overwhelmingly supports Baxter's conclusion that suffering is the church's normal lot. When his party was doing well in the world, Baxter could not see the heavenly city. The crucible of persecution opened his eyes to a more biblical eschatology—an eschatology of waiting, an eschatology of humility.

Believers do have victory and glory in Christ already. Paul says that somehow, believers are already seated with Jesus in the heavenly places (Ephesians 2:6). However, too much focus on victory in Christ can lead to what theologians call an "over-realized" eschatology. And such an over-realized eschatology can easily lead to pride.

The Corinthians appeared to have fallen into this error, which is why Paul sarcastically rebukes them when he writes, "Already you have all you want! Already you have become rich! Without us you have become kings!" (1 Corinthians 4:8). The Corinthians were living as if they had already arrived and thought that they were God's greatest church on earth. This is Paul's chief complaint about their focus on tongues and prophecy and miracle working: they were living by sight, not faith, and thus taking great pride in these kinds of glorious, visible gifts. They had an over-realized eschatology, exulting in power and victory and strength rather than celebrating gifts of service and suffering, putting others first while waiting a future reward and a future city.

This is the test: if a view of eschatology leads to pride, there is error and perhaps much worse. Peter, instead, admonishes believers to prepare their minds for action, to be sober-minded, and to set their hope fully on the grace that will be brought to them at the revelation of Jesus Christ (1 Peter 1:13). That is biblical eschatology; that is humility.

Why Should Cross and Trial Grieve Me?

You know I got trouble, I got trouble, I got trouble, but:
  Trouble don't last, God's got your back,
  Trouble don't last, God's got your back,
  Trouble don't last, God's got your back.
—Prisoner Choir, Bulloch County Correctional Institute[5]

Having a humble, biblical eschatology is essential for believers to make sense of the trials and suffering they endure in this life. The New Testament speaks of suffering as a normal part of the Christian life, and a chief means God uses to sanctify His followers.

> Therefore, since we have been justified by faith, we have peace with God through our Lord Jesus Christ. Through him we have also obtained access by faith into this grace in which we stand, and we rejoice in hope of the glory of God. Not only that, but we rejoice in our sufferings, knowing that suffering produces endurance, and endurance produces character, and character produces hope, and hope does not put us to shame, because God's love has been poured into our hearts through the Holy Spirit who has been given to us. (Romans 5:1–5)

Paul has just proven to the Romans that believers are justified by faith alone, and then he describes the Christian life as one of rejoicing in sufferings because they produce qualities far more precious than comfort—endurance, character, and hope. James writes, "Count it all joy, my brothers, when you meet trials of various kinds, for you know that the testing of your faith produces steadfastness" (1:2–3). Suffering reminds those who are in Christ to place their hope in heaven, not in their material lives here. Peter makes the same point in this beautiful passage (which is well worth memorizing):

> Blessed be the God and Father of our Lord Jesus Christ! According to his great mercy, he has caused us to be born again to a living hope through the resurrection of Jesus Christ from the dead, to an inheritance that is imperishable, undefiled, and unfading, kept in heaven for you, who by God's power are being guarded through faith for a salvation ready to be revealed in the last time. In this you rejoice, though now for a little while, if necessary, you have been grieved by

various trials, so that the tested genuineness of your faith—
more precious than gold that perishes though it is tested by
fire—may be found to result in praise and glory and honor at
the revelation of Jesus Christ. Though you have not seen him,
you love him. Though you do not now see him, you believe in
him and rejoice with joy that is inexpressible and filled with
glory, obtaining the outcome of your faith, the salvation of
your souls. (1 Peter 1:3–9)

Suffering refines faith and reiterates that the Christian's true inheritance is kept in heaven. When people are doing well, they do not think
they need God's help; they may forget their sheer dependence on Him
for every good thing. But then some trial arises, whether external or
internal, and suffering drives believers to their knees. Christians once
more come to God in their pain and weakness. A biblical eschatology
reminds believers that the ultimate outcome of their faith is the salvation of their souls, not earthly prosperity.

None of this is to say that Christians should seek suffering, but
they should expect it. God has ordained days of suffering so that believers may be blessed in an even greater way: growth in faith and meekness. "Humility is a strange flower; it grows best in winter weather, and
under storms of affliction," says Samuel Rutherford.[6]

However, Christians are not automatons, and trials do not always
lead to a godly response, at least not initially. What I have found is that
suffering never leaves people neutral; it causes them to go one way or
the other. Some grow bitter and dark, taking their complaints to the
world rather than to the foot of the cross. Other Christians may define
their good in a worldly sense, forgetting that the greatest good is to be
conformed to the image of Christ (Romans 8:28–29). Other believers,
however, take Paul and James and Peter to heart, and let their suffering work a great humility and joy in them. Indeed, the godliest and
humblest Christians I have ever met are those who have suffered many
years in various forms of trials. How can it be otherwise with Christ as

our Lord and model? As Annie Dillard writes, "You do not have to sit outside in the dark. If, however, you want to look at the stars, you will find that darkness is necessary."[7]

Today's culture shutters away suffering as best it can. For many reasons, we keep death distant and sanitized. It is rare for the elderly to live and die in the family home, surrounded by loved ones. There are excellent medical reasons for this, but death and suffering are not as ever-present as they once were—not until some tragedy brings them home, suddenly and across all media outlets. People are shocked that human beings might actually die unbidden. People no longer sing of sickness and death as if they awaited them tomorrow like previous generations did, who did not live in such comfort and prosperity. Of course, it is true that on average we live longer than ever before. But what are a couple of decades in light of eternity? Our ancestors knew better the reality and value of suffering, as this beautiful seventeenth-century hymn so well illustrates, "God oft gives me days of gladness; shall I grieve if He give seasons, too, of sadness? God is good and tempers ever all my ill, and He will wholly leave me never."[8] God-ordained suffering plays an indispensable role in humbling believers and reminding them of their true hope. Heaven will be a wonder. I cannot wait.[9]

By the grace of God, I have been given a blessed life: wonderful, godly parents; tremendous teachers in school; the ability to serve my country; fellowship at some wonderful churches; and above all, a faithful wife who has given me two amazing, fun, talented daughters who love Jesus. I, however, would not have grown as I have without various trials that have softened my character and made me gentler to fellow sinners. An early, unexpected military deployment strained my marriage so that it was the sheer grace of God that held us together. After finishing at the top of my seminary class, I was fired by my first church after one year, already washed up in my pastoral career right out of the gate. Nagging health issues have sapped my energy and kept me prayerful, often in the middle of the night. Through it all, the same sins that first brought me to Christ are my constant companion. I know that there will be no victory lap until glory.

Suffering is so important in the Christian life that Paul even speaks of believers sharing in the afflictions of Christ, "Now I rejoice in my sufferings for your sake, and in my flesh I am filling up what is lacking in Christ's afflictions for the sake of his body, that is, the church . . . to make the word of God fully known, the mystery hidden for ages and generations but now revealed to his saints" (Colossians 1:24–26). What could be lacking in Christ's afflictions? Paul does not mean he can add to the atonement for sin, which only the Son of God could accomplish. Yet, after His crucifixion and resurrection, Jesus did not choose to bring the gospel to the ends of the earth Himself, but gave that mission, that privilege, to His followers. As they take part in that great project, they will find it to be cross-shaped. Bringing Christ to the world means to share in His sufferings.

As believers share in suffering, they also share His God's comfort (2 Corinthians 1:3–6). Christians then turn around and pay forward that same comfort to others in their affliction. Who is better able to sympathize with the cancer patient than a cancer survivor? Who is best able to help an alcoholic than one who has felt the same addictive pull? Why, as a general rule, are the poor proportionately more charitable than the wealthy? In all these cases, someone who has experienced an affliction is able to comfort others who are experiencing the same. *Trouble won't last; God's got your back.*

Weakness Is the Way

The church is compared to weak things:
to a dove amongst the fowls; to a vine amongst the plants;
to sheep amongst the beasts; to a woman, which is the weaker vessel.
God's children are bruised reeds
before their conversion and oftentimes after.
—Richard Sibbes[10]

When I reported to my first unit at Ft. Stewart, Georgia, as a young Second Lieutenant in the U.S. Army, I wanted to make a good impression. This is hard enough as a new wet-behind-the-ears officer, but even harder given my situation. I was the lone Medical Service Corps officer assigned to a hard-charging infantry battalion. That meant I was a rear echelon pencil pusher in the midst of warriors.

My first morning I reported to physical training at zero dark thirty, and walked up to my place behind the formation with the rest of the officers and senior sergeants. Before I could say anything, the grisly, old platoon sergeant from the Scout Platoon sauntered up to me. The Scouts were the elite platoon in our battalion, the best of the infantry. This old sergeant looked at me, and with everyone watching, pointed to a spot on his thigh and said loudly, "See that, sir? Gunshot wound. Grenada." Right off, he was letting me know my place. He was showing his strength and my inexperience. Well, I was not going to have that. Without missing a beat, I pointed to my heart and said, "See that, Sergeant? Emotional scar. Junior high."

That was probably the cleverest retort of my entire life. And yes, I am proud of it. But it had a point that I think was vaguely scriptural. Natural human tendency is to lead with strength, letting others know straight off about one's abilities and experience. People want respect. Showing any weakness or failure makes people feel vulnerable. At the start, I wanted my men to see that I was comfortable with who I was: I was not old enough to have fought in Grenada, but I had survived junior high. Some lead with strength; others with weakness. Either way, everyone has a war story.

The Corinthians believed that the apostle Paul was a weak leader whom they compared to their own super-apostles, who confidently asserted their own authority and gifts. The Corinthians boasted of these strong leaders in comparison to Paul. This poor thinking goaded Paul to respond with some boasting of his own, in what has to be one of the most startling passages in all of church history.

Since many boast according to the flesh, I too will boast. . . .
Are they servants of Christ? I am a better one—I am talking
like a madman—with far greater labors, far more imprison-
ments, with countless beatings, and often near death.

Five times I received at the hands of the Jews the forty
lashes less one. Three times I was beaten with rods. Once I
was stoned. Three times I was shipwrecked; a night and a day
I was adrift at sea; on frequent journeys, in danger from rivers,
danger from robbers, danger from my own people, danger
from Gentiles, danger in the city, danger in the wilderness,
danger at sea, danger from false brothers; in toil and hardship,
through many a sleepless night, in hunger and thirst, often
without food, in cold and exposure.

And, apart from other things, there is the daily pressure
on me of my anxiety for all the churches. Who is weak, and I
am not weak? Who is made to fall, and I am not indignant?
If I must boast, I will boast of the things that show my weakness. (2 Corinthians 11:18, 23–30)

Paul recited all of his hardships not to show that he was some kind
of superhero who could somehow endure it, but to show what a true
Christian leader looks like: someone who suffers for the cause of Christ.
When one's ultimate hope is in heaven and its glory, there is no need
to boast. Believers who are justified in Christ have no need to try to
appear strong, or to act as if this life is all they have and that they must
somehow show everyone how well things have turned out for them.
If believers must talk about themselves, they should do so in ways
that show their weaknesses. Others may then see that their strength is
from the Lord. Paul concludes his list of achievements saying, "For the
sake of Christ, then, I am content with weaknesses, insults, hardships,
persecutions, and calamities. For when I am weak, then I am strong"
(2 Corinthians 12:10).[11]

Sin and weakness is not to keep people on the ground but rather on their knees—dependent on God's power. Therefore, Paul realized that when he went through these various hardships, God's power was made perfect. These times of weakness were precisely when he was strongest, for that was when Christ most rested upon him. Therefore he boasted all the more gladly of his weaknesses (2 Corinthians 12:9).

Think about those chronic, unresolved issues of pain and struggle in your life, whether physical or mental or relational; that "thorn" which keeps you in distress and bent before God. I know of people who have everything in their lives together except for some nagging, chronic ailment that keeps them off balance. I know of others whose careers and personalities are brilliant, but who must deal with relatives who are simply beyond human help. I have friends who are made involuntary monks each night, praying for the woes of the world as they toss and turn in anguished insomnia—with answers only heaven will reveal.

In Christ Alone

For no one can lay a foundation other than
that which is laid, which is Jesus Christ.
—1 Corinthians 3:11

Humble yourselves, therefore, under the mighty hand of God
so that at the proper time he may exalt you. . . .
And after you have suffered a little while, the God of all grace,
who has called you to his eternal glory in Christ,
will himself restore, confirm, strengthen, and establish you.
—1 Peter 5:6, 10

Why is it important for Christians to place their primary hope in heaven? So that they may not grow discouraged when life turns out differently than they expected. So that they would not discourage other people when they suffer, as if something were wrong with them.

And so that when they experience seasons of blessing and prosperity, they would not grow proud. Their hope remains in heaven and there alone. Not until Christ returns again will all things be made new (cf. Revelation 21:5). Remembering that key fact helps keep Christians humble before God and neighbor, no matter their lot.

If believers are to grow in humility, then it will be through Christ alone. Humility is not a person or virtue of its own but has its existence on earth only through the Son of God, who made all things. Humility keeps believers focused on what matters most. Humility keeps believers from becoming distracted. Nothing is more important than for people to grow in faith and humility through Jesus Christ. This life is not all there is.

The famous author John Updike illustrates this point well in his breakout novel, *Rabbit, Run*. One of the main characters in the novel is a young Episcopalian priest named Jack Eccles. Eccles is a smart and urbane minister who is devoted to improving people's lives through his calling. But Harry "Rabbit" Angstrom and his wife prove too difficult for him, and so Eccles seeks out the help of another pastor who is involved with the family, an older, German Lutheran pastor named Fritz Kruppenbach. Eccles visits the home of Kruppenbach, who interrupts his lawn-mowing to receive the younger minister. After Eccles suggests they try to intervene in the couple's marriage together and employ various tactics to help them patch things up, Kruppenbach can take it no longer:

> If God wants to end misery now, He'll declare the Kingdom now. . . . I say you don't know what your role is or you'd be home locked in prayer. *There* is your role: to make yourself an exemplar of faith. *There* is where comfort comes from: faith, not what little finagling a body can do here and there; stirring the bucket. . . . Make no mistake. Now I'm serious. Make no mistake. There is nothing but Christ for us. All the rest, all this decency and busyness, is nothing. It is Devil's work.[12]

If God wanted to end all misery now, He would declare the kingdom fully today; Jesus would come again. His purposes are something greater. In the meantime, those who know Christ should do all they can to serve their neighbors and point them to the only One who can fix them—God. Believers can give the gospel of hope—for this life and the life to come. They can proclaim a city that is not yet here. And believers can assure their loved ones that their suffering is the normal warp and woof of this world, so they should not despair. It is because of this good news that Jesus tells His followers to invite the poor to dinner, to feed them, and to show them a bit of Himself. Christian humility gives a small foretaste of that great banquet that awaits the meek.

Believers do this for a heavenly reward. To live like this is to live by faith. To live like this is to live humbly, setting one's hope fully on the grace to be given when Christ Jesus is revealed.

PRAYER

Christ, as You had ceased not to be a King
because You art like a servant,
nor to be a lion because You were like a lamb,
nor to be God because You were made man,
nor to be a judge because You were judged;

So grant us remembrance
that we will not lose honour by our humility,
but shall, like You, be honoured for our humility
when You come again to make all things new.
—Henry Smith (altered)[13]

CHAPTER NINE

. . . .

TALES FROM THE LOWER TOTEM POLE: HUMILITY TOWARD OTHERS

The Virgin Mary did not vaunt herself but went back and milked the cows, scoured the kettles, and swept the floors like any housemaid.
—**Martin Luther**[1]

Believers can seek to be humble before God, but the real proof is in how they treat others. After all, Christians do not see God, but they do see their neighbors. How believers treat other humans reveals what is actually in their hearts (cf. Matthew 25:31–46; 1 John 4:20). Faith without works is dead. It is impossible to love one's neighbors without practicing humility toward them. If believers are meek before God and modest about themselves, they will increasingly behave humbly toward their neighbors as well. As Murray writes, "Humility before God is nothing if not proved in humility towards men."[2]

Settling at the Bottom by Lifting Others Up

It would be a good contest amongst Christians,
one to labour to give not offence,
and the other to labour to take none.
The best men are severe to themselves, tender over others.
—**Richard Sibbes**[3]

All sorts of biblical injunctions to love others well require believers to display humility. What does it look like to humbly serve others? Let me suggest five areas:

1. Serve One Another in Menial Tasks

This is perhaps the most obvious, and for many, the most difficult way to humble oneself and love others. Since Adam's fall, menial work has become difficult, and naturally, people shy away from it. How often do I put off a chore at home or work hoping someone else will get to it first? Plenty. This is why Paul writes, do not be haughty, but give yourselves to lowly tasks (Romans 12:16). Paul's Greek here is ambiguous, and may read, "but associate with the lowly," which is much the same thing. After all, don't Christians wish to associate with Jesus, the son of a carpenter, born in a stable? Then they will give themselves to lowly tasks. Jesus says as much as He famously washed His disciples' feet:

> "Do you understand what I have done to you? You call me Teacher and Lord, and you are right, for so I am. If I then, your Lord and Teacher, have washed your feet, you also ought to wash one another's feet. For I have given you an example, that you also should do just as I have done to you. Truly, truly, I say to you, a servant is not greater than his master, nor is a messenger greater than the one who sent him." (John 13:12–16)

My church has monthly potluck lunches after worship, which by itself is an appreciated service to the many college students who attend. The church body works hard on the logistics of these lunches, but for my part, I try to do as little as I possibly can. After all, I just served by preaching, I reason. One time, however, we were short-handed during cleanup, and I found myself sweeping the floor. Visiting missionaries saw me and insisted on taking a photo to show their church in the country where they ministered. I asked why and they replied that in that culture, no leader—including pastors—would dream of doing something so menial. It was beneath their dignity. I am glad they caught me on the one Sunday I actually looked like I was working!

Of course, I am being a bit facetious. Menial work obviously includes such things as sweeping floors, but it also includes work done in a cubicle—that tiresome email or flowchart or phone call you do in service to others. When such things are done in humility and love, it is just like washing someone's feet.

2. Defer One's Personal Agenda

One of the greatest sources of conflict between humans is their natural willfulness, which leads them to insist on their own way. People should have opinions and desire excellence, but often what they really want is control. People want to be the ones who call the shots and who take credit when something goes well. A telltale sign of this is the kind of severe micromanaging where someone not only picks the menu but instructs that the napkins should be folded like swans; and if one napkin looks like a wilted duck instead, they blow their tops. One of the cures for such control issues is simply to grow in humility.

Christ is the example. He did not consider equality with God something to be grasped, but emptied Himself, becoming a servant (cf. Philippians 2:3–8). "Not my will, but thy will be done," He prayed at Gethsemane. When believers bear their cross, it often means sacrificial service and also deferring their wills—letting others get their way, especially in minor matters. That is why many scholars believe that the whole letter of Philippians was aimed at two women in particular, as Paul writes toward the end, "I entreat Euodia and I entreat Syntyche to agree in the Lord" (Philippians 4:2). Why? So they can follow the example of their Lord, to "do nothing from rivalry or conceit, but in humility count others more significant than yourselves" (Philippians 2:3).[4]

Sometimes people need to let go of their own opinions or who gets credit for them. Humility always puts the common good ahead of ego. George C. Marshall was the top U.S. Army general in World War II, and then later Secretary of State. Even with such unrivaled accomplishments, he was known for saying, "There is no limit to the good you can do if you don't care who gets the credit."[5] In other words, even if one's ideas are the best, the important thing is seeing them implemented, not getting another feather in one's vanity cap.[6]

Closely connected is the need to remain open-minded and be correctable. After all, "A rebuke goes deeper into a man of understanding than a hundred blows into a fool" (Proverbs 17:10). And when others insist on getting their own way, consider what Paul wrote to the Corinthians concerning lawsuits among believers, "Why not rather suffer wrong?" (1 Corinthians 6:7). What a revolutionary thought for today's litigious society: there might be something more important than getting all that we think is owed us.

3. Do Not Glory in Successes

Believers should boast in their weaknesses, not in their perceived strengths. But how could glorying in one's successes hurt others if the glory is given to God? Suppose two friends studied hard for the same exam, and one received a perfect score while the other barely passed. The one with the good grade may wish to thank God for the success, but if it is done in such a way that the struggling student hears it, it may become a source of great discouragement. It is little different than a football player who catches a touchdown pass, kneels down to credit God but then mockingly points his finger in his opponent's face. Do one or the other, but not both. In fact, maybe doing neither would be an even better policy.

Be careful, especially when God grants success. As Jesus told the seventy-two when they rejoiced that God had given them power to cast out demons, "do not rejoice in this, that the spirits are subject to you, but rejoice that your names are written in heaven" (Luke 10:20).

The proverb says, "He that blesseth his friend with a loud voice, rising early in the morning, it shall be counted a curse to him" (27:14 KJV). The context of words matter, even when the words are good. Do not glory in God's blessings in such a way that one's neighbor is hurt by it. Humility glorifies God precisely by first loving one's neighbor.

4. Speak Only to Bless

Few things reveal pride or humility more than conversations with one another. A straightforward, simple way for believers to show humility toward others comes from James 1:19, "Let every person be quick to hear, slow to speak, slow to anger." This is one of those verses that doesn't need a lot of subtle interpretation: just do it. Listen before talking. Ask questions to try to understand someone rather than as a method of turning the conversation back to oneself. Ask open-ended questions, and in time, questions that go beneath the surface that will enable people to think and express their thoughts. Listening—really listening—is hard work. Often when I meet someone for coffee and they begin to pour out their problems or life story, I find my mind wandering back to my own worries and I have to remind myself to work hard at listening.

This verse does not command believers never to talk but to be slow in doing so. Having led many meetings over the years, I attest that the participants who hold their fire longest are often most listened to when they speak. They have listened to the arguments from all sides, and then weigh in with their considered, dispassionate opinion. This type of speaking shows a wisdom that often carries the day, but more importantly, it shows a sincere love of others.[7]

A close corollary to this principle is that believers should speak only to bless, "Let no corrupting talk come out of your mouths, but only such as is good for building up, as fits the occasion, that it may give grace to those who hear" (Ephesians 4:29). Paul does not just tell believers to watch their mouths, in terms of not cursing or telling off-color jokes, but that they should always speak in such a way that builds others up and gives them grace.

At the same time, this principle of gracious speech does not mean that Christians cannot rebuke someone if it fits the occasion, since love "rejoices with the truth" (1 Corinthians 13:6). Yet Paul is also clear that correction still needs to be in a way meant to build others up, not just to humiliate. Rebukes have their place in slow, godly, gracious speech: "Faithful are the wounds of a friend; profuse are the kisses of an enemy" (Proverbs 27:6).

In Colossians, Paul tells believers to let their "speech always be gracious," and yet "seasoned with salt" (4:6). Think about baking a loaf of bread, for instance. How much salt is added? Just enough. Too much salt will ruin the recipe; and yet no salt at all would make for some bland bread. Let grace be the main ingredient, but scatter in salt as needed.

5. Always Forgive Others

Forgiveness is perhaps the most important and telling marker of humility. Jesus gives a direct warning that if believers do not forgive others they cannot consider themselves saved, "For if you forgive others their trespasses, your heavenly Father will also forgive you, but if you do not forgive others their trespasses, neither will your Father forgive your trespasses" (Matthew 6:14–15). If believers know the depth of their own sins and how they have offended a holy God, they dare not withhold the same forgiveness they themselves have received. Grace not only saves, but it also softens and makes Christians merciful.

Notice how Paul frames the command to forgive in terms of treating one another in the same manner of grace that God has treated us.

Put on then, as God's chosen ones, holy and beloved, compassionate hearts, kindness, humility, meekness, and patience, bearing with one another and, if one has a complaint against

another, forgiving each other; as the Lord has forgiven you, so
you also must forgive. (Colossians 3:12–13)

Forgiveness begins by clothing ourselves with the character of Christ.
In this clothing, Paul uses two different Greek words for humility
(ταπεινοφροσύνην) and meekness (πραΰτητα), for emphasis, I suppose, in light of what follows: forgiving each other; as the Lord has
forgiven you, so you must also forgive. There are two words for humility, followed by two commands to forgive. One does not need to be a
biblical scholar to see the link.

Some have said that believers do not have to forgive until the
offending party has asked for it. I can see some practical wisdom in
such a view. A wife probably does not do her marriage any favors if
she preemptively says to her husband, "I forgive you for burning the
dinner." A better approach is to be quick to listen, slow to speak in
such instances. However, if the idea is that believers do not have to
forgive until they receive an apology, I think such is counter to the
gospel and humility. Jesus's whole point is that we should forgive as the
Lord has forgiven. God's grace is preemptive and unmerited. Believers
should have hearts of gentleness, humbled by grace, instantly ready to
forgive others their sins.

One of the most productive and brilliant pastors was my pastor
during my seminary years. He has had an extraordinary career of scholarship and ministry, serving for decades at a small, blue-collar church
before taking his last call to a large, historic church in downtown
Boston. But it is not his scholarship or preaching skills or leadership
that leave a lasting impression; it is his humility. He often repeated
the idea, "A Christian is someone who is always more offended by his
own sins than those of everyone else." All Christians who have drunk
deeply from the well of grace can confess their faith along with Paul in
this early Christian creed: "The saying is trustworthy and deserving of
full acceptance, that Christ Jesus came into the world to save sinners,
of whom I am the foremost" (1 Timothy 1:15).

Now, objectively speaking, that may not seem true. "What about Hitler?" I can imagine someone asking. No one is responsible before God for anyone's sins except their own. A person's own sins are always the worst they experience because they come from within their own hearts. Yet, remarkably, all of a believer's sins are forgiven through the blood of Christ. There is no higher joy or peace for believers than to be able to forgive others who sin against them as Christ has forgiven them.

This is true with small sins as well as large. As Proverbs tells us, "Good sense makes one slow to anger, and it is his glory to overlook an offense" (19:11). Everyone deserves hell for all eternity apart from God's grace, so who are we to get angry when someone is five minutes late or the waiter brings us a dirty fork?

I anticipate one more question. Must believers forgive their enemies, even their mortal enemies? Jesus answers plainly,

> "You have heard that it was said, 'You shall love your neighbor and hate your enemy.' But I say to you, Love your enemies and pray for those who persecute you, so that you may be sons of your Father who is in heaven. . . . For if you love those who love you, what reward do you have? Do not even the tax collectors do the same?" (Matthew 5:43–46)

Jesus says to love one's enemies, and part of that love is forgiveness. Paul makes it clear that Jesus died for believers while they were yet God's enemies (cf. Romans 5:6–11), and believers are to forgive as the Lord has forgiven them. Vengeance belongs to the Lord. The believer's duty is to obey Jesus by lovingly forgiving their enemies, wishing for them the same grace they have received. Gospel humility demands and enables such love and forgiveness.

Jesus once ate at the home of a Pharisee named Simon, and an unknown woman greeted Jesus by anointing His feet with oil and her own tears. The oil was an expensive way of honoring Jesus as her king; the tears were a heartfelt expression of pure love. When Simon criticized the woman, Jesus responded,

> "You gave me no kiss, but from the time I came in she has not ceased to kiss my feet. You did not anoint my head with oil, but she has anointed my feet with ointment. Therefore I tell you, her sins, which are many, are forgiven—for she loved much. But he who is forgiven little, loves little." (Luke 7:45–47)

If believers know they have been forgiven much, they will forgive much. What else can they do but to live as Christ?

Inviting the Needy into Our Lives

A church in which there are no poor would do well
to raise the question, whether it does not lie outside the pale
of God's election. For "hath not God chosen the poor
of this world rich in faith, and heirs of the kingdom,
which he hath promised to them that love him?"
—John L. Girardeau[8]

As we looked at the brief survey above of what it means to act humbly toward one another, I hope it was obvious that each of these practices stem only from Christ's work in us, as we strive to imitate Him. It stands to reason. As Jesus works a greater holiness in His people, it will cause them to treat others as He has treated them. They will grow in humility toward one another.

As believers wash each other's feet, speak to bless, and forgive others, so they should imitate Jesus in deciding with whom to spend time and minister with their lives. In Luke 14, Jesus instructs His disciples about whom they should invite when they throw a banquet. First, Jesus taught what their attitude ought to be when they are the invited guests (14:7–10). Then Jesus summarizes, "Everyone who exalts himself will be humbled, and he who humbles himself will be exalted" (Luke 14:11). Right after this maxim, Jesus then gives instructions on what believers' attitudes ought to be when they are the ones blessed enough to do the inviting.

> He said also to the man who had invited him, "When you give a dinner or a banquet, do not invite your friends or your brothers or your relatives or rich neighbors, lest they also invite you in return and you be repaid. But when you give a feast, invite the poor, the crippled, the lame, the blind, and you will be blessed, because they cannot repay you. For you will be repaid at the resurrection of the just." (Luke 14:12–14)

Clearly, Jesus is not telling His followers to neglect friends and relatives. Jesus instead emphasizes that when believers serve others, they must not do it in order to be repaid. Do not scratch other people's backs in order to receive something in return. Rather, spend time, energy, and money on those who cannot repay. Take care of the needy.[9]

What does this mean practically? It certainly has financial implications. Christians ought to be about ten percent poorer than their pagan neighbors, if they are faithful in tithing and giving to their local churches. These churches, in turn, should spend the money on God's kingdom causes. In addition, believers may also be prompted to give to worthy charities or persons in need as occasions arise.

There are other ways to give. Pick up the phone and talk or text—check in on someone. Write an email or handwritten note of encouragement or sympathy for those experiencing pain. Cook a meal, loan a car, volunteer in the nursery. Visit a shut-in, just to listen and be present. These all are ways that believers can "invite to a banquet" those who are not able to repay.

Likewise, when believers do gather, they should look around and ask whom they have invited and why. Is there some person or group they are inadvertently excluding because they would not fit?

Have Christians thought through how to include as many people as possible, taking into account things like dress, transportation, work hours, and so forth? Now there may be sound reasons to limit who is invited, depending on the purpose of the group. If a group of financial advisors is meeting to discuss the stock market, I am not sure they need to invite folks from the local dentist association. But when it comes to purely social gatherings—especially those that are church related—Christians should ask if they are only including people like themselves, or if they also invite the "poor, crippled, lame and blind," both literal and figurative.

Early on, a few negative experiences shaped my life and ministry. When I was a young unemployed pastor, after being fired with only one year at my first church, I remember going to ministerial conferences and being introduced to folks. People wanted to know right away who I was and what I did. I would not waste any time and immediately told these older ministers that I was unemployed. Almost always, I could detect two different sets of reactions. Some men were immediately sympathetic and began to ask a series of questions about what they might do to encourage and assist me. Others abruptly began to look past me toward someone else. I could see the calculations in their eyes that they had quickly sized me up and realized I could do nothing useful for them.

Because of this experience, I have made it a goal when I go to conferences and presbytery meetings to meet others simply to get to know them—not to be repaid in my career. I have often failed at living up to this goal, but I try to be aware that there are more ways than one to invite people to a banquet, and more ways than one to exclude them.

Key People or Precious Souls?

When I preach I regard neither doctors nor magistrates,
of whom I have above forty in my congregation;
I have all my eyes on the servant maids and on the children.

And if the learned men are not well pleased
with what they hear, well, the door is open.
—Martin Luther[10]

The church slips into worldly, exclusive thinking at times. I believe Christian organizations can inadvertently ignore Luke 14:12–14 by structuring ministries to target certain sorts of people. Church growth methodologies look for "key people" to invest in—people who can repay the church. New members classes spend considerable time on "spiritual gifts," complete with handy charts that show people just where they can plug in to help the church. Pastors who are really on their toes will get a commitment from new members for a specific area of service before they complete the class. Pastors may soon come to think, *I need to pour myself into that energetic young couple because they can help lead our youth ministries*, rather than thinking, *I need to pour myself into that young couple because they need Christ, period.* But when church leaders get it right, they invite others to the banquet for the right reasons. Then, as part of their discipleship, these new members might be encouraged to serve the wider body with the motivation of love, not plugging some ministry hole.

One of my happiest church members is a young lady who, along with her mother, came to Christ through our body several years ago. This young lady is full of joy and prayer and has tremendous zeal for those still outside of Christ. She also has autism. When I first met her, before her conversion, she was obsessed with Maleficent from Disney's *Sleeping Beauty*, and she had made hundreds of paper cutouts of the villain, which were scattered throughout her house. Now, after having grown in Christ, she is a typical young lady in many ways, but because of her autism and different set of social skills, she is unlikely to become a leader in the normal sense. However, she is always praying, often out loud and with great sincerity during the Sunday worship service. She never tries to hide her sins or moderate her concerns for unbelievers, just stating straight out, "I would like it if you would come to Christ and not have to go to hell." She is pure gold, and I would not trade her for anyone.

Had I or our church looked at her and decided she was not worth the investment of our time, we would be far poorer for it. If we had said she will never be a leader or a people magnet, or a good evangelist, we would have missed out and insulted Jesus at the same time, for He lives in her. As time has passed, we have learned that this young lady is the one throwing a banquet, and we are lucky to get a place at her table. We just have to have eyes to see it. Such is the nature of God's kingdom—a kingdom the world simply cannot understand.

When I was at Army training at Ft. Bragg, North Carolina, as an R.O.T.C. cadet, I was worn out from weeks of constant activity without enough sleep. Cadets were kept busy and rarely allowed time for worship. Most Sundays we were given one minute to pray silently to the "god of our own choosing," as we stood together in formation. I was starved for Christian fellowship and encouragement. Then one week we had an hour of free time, and amazingly a cadet Bible study led by local Ft. Bragg officers was scheduled during that same hour. I eagerly made my way to the chapel and sat down next to a major and colonel. After ten minutes of waiting, no one else showed up so they looked at their watches and one said to the other, "Well, do you want to try again next week?" They got up and went to their cars. One cadet was not enough for them.

Since that experience I have determined never to despise whomever God would send me, no matter how few in number. I have not been entirely perfect in this, but almost always when I lead a Bible study or teach a lesson, if one or two show up, that is enough for me; it is whom God has ordained. Jesus limited Himself to twelve men and often just to Peter, James, and John. Am I greater than my Master? When throwing a feast, invite those who cannot repay.

Humility and Social Status

Again I saw that under the sun the race is not to the swift,
nor the battle to the strong, nor bread to the wise,
nor riches to the intelligent, nor favor to those with knowledge,
but time and chance happen to them all.

—**Ecclesiastes 9:11**

Luke 14 could not be applied thoroughly without addressing the sensitive subject of how various social classes should relate to each other in the church. Not everyone will agree on how this should work out, and so we should all maintain our opinions gently and learn from one another. As we have seen, Christ's kingdom is "already, and not yet" fully here. Thus, the New Testament's teaching on social justice is nuanced and much debated. Christians should, however, resist the mind-set of secular culture, which evaluates happiness primarily in terms of material and economic well-being. The study of history is reduced to power struggles between classes and interest groups. Believers must resist such a simplistic impulse, even as they seek a more just society. Humility suggests a deeper way.

In order to love people, Christians know they must treat others fairly and with dignity as those equally created in the image of God. Must they also aim to make everyone equal in terms of wealth and power? The New Testament's answer is an unambiguous no. Class distinctions are clearly maintained, and believers are to seek humility in accordance with their own stations. Obviously, how this works out is tricky business since Christians are called to care for the poor. "They asked us to remember the poor, the very thing I was eager to do," Paul says in Galatians 2:10. Paul harshly rebukes the Corinthians for the class distinctions within the church that exclude the poor from their celebration of the Lord's Supper (1 Corinthians 10:16–17; 11:17–34). The New Testament is clear that in the church, "there is neither Jew nor Greek, there is neither slave nor free, there is no male and female, for you are all one in Christ Jesus" (Galatians 3:28). All believers are royal priests, equal together in Christ (1 Peter 2:9).

The New Testament, however, is not interested in upending social structures as a whole. Husbands and wives are coequal in Christ but maintain their distinct roles (Ephesians 5:21–33; Colossians 3:18–19; 1 Peter 3:1–7). The elderly are to be given particular honor and respect (1 Timothy 5:1–2; Titus 2:2–4). For the most part, servants and masters stay servants and masters (Ephesians 6:5–9; 1 Timothy 6:1–2; 1 Peter 2:18–21). The gospel has come to do greater things than to restructure current social structures. As Peter writes,

> Be subject for the Lord's sake to every human institution, whether it be to the emperor as supreme, or to governors as sent by him to punish those who do evil and to praise those who do good. . . . Honor everyone. Love the brotherhood. Fear God. Honor the emperor. (1 Peter 2:13–14, 17)

Peter presents a priority of ethics: honor all, love believers, fear God, and in all this, obey human government. Remember that Peter wrote this to Christians under the rule of the brutal, cruel, pagan Roman Empire. But what about those in the lowest dregs of society, those who were unjustly owned by other men? Peter goes on,

> Servants, be subject to your masters with all respect, not only to the good and gentle but also to the unjust. For this is a gracious thing, when, mindful of God, one endures sorrows while suffering unjustly. For what credit is it if, when you sin and are beaten for it, you endure? But if when you do good and suffer for it you endure, this is a gracious thing in the sight of God. For to this you have been called, because Christ also suffered for you, leaving you an example, so that you might follow in his steps. (1 Peter 2:18–21)

So Peter tells believers in unjust social situations to endure their suffering and not seek political revolution. Why? Because such service imitates their Lord. In order to drive home his point that the gospel came to do something different and greater than social restructuring, Peter explains what Christ did by His suffering:

> He committed no sin, neither was deceit found in his mouth. When he was reviled, he did not revile in return; when he suffered, he did not threaten, but continued entrusting himself to him who judges justly. He himself bore our sins in his body on the tree, that we might die to sin and live to righteousness. By his wounds you have been healed. For you were straying like sheep, but have now returned to the Shepherd and Overseer of your souls. (1 Peter 2:22–25)

Jesus came to save souls for all eternity. What can be more important or wonderful? The church must resist the impulses of its surrounding secular culture to measure importance by money, power, and social status. Paul presents the same social ethics in such places as Romans 13, Ephesians 6, and Colossians 3.[11] The gospel radically restructures relationships within the church, but not in society as a whole—at least, not yet.

Of course, whole libraries have been written about the impact Christianity should have upon society, and almost every Christian tradition holds that the gospel has at least some positive leavening impact wherever it goes. As a rule, Christianity lifts people up, promotes human rights, opposes tyranny, ends slavery, and so forth. Many believers have professional callings devoted to such good ends and deserve the church's support and respect. This book is not the place to explore further that dynamic or to describe the differences between New Testament-era slavery and later, race-based chattel slavery. Yet, despite these differences, New Testament slavery was still an inequitable system. Paul pleads with Philemon to release the runaway slave, Onesimus, and he tells slaves to gain their freedom if they can (1 Corinthians 7:21).

Paul, however, does not command Philemon to release Onesimus; rather he wants Philemon to do so willingly, out of love and from a sanctified heart (cf. Philemon 8, 9, 21). In Corinthians, Paul tells slaves that if they cannot gain their freedom, "do not be concerned about it." Why? Because "he who was called in the Lord as a slave is a freedman of the Lord. . . . So, brothers, in whatever condition each was called, there let him remain with God" (1 Corinthians 7:20–24). In other words, slaves (or bondservants) should not be overly concerned about their social status because they belong to Christ and have a heavenly inheritance. The biblical eschatology of hope keeps believers from becoming consumed with social restructuring, even as they care for the poor and advocate for the rights of the oppressed.

Paul tells both slaves and masters to treat one another with respect and humility (Ephesians 6:5–9; Colossians 3:22–4:1). He does not tell them to switch positions. Paul pleads with Philemon to do the right thing, but he does not require it. Why not? Because the more imperative ethic in the New Testament is that of growing in grace—not social justice, as important as that is. When change does come, it comes from the heart. Whatever injustice is not corrected will be recompensed in glory. That is the kind of humility that the gospel calls believers to when it comes to grappling with social status and power. Christians must stand up for others when they are oppressed, but when it comes to their own unjust situations, they are to imitate their Lord, who Himself was oppressed. This does not mean that believers cannot use the legal system to the best of their advantage; Paul does just that in Acts. However, they are never to use violence for their own advancement, nor seek to make the social structures of this world perfectly imitate the equality and love they find within the church.[12]

In his seminal essay, "Charity and Its Fruits," Jonathan Edwards describes the biblical attitude regarding social status this way:

Humility will further tend to prevent a leveling behavior. Some persons are always ready to level those above them down to themselves, while they are never willing to level those below them up to their own position. But he that is under the influence of humility will avoid both these extremes. On the one hand, he will be willing that all should rise just so far as their diligence and worth of character entitle them to, and on the other hand, he will be willing that his superiors should be known and acknowledged in their place, and have rendered to them all the honors that are their due. He will not desire that all should stand upon the same level, for he knows it is best that there should be gradations in society: that some should be above others, and should be honored and submitted to as such. And therefore he is willing to be content with this divine arrangement.[13]

Humility accepts one's station in life, knowing that in God's sight, social status in this life is far secondary to the matters that will last into eternity. Why else would Jesus say, "But many who are first will be last, and the last first" (Mark 10:31)?

Believers in positions of privilege should still use their power to assist those in need. The wealthy are to be especially generous and ready to share (1 Timothy 6:17–19). Bosses and magistrates should treat their employees and subjects with equity and respect. My first Army boss gave me sage career advice. We can look to those above us and try to impress them or we can look to those under our care and try to do right by them. Always, he said, look below. I think such advice is in accord with Christian ethics and humility. Those in positions "above" should do all they can to rule well in service to those they lead. Others have callings to public service or to lead societal reform for the common good. But if such service is to last into eternal reward, it must come from sanctified hearts doing it first for Christ.

Remembering this biblical set of priorities helps believers to remain humble in light of so much social injustice. In America, obviously, it is impossible to talk about matters of social justice without considering the even more sensitive subject of race relations, particularly between whites and African-Americans. This is not the book for a discussion on race, and frankly, as one with a white, middle-class suburban upbringing, I am not able to talk much about what it means to be humble in these matters. Believers who have not experienced much racial prejudice must humble themselves and learn about suffering from those who have. What I can do is tell the stories of those who have suffered racial oppression and emerged from it with a Christ-laden humility, rather than the hatred and anger the world tells them is their birthright.

I think of the African-American inmates in that prison in the Deep South who welcomed me in to preach, even though I did not have the slightest idea how to relate to them. They received me with joy and treated me like I was one of them, their brother in Christ. I think of the black pastor who also served as the janitor for our predominantly white congregation. I knew a bit about his background, how he had grown up poor and gotten into trouble with the law, spending his youth in and out of jail. The Lord had captured him, prospered him, and called him to be a pastor of a growing church. I knew he was doing well enough financially that he did not need to be our church's janitor. When I asked him why he worked for us even though he did not need the money, he told me, "I don't ever want to forget where I came from. It is my privilege to serve your church." A white brother could never have suggested such a regimen; it had to come from within, from Christ. Nor does the world understand such a mind-set in light of so much racial injustice. Only the gospel can work this kind of humility in human hearts.

I think of the ninety-three-year-old African-American saint who lived in my neighborhood and allowed me the great privilege of administering her last communion before she went home to glory. She had grown up in rural Virginia during the era of segregation and Jim Crow, educated with hand-me-down books in a Negro public school that met in the basement of her Presbyterian church, broken windows and all. She studied and worked hard, leaving a legacy of accomplished children, all of whom earned advanced degrees in the field of education and had distinguished careers.

I love history and talking to older folks about their experiences. Time and time again, I pressed her and her children for details on the prejudice and racial hatred they must have undergone for decades. They each had stories—stories of humiliation and injustice, stories which made me rage inwardly.

This was also a family who loved their Lord and embodied His sweetness, and so they also had the story of the gospel. As much as I pressed them and gave them permission to express their anger freely, I never heard a word of resentment, bitterness, or even frustration about their past. They said they tried to make the most of the situation they were born into. All they displayed was a humble gratitude to God for His many blessings. I hardly knew what to do. What does one do in the midst of such love in the face of such injustice? Nothing but to soak it in and hope some of it rubs off a little.

The View from the Bottom

*Who knows? Perhaps if God had given us
greater talent, better health, a more personable appearance,
we might have lost our souls! Let us then be content
with what God has given us.*
—Alphonsus de Liguori[14]

When I was a boy playing outside with other kids, occasionally without warning some rascal would yell, "Dog pile!" This compelled us to immediately jump on top of one another until our collective weight collapsed and some poor sap ended up at the bottom, hoping it did not last too long. The view was never scenic.

That is the way a number of believers still view life, even among Christian brothers and sisters. Some believers push and pull and strive to end up on top, looking down at everyone. They want to sit atop life's totem pole, monarch of all. But when folks are in Christ and have His heart, such a lofty perch will soon grow lonely. Believers are made in Christ to serve, to put others first. If they do not, they have no health, no joy. Sin takes Christians away from others, isolates them, and feeds their pride. They can grow callous and hollow, serving only themselves, even if it seems they are at the top of a great company of admirers.

But when focused on Christ, when believers find themselves at the top of the totem pole in their worldly office—perhaps a worksite foreman or church elder or exhausted mother—they will see it as Jesus sees it: a way to serve those beneath them as they try to lead faithfully. Believers grow in their humility toward one another by remembering Jesus and His love. He is in charge and puts people just where He means to, whether rich or poor, slave or free, black or white. Humanly speaking, the pole stays upright, and the people on top remain in charge. Spiritually speaking, believers understand that the way up is the way down. Soon enough, they will find themselves yelling "Dog pile!" hoping that somehow they will end up at the bottom, smothered and happy.

PRAYER

Lord, truly humble us
so that we do not become so easily angry,
nor so harsh or critical of others.

Keep us compassionate and tender
to the infirmities of our fellow-sinners,
knowing that if there is a difference between us,
it is by your grace alone.

Remind us that we have the seeds
of every evil in our own hearts.

And under all our trials and afflictions,
cause us to look to thy hand,
to lay our mouths in the dust,
acknowledging that we suffer much less
than our iniquities have deserved.

—adopted from John Newton[15]

Humility Applied—Love

*Then Jesus said to the crowds and to his disciples,
"The scribes and the Pharisees sit on Moses' seat, so practice and
observe whatever they tell you—but not what they do. For they
preach, but do not practice. They tie up heavy burdens, hard to
bear, and lay them on people's shoulders, but they themselves are not
willing to move them with their finger.*

*They do all their deeds to be seen by others.
For they make their phylacteries broad and their fringes long,
and they love the place of honor at feasts and the best seats
in the synagogues and greetings in the marketplaces
and being called rabbi by others.*

*But you are not to be called rabbi, for you have one teacher,
and you are all brothers. And call no man your father on earth, for
you have one Father, who is in heaven. Neither be called instructors,
for you have one instructor, the Christ.
The greatest among you shall be your servant.*

***Whoever exalts himself will be humbled,
and whoever humbles himself will be exalted."***

—JESUS, THE CHRIST,
MATTHEW 23:1–12 (EMPHASIS ADDED)

CHAPTER TEN

· · · ·

THE ASSEMBLY OF EGOS: HUMILITY TOGETHER

Solitude is not the scene of Pride;
the danger of pride is in company, when we meet to look upon another.
—**John Donne**[1]

And they devoted themselves to the apostles' teaching
and the fellowship, to the breaking of bread and the prayers.
—**Acts 2:42**

In his classic book *Life Together*, the German pastor Dietrich Bonhoeffer is sometimes uncomfortably specific in his applications. For instance, on the importance of singing in unity, Bonhoeffer writes,

> There are some destroyers of unison singing in the fellowship that must be rigorously eliminated. There is no place in the service of worship where vanity and bad taste can so intrude as in the singing. . . . There is the bass or the alto who must call everybody's attention to his astonishing range. . . . There is the solo voice that goes swaggering, swelling, blaring, and tremulant from a full chest and drowns out everything else to the glory of its own fine organ. . . . and finally, there are often those also who because of some mood will not join in the singing and thus disturb the fellowship. Unison singing, difficult as it is, is less of a musical than a spiritual matter.[2]

As someone who loves to sing loudly—if not always well—I cringe when I read this critique, and frankly, I am not sure I entirely agree. But at least Bonhoeffer is asking the question of what humility should look like in the church together.

That is not a question the church often asks today. How should Christians gather in a way that reflects the humility of the gospel? What does it mean for believers to be humble together, meek as a group? If humility should be the chief hallmark of the faithful Christian, surely the same should be said of Christians living together—the church. Humility should mark the congregation as a whole. What do humble churches look like? That is what this next section attempts to answer.

Humility and Membership in Christ's Body

Likewise, you who are younger, be subject to the elders.
Clothe yourselves, all of you, with humility toward one another,
for "God opposes the proud but gives grace to the humble."
—1 Peter 5:5

People were made to be in community, and the only way believers can grow in any lasting way is in close communion with other believers. The Scriptures are crystal clear on this point, from Genesis 1, where God made man with the command to multiply, to Revelation, where heaven is portrayed as a banquet and a city and a vast worship service with the saints gathered around God's throne together. In a very real and formal sense, Christians should therefore belong to a local body of believers who mutually submit to one another in love.

This local body is one that has structure and authority under Christ. The author of Hebrews commands believers to "obey your leaders and submit to them, for they are keeping watch over your souls, as those who will have to give an account" (Hebrews 13:17). Presumably, these leaders are the elders of the local congregation, as seen in Acts 20, 1 Timothy 3, and elsewhere. Hebrews assumes that Christians actively participate in a congregation with some sort of structure and leadership. Paul likewise assumes some kind of formal membership in the local church when he instructs the Corinthians to expel an unrepentant immoral man from their body in 1 Corinthians 5. If they did not have some kind of church membership roll, how would removing a man be possible? Certainly not by physical force; the church is never enjoined to do this, for its weapons are not the weapons of this world. There must have been formal membership in the church at Corinth.

This sense of community and dependency comes with difficulty to many Americans, with our tradition of rugged individualism and moral relativism. Henry Fairlie observes,

> "Doing one's own thing," or any of the other similar passwords of our time, such as "I'm OK, you're OK," may seem to have little Pride in them. Where is the claim to superiority in them? Do they not merely ask to be allowed to live and let live? But what we eventually find in them is an assertion of self-sufficiency—a denial of one's *need for community* with others, which is in fact a form of selfishness, since it is always accompanied by a refusal of one's *obligation of community* with others.[3]

So it is with believers who claim they are trusting Christ, but proudly refuse to join with His body, preferring their own authority and opinions over those of the assembled saints. If believers are to grow in humility in any sort of serious and lasting fashion, it will almost always be through membership and participation in a local, faithful church.

Augustine tells the story of a famous pagan rhetorician named Victorinus who converted to Christianity at the height of his career, "bending his neck under the yoke of humility and his forehead to the ignominy of the Cross." Yet he chose to keep his faith private in order to protect his reputation among his pagan colleagues. His friend Simplicianus answered, "I shall not believe it nor count you among the

Christians unless I see you in the Church of Christ," to which Victorinus replied, "Then is it the walls that makes Christians?" Soon enough, Victorinus knew he must publicly confess his faith before men if he were to be faithful to Christ. Augustine describes his change of heart:

> He felt that he was guilty of a great crime in being ashamed of the sacraments of the lowliness of Your Word, when he had not been ashamed of the sacrilegious rites of those demons of pride whom in his pride he had worshipped. So he grew proud towards vanity and humble towards truth.[4]

When believers grow proud toward vanity and humble toward truth, the expectation is that the newly humbled believers will profess their faith publicly and join Christ's church. God's grace is great, and there are certainly many who will be in heaven who for various reasons never take this step. However, publicly professing faith and joining a local congregation are a normal outworking of the humility formed and cultivated by saving faith.

There is a delightful older man in my congregation who took a while to make this step. His wife had joined and become involved in the church years earlier, but he politely declined. When I visited him, it was obvious that he understood and believed the gospel. He read his Bible every day. For various health and social reasons, he had never been baptized or regularly attended worship. The day came when he decided it was time to make his faith public. Due to his health, he told me he would do his best to get through the ninety-minute worship service in which he was baptized, but he could not promise me much after that. That was fine, the elders told him, as we interviewed and approved him for baptism. We baptized him on the first Sunday of January several years ago, and he has barely missed a Sunday service since. Joining the church did not save him, but his saving faith led to a humility that naturally submitted itself to baptism and church membership. Once he joined, he did not want to leave.

Humility Submits to the Means of Grace

"Abide in me, and I in you. As the branch cannot bear fruit
by itself, unless it abides in the vine, neither can you,
unless you abide in me. I am the vine; you are the branches.
Whoever abides in me and I in him, he it is that bears much fruit,
for apart from me you can do nothing."

—Jesus, John 15:4–5

So how practically does growth in humility occur in the church, besides the occasions of service and conflict that community inevitably provide? Very simply, believers grow in humility together under the three clear means of grace God provides: Word, prayer, and sacrament.

I would argue that one criterion for judging a church's humility is the degree it trusts these simple means of grace from God, compared to its own programs, its own wisdom. Fancy programs and performances may look impressive, but anything not built upon Christ will simply burn up in the end (1 Corinthians 3:10–15). This is part of what it means to live by faith and not sight. It is pride that feeds the eyes. In my current church, the leaders try not to promote anything not in accord with these three means of grace, adopting the simple motto that "we grow in grace through the Word, Sacraments and Prayer, along with discipleship, fellowship and care." But here is the key: a church that focuses on the Word, prayer, and sacraments alone will be utterly boring—unless the Holy Spirit is on the move. He alone keeps it humble and vibrant.

Humility under the Word

Since faith comes by hearing the Word of Christ (Romans 10:17), and the beginning of wisdom is the fear of the Lord (Proverbs 1:7), it stands to reason that growing in humility together begins with sitting under God's Word together. A church that has abandoned the Bible as its authority, either formally or practically, is, by definition, proud. They lean on their own understanding, are wise in their own eyes, and will not be spiritually healthy until they turn again to the authority of the written Word (Proverbs 3:5–8).

In contrast, a humble church yearns and thirsts for what God has for them in the Bible, receiving "with meekness the implanted word, which is able to save your souls" (James 1:21). God's Word should play a central part in Christians' worship, being read and sung throughout the service in the calls to worship, the confessions of faith and sin, the singing of psalms and hymns, and the benedictions. The members are Bereans, searching the Scriptures daily to discover the truth (Acts 17:11). Like the Bereans, they will do this search together, in community, as the church. Studying the Scriptures together helps protect one another from idiosyncratic and dangerous interpretations. Insights arrived at individually can easily lead to heresy.[5]

I once received a call from a man who had apparently been excommunicated from another local church. The man knew I was familiar with this church's leaders, and he wanted me to appeal his case with them. I allowed that they might be in error, since no church is perfect. However, before I would consider helping him in this matter, I needed to know his current church attendance situation. He was not worshiping anywhere. I invited him to attend our church, with the promise that after faithful attendance of a few months, I would talk to him about his case. He told me had no need to attend any church. "What about learning God's Word?" I asked. He replied, "Why would I need to sit under a pastor for that? I have my own Bible." I bid him farewell and wished him well. I couldn't help him; no intervention can supersede the pride that thinks it cannot learn truth from others—especially God's Word entrusted to His church.

At the same time, it is vitally important that preachers likewise sit under the authority of the Word. One of the earliest battles I lost in my current congregation was a discussion about who could read Scripture during the worship service. I still remember one elder telling me that it was important for the congregation to see that "the pastor did not own the Bible—that they see you sitting under it with the rest of us while a regular member ascends the pulpit to read." That is a battle I am glad I lost; I love first sitting under God's Word before having the privilege of standing and proclaiming the gospel from the text. I am but a steward of these mysteries.

That is why preachers must not come before God's people in self-confidence, puffed up with their own studies, but they come with weakness, fear, and trembling. Their confidence must be solely in the Spirit of the crucified Christ working through their weakness (1 Corinthians 2:1–4; 8:1). Why? Paul says, "so that your faith might not rest in the wisdom of men but in the power of God" (1 Corinthians 2:5). Preachers are mere messenger boys proclaiming tidings of great joy. They dare not rely on charming anecdotes or personal charisma. After all, they preach not themselves, but Christ as Lord.

Humility in Prayer

If one evaluation of a congregation's humility is how much it heeds God's Word together, then surely another is how much it prays together. The practice of prayer is hard to quantify, since God alone knows the heart, and yet the amount of time spent in prayer is not irrelevant. For instance, is there a church-wide prayer meeting open to all? Do small groups spend time in prayer together? Are business meetings opened and closed in prayer? Do the elders pause at crucial parts in their meetings to seek the Lord's mind? Most significantly, are the worship services themselves full of prayer? After all, believers are meeting with God, which means in part actually talking to Him.

Second Chronicles 7:14 is talking about the church, not the United States, when it says, "If my people who are called by my name humble themselves, and pray and seek my face and turn from their wicked ways, then I will hear from heaven and will forgive their sin and heal their land." Believers are the New Israel (cf. Acts 2, 15; Galatians 6:16), and the land is the church. Before they can address their fellow countrymen, Christians first need to humble themselves, repent, and pray. A humble church is a praying church.

A church that does not pray much does not sense its need for God's grace much. I say this from personal experience because disciplined prayer has never come easily for me. One of the greatest marks of my own pride has been not praying as I should.

Two things have kept me going. First, as I have become older I have more clearly seen my own weaknesses and vulnerability in daily life. So what do I do? I pray more, throughout the day, about all sorts of things, big and small. What else can I do? I need God more than I once did, or at least I know that now. I know that I must fight my spiritual battles in weakness, wearing Christ's armor, not my own (Ephesians 6:10–20).[6] So I pray. Perhaps this is precisely what means to grow in humility.

Second, when my own prayer life has been deficient, praying in community with my Christian brothers and sisters has kept me growing. Weekly and sometimes daily prayer meetings have kept me close to Christ when my own walk was weak. I cannot tell you the number of times I have tried to tackle in prayer a personal problem of mental anguish—perhaps even a demonic attack—to no effect, but as soon as I humbled myself to ask my wife or a brother to pray, the resolution was almost instantaneous. Surely, Christ alone is my mediator and God can answer any prayer, but perhaps God was making my humility concrete. After all, even the great apostle Paul asked prayer for boldness and for clarity (cf. Ephesians 6:19; Colossians 4:4). "No man is an island, entire of itself," writes John Donne, and perhaps that is about prayer as much as anything.[7]

A humble church is a house of prayer, a place where believers lower themselves before one another in their need, and then lift one another up in love to the loving Savior. A humble church is a dependent church, trusting God alone to bless its simple efforts, so that when they prosper, they know it was only by His hand. *Soli Deo gloria.*

Humility in the Sacraments

There is a sense in which discussing one's need for humility in the sacraments is altogether backwards; in the sacraments God humbles Himself before His people. In His Word, God speaks, and believers are to submit to what He commands and promises. In the sacraments, God condescends to His people's weakness by giving them visible signs and seals of the gospel to reinforce their faith. The Word remains primary in forming and nurturing faith, but the sacraments strengthen faith by visibly confirming God's promises to believers in Christ.[8] The sacraments are ordinances of humility also because God participates with believers in their weakness. Jesus gives believers Himself. Baptism and the Lord's Supper both point to Christ's weakness on believers' behalf, to His death on the cross in their place. They are also wonderful reminders that heaven is real and corporeal, that our bodies will be physically resurrected as surely as Christ's.

So to talk about the believer's need for humility in the sacraments is almost ridiculous. It is due to Christ's humility that the church even has sacraments. It is simply impossible to participate faithfully in the sacraments apart from humility, for in them, believers embrace Christ's life. They bury themselves in Christ (Romans 6:3–4) and claim His life as their own. To be baptized and to take the bread and the wine is precisely to ask for Christ's humility to be embodied in oneself, more and more.

Paul offers the following warning about taking the Lord's Supper proudly and without proper self-examination:

> Whoever, therefore, eats the bread or drinks the cup of the Lord in an unworthy manner will be guilty concerning the body and blood of the Lord. Let a person examine himself, then, and so eat of the bread and drink of the cup. For anyone who eats and drinks without discerning the body eats and drinks judgment on himself. (1 Corinthians 11:27–29)

What does Paul mean that believers must "discern the body"? Certainly, in part, it means to look at the bread and recognize that it is holy, part of a sacred meal in communion with God Himself. The context suggests that much more is involved. Apparently, the Lord's Supper in Corinth was part of a larger meal (1 Corinthians 11:18–22, 33–34), and the rich were eating lavishly and not sharing their food with the poor. Paul says the Corinthians eviscerated the sacrament altogether with this practice (verse 20), and God was not with them in this meal. Paul's warning to "discern the body" echoes what he had already written, "The bread that we break, is it not a participation in the body of Christ? Because there is one bread, we who are many are one body, for we all partake of the one bread" (1 Corinthians 10:16b–17). The "body," then, is not just Christ symbolized by the loaf of bread, but also the body of Christ, the church.

To discern the body in the Lord's Supper then means to consider the whole body of Christ. The sacrament is communal in its very essence. Baptism and communion are always to be public, except perhaps in rare and extreme circumstances. The whole congregation is to celebrate the sacrament together. It is impossible to be baptized or take the Lord's Supper without an attendant humility toward one another, by participating in the church together.

Several applications arise from this teaching. Every part of Christ's body is valuable, no matter how seemingly insignificant and marginal (1 Corinthians 12:22). This is one reason why many Christian churches baptize the infant children of their members, understanding them as part of Christ's visible body. Paul says Christians need each part of Christ's body, not valuing one member over another, so "that there may be no division in the body, but that the members may have the same care for one another" (1 Corinthians 12:25). Believers should feel that mutual dependence every time they break the bread together, excluding none who have confessed their faith and belong to Christ, no matter how marginal they may seem.

At the same time, Paul says, "If one member suffers, all suffer together; if one member is honored, all rejoice together" (1 Corinthians 12:26). Rejoicing in another's success when one suffers is a difficult task. As Pastor Ames in *Gilead* confesses, "'Rejoice with those who rejoice.' I have found that difficult too often. I was much better at weeping with those who weep."[9] Yet, taking the supper together unites believers in Christ as one body. Believers suffer and rejoice with one another, whether they feel it or not. The key is to let one's feelings and affections catch up with reality by sharing one cup and loaf.

Sharing one loaf does not, however, mean all Christians are just one bland lump of dough, indistinguishable from one another. Paul explains, "Now there are varieties of gifts, but the same Spirit; and there are varieties of service, but the same Lord. . . . For the body does not consist of one member but of many" (1 Corinthians 12:4–5, 14). Each believer plays a part. Humility embraces one's own role, while encouraging others in theirs. This may involve recognizing the varying measure or degree of those gifts, "Grace was given to each one of us according to the measure of Christ's gift" (Ephesians 4:7). Believers' roles in Christ's body are varied, but their goal and their Lord are the same. Humility accepts and rejoices in this great grace, the privilege of life together in Christ.

Humility in Church Discipline

The end of all things is at hand; therefore be self-controlled and sober-minded for the sake of your prayers. Above all, keep loving one another earnestly, since love covers a multitude of sins.
—**1 Peter 4:7–8**

Church discipline is not well known or practiced today, but historically it was considered one of the three marks of the visible church, along with the Word and sacraments. In other words, a congregation was part of Christ's one, holy, apostolic, and catholic church if it preached God's Word faithfully, administered the sacraments, and exercised church discipline. This last mark is the means by which a church maintains the integrity of its membership, so that those who openly reject the gospel are warned, and if need be, removed from membership, excommunicated (cf. Matthew 18:15–18). The purpose of such church discipline is a form of discipleship, teaching the baptized to obey all that Jesus commands, which is, after all, part of the Great Commission (Matthew 28:18–20). But Jesus's main command is that believers simply trust Him to save their souls, apart from their own works (John 6:29). Thus, the ultimate purpose of church discipline is always an attempt to reclaim sinners, to exhort them to believe the gospel, and cast themselves on Christ's mercy, "for everyone who calls on the name of the Lord will be saved" (Romans 10:13).

The practice of such church discipline is indispensable to a faithful, humble church as they pursue Christ together. How can a church remain faithful if it tolerates the stiff-necked and high-blown within its midst? A humble church insists that all its members be humble, which is to say, trusting Christ, despite their ongoing struggles with various sins and prides. At the same time, leaders must pursue all such discipline gently and humbly themselves, keeping a close watch on their own hearts (Galatians 6:1).

Church discipline can work remarkable humility in its recipients, and it often brings encouragement to the whole congregation. When sinners are restored by the grace of God, the whole church is reminded of their own salvation that is by that same grace alone. In this sense, James 5 can apply to the case of a man or woman caught in great sin.

> Is anyone among you sick? Let him call for the elders of the church, and let them pray over him, anointing him with oil in the name of the Lord. And the prayer of faith will save the one who is sick, and the Lord will raise him up. And if he has committed sins, he will be forgiven. Therefore, confess your sins to one another and pray for one another, that you may be healed. (James 5:14–16a)

This is largely an instruction to those who are physically ill, not those caught in sin. Note, nonetheless, that James introduces the confession of sin. Physical illnesses are not connected to specific sins in most cases (cf. Job 1; John 9:3). Somehow, however, confession of sin is related to coming before the elders for prayer. Why? Look at the specific vocabulary that James uses. He promises that the "prayer of faith will save the one who is sick, and the Lord will raise him up." The word for "saved" here is the same for spiritual salvation, although some translations prefer "heal" or "restore." Physical healing is not promised each time believers pray in faith. Rather, James is promising spiritual salvation to any who come before the elders in weakness and faith, asking for prayer. Very often, I believe, they will be physically healed as well (at least I have often seen it), but the one promise we can absolutely bank on is that, no matter what happens, "they will be raised up" in Christ one day. "If he has committed sins, they will be forgiven." Whether sick or sinful, could anything be more encouraging than that?

It is in view of that encouragement that James then says, "confess your sins to one another and pray for one another, that you may be healed." Such public confession requires great humility. That is why James also tells the elders to anoint with oil. What function did the oil perform? In Mark 6:13 Jesus sends out the Twelve to heal the sick and anoint them with oil, all in light of the promises found in Isaiah 61, that the coming Messiah would "proclaim the year of the Lord's favor . . . to comfort all who mourn . . . to give them a beautiful headdress instead of ashes, the oil of gladness instead of mourning" (verses 2–3). Oil represents nothing less than the gospel—that those who are cast down and brokenhearted will be lifted up in Christ. The elders represent Jesus's goodness to those who come in humble confession by granting them prayer and a beautiful headdress— the oil of gladness.

Believers may be poor, brokenhearted, mournful, and sick, but they are blessed in God's sight, highly exalted in Christ. It takes great humility to receive this blessing, to come and formally ask for the congregation's leaders to pray. But believers will not regret it if they do. The whole purpose of church discipline is to restore the offender to God's grace, the very thing that will not be denied to any who seek it. When those caught in sin come in sincere faith and repentance to their church, there should be nothing there for them but grace, forgiveness, and love.

I think of church members who struggled over and over with sin, even serious and life-threatening sins. However, they confessed it and submitted to whatever discipline the elders deemed wise. Despite their transgressions, they continued to love Jesus and to need His grace. In time, in every case, as they humbled themselves through the process of church discipline, God has exalted and prospered these struggling members. I count their restored lives as the greatest joy of my pastoral ministry. Love covers over a multitude of sins (1 Peter 4:8), just as Christ's blood has done for me. What a joy it is to serve communion to those who have thought themselves disqualified, to put my arm around them as I give them the bread and wine, to remind them that the work of Christ is sufficient. They are now perfectly loved and accepted by His grace alone. Church discipline, indeed.

The Humble Church

For what we proclaim is not ourselves, but Jesus Christ as Lord,
with ourselves as your servants for Jesus' sake.
—2 Corinthians 4:5

A humble church relies on God's simple means of grace, trusting His wisdom more than their own. It is a church that loves God's Word and submits to it in all its precepts. It is a church that is desperate for God's strength and so spends much of its time together on its face in prayer. It is a church that boldly feeds on Christ in the sacraments, grabbing all the grace they can and reveling in it together, knowing they are one body, all sinners saved by Christ alone. It is a church that helps one another grow in godliness by humbly confronting one another in love, and gladly submitting to gracious church discipline. For everyone who humbles themselves will be exalted.

In doing all these things, the humble church will constantly point everyone to Christ and His glory. They will also be aware of the subtleties of pride, which puffs them up with the thought that they alone are the ones getting it right, in the face of so many worldly churches around them. Aware of this danger, they will not promote themselves as anything special. They will promote no brand except Christ and the gospel of grace for all kinds of sinners. If no one notices them in the process, what does it matter, as long as souls are being saved, lives restored, and God glorified? That is the humble church.

I am grateful that I have had this modeled for me in several congregations in my life. I have seen it in the flesh. Such congregations exist and are wondrous places of beauty and joy. They are gardens in a world of factories.

PRAYER

Blest be the tie that binds
our hearts in Christian love;
the fellowship of kindred minds
is like to that above.

Before our Father's throne
we pour our ardent prayers;
our fears, our hopes, our aims are one,
our comforts and our cares.

We share our mutual woes,
our mutual burdens bear,
and often for each other flows
the sympathizing tear.

From sorrow, toil, and pain,
and sin, we shall be free;
and perfect love and friendship reign
through all eternity.

—John Fawcett[10]

CHAPTER ELEVEN

· · · ·

LIKE MEN SENTENCED TO DEATH: CHRISTIAN LEADERSHIP AS HUMILITY

Are you thinking to construct some mighty tower in height?
First think of the foundation of humility.
So then you see even a building is low before it is high,
and the top is raised only after humiliation.

—**Augustine**[1]

So let no one boast in men. For all things are yours.
—**1 Corinthians 3:21–23**

Authentic Christian leadership needs to be relentlessly meek—consistently and self-consciously humble in all its endeavors after the model of Christ. Indeed, humility is the goal of all true Christian leadership. In the last week of His earthly ministry, Jesus again gives the maxim, "Whoever exalts himself will be humbled, and whoever humbles himself will be exalted" (Matthew 23:12). He follows this recitation with the famous "Seven Woes" pronounced on the Pharisees and other Jewish leaders.

Previously, Luke 14 flanks the maxim with two positive teachings on humility, both concerning banquets. Luke 18 does much the same, as Jesus teaches about the publican's self-deprecation and the need to become like a child. This time Jesus surrounds His teaching on humility with only rebuke; it is humility taught as prophecy, as the pronouncement of God's judgment upon the proud. This chapter will explore the rebukes (Matthew 23:1–11) and attempt to turn them into positive remedies. Chapter 13 will focus upon the later woes (Matthew 23:13–36).

Scum and Dregs

Indeed he was ill, near to death. . . .
So receive him in the Lord with all joy, and honor such men,
for he nearly died for the work of Christ.
—Philippians 2:27, 29–30a

Most of Jesus's rebukes in Matthew 23 focus on the poor and prideful leadership of the scribes and Pharisees—how they led with their own strength, thus working against God's real purposes in the world. The scribes and Pharisees focused on outward appearances rather than on the grace of God toward needy sinners. Though they may have looked like strong leaders, Jesus tells the faithful not to follow their example. "So practice and observe whatever they tell you—but not what they do. For they preach, but do not practice . . . they do all their deeds to be seen by others" (Matthew 23:3, 5). They wanted to look good up front, so they wore large phylacteries and long fringes as visible symbols of their own piety. Outward show is never true, God-focused leadership.

In contrast we see Moses—Israel's great liberator and the first prophet of God. He led his people from slavery in Egypt, all the way to the borders of the Promised Land, a forty-year pilgrimage of hardship, opposition, and warfare. Moses was a great leader. According to the Bible, he was also "very meek, more than all people who were on the face of the earth" (Numbers 12:3). Leadership and humility are not mutually exclusive.

The character of Christian leaders will influence the whole church. Prideful leaders will cultivate prideful church bodies. Humble,

Christ-centered leaders will cultivate humble church bodies. After all, Paul tells the Corinthians to imitate him as he imitates Christ (1 Corinthians 11:1).

What does biblical leadership in the church look like? Jesus gives us a clue in His response to the twelve apostles about their bickering regarding who would sit at His right hand in glory.

> And Jesus called them to him and said to them, "You know that those who are considered rulers of the Gentiles lord it over them, and their great ones exercise authority over them. But it shall not be so among you. But whoever would be great among you must be your servant, and whoever would be first among you must be slave of all. For even the Son of Man came not to be served but to serve, and to give his life as a ransom for many." (Mark 10:42–45)

Jesus makes similar points in Matthew 18:1–4 and Luke 22:24–30. These famous passages need almost no elaboration; they are clear. Jesus teaches that the church's leadership values should be the polar opposite from those in the world. Authority is always to be that of service, of doing what is best for the sheep they pastor and serve. Jesus, of course, is the great model in this.

In my senior year of Army R.O.T.C., it came time for graduates to choose in what branch of the Army we wanted to serve—infantry, artillery, quartermaster, ordnance, and so forth. There was more than a score of possible branches. During this process, a young infantry officer came to class to try to sell us on his branch. After showing us a stirring slideshow of his unit in action, he told us, "You want to go infantry, because when you are infantry, everyone works for you." His point was that the Army was structured in such a way that all the other branches, including the sister combat branches, were set up to serve the infantry in its mission.

That stayed with me because as a young Christian, his speech helped me think about what it meant to serve as a believer in the military. In fact, it helped steer me toward another Army branch whose motto was "service above self." What he might have said was, "You want to go infantry because there is no higher form of service than to put yourself on the front line, taking the bullets for all those behind you." That would have been more in accord with Jesus's teaching, understanding a position in a combat unit as a form of sacrificial service.

Paul also confronts a worldly attitude among the Corinthians with their view of good, successful leadership. The Corinthians loved glory and strength and prosperity in their leaders. His rebuke contains a description of true Christian leadership in their day.

> For I think that God has exhibited us apostles as last of all, like men sentenced to death, because we have become a spectacle to the world, to angels, and to men. We are fools for Christ's sake, but you are wise in Christ. We are weak, but you are strong. You are held in honor, but we in disrepute. To the present hour we hunger and thirst, we are poorly dressed and buffeted and homeless, and we labor, working with our own hands. When reviled, we bless; when persecuted, we endure; when slandered, we entreat. We have become, and are still, like the scum of the world, the refuse of all things. (1 Corinthians 4:9–13)

Some translations put it even more powerfully, translating "refuse" as "dregs" or "offscourings," but the idea is the same (cf. Lamentations 3:45). The apostles were considered society's leftovers or throwaways, like the thin film that people rub off the top of their ale or the tea leaves at the bottom of their cup—worthless and gross. This is what true Christian leadership looks like in the eyes of the world. Christian leaders live to serve a crucified Lord rather than to impress the surrounding culture. They recognize they will never fully fit in with any secular inner circle.

Now think of how many Christians want their church leaders to appear. They want leaders to be well respected in the upper echelons of society, on advisory boards and in cahoots with the power brokers of the community. If Christian leaders can achieve those while somehow remaining scum and dregs, such positions provide tremendous opportunities. Erastus, the city treasurer of Corinth, was likely a member of the church, and for him, Paul has only commendation (Romans 16:23). If the choice ever came to Erastus to choose the way of Christ or to choose the way of the world in his service as city treasurer, Paul would tell Erastus to choose Christ, to remain as a scum and dreg, even as he lost his social status and influence.

As staggering as calling Christian leaders scum and dregs is, what Paul says earlier in the passage is even more startling. Paul says that God has exhibited the apostles—the early church's most important leaders—"as last of all, like men sentenced to death, because we have become a spectacle to the world, to angels, and to men" (1 Corinthians 4:9). Paul has in mind a Roman military parade after a great victory. Leading the parade would be the triumphant general, resplendent in glory. Following the general would be his victorious troops. Last of all would be their prisoners, "those sentenced to death," almost certainly by brutal torture in the Coliseum as part of the gladiatorial games that were the sadistic hallmark of Roman culture. Paul says that this last place in the parade is the place true Christian leaders occupy, as those who are about to die, those with the least outward glory.

Do churches today seek leaders who are last in the parade or who are outwardly glorious and given special privileges, things like distinctive parking or the first place in line at the potluck? Do today's church leaders have especially large chairs at the front of the sanctuary for only their use? Do these leaders demand large offices for the express purpose of displaying the size of their personal libraries? I have seen all of this, as if Matthew 23 were not in the Bible at all. Jesus says that the scribes and Pharisees "love the place of honor at feasts and the best seats in the synagogues and greetings in the marketplaces and being called rabbi by others" (Matthew 23:6–7).

Sadly, Jesus's words describe much of Christian leadership today. When believers thumb through a typical Christian magazine, they see leaders portrayed in advertisements as speakers for conferences or in promotional material for their new must-read book. Sometimes, the adulation is almost to the point of satire; *The Onion* or *The Simpsons* could not do better. Admittedly, this is hardly a scientific survey, and most of those leaders are featured because someone paid for it—there are commercial interests involved. Still, they are given full-sized, glossy displays of eminence, rather than assigned a place at the end of the parade. And while many of us pastors would never seek this kind of fame, we continue to read the magazines, jealous that these people are recognized more than we are.

When I preside over the ordination of new officers in our church, I sometimes bring out a staff of authority to give them, like those carried by Roman generals or Napoleon's marshals. It is a symbol of their authority to lead. But the staff I give them is a bit different—a plain, black toilet plunger. It reminds them that they have authority to imitate Christ, to serve as He did. They are being ordained to a position of self-abasement and servitude, not one of privilege and glory.

One small way I apply this is refusing to use a preset email signature with my title below my name. I do not ever want to take my calling for granted. I am a pastor merely by the grace of God, and every day I get to serve in such an office is a mercy and a grace to me. Glory will come, for even the apostles were promised seats in heaven to judge the twelve tribes of Israel. However, they endured tribulation first (Luke 22:28–30). The way up is always the way down, especially for Christian leaders. Christian leader, take your plunger and find your place at the end of the parade.[2]

Paul illustrates this principle wonderfully in Philippians 2 when he commends the work of Timothy and Epaphroditus. If one looks at the structure of the chapter, Paul has first presented Jesus Christ as the supreme model of sacrificial service in the famous hymn (2:5–11). He then gives Timothy and Epaphroditus as living examples of following the same pattern Christ did: emptying themselves by becoming servants and humbling themselves even to the point of death. Timothy did not "seek his own interests" (2:21; also verse 4) but those of others. Epaphroditus left the comfort of his own home to come serve Paul, and during that service, he got sick and "nearly died for the work of Christ" (2:27, 30). Paul says to honor such men as this (2:29). Not because they had loads of accomplishments, but simply because they were servants for the sake of Christ.

Our mid-sized church has decided to operate without a church secretary, at least for the time being. In part, this is for budget reasons. In part, it is from a biblical conviction that the work of administration should be done by our deacons and other church members they oversee. One of the benefits of not having a secretary is that most weeks, I get to type up the bulletin for Sunday worship. It is tiring some weeks, but as I type in each name of the nursery volunteers, or potluck cleanup crew, or the home fellowship group hosts, I am reminded to pray for and be thankful for each of them. I am part of a great host of noble sisters and brothers who give themselves to the work of Christ, all without pay. It keeps me in my place as their pastor, and I am grateful to do the small work of typing each of their names.

Of Titles and Children

The fullest and best ears of corn hang lowest towards the ground;
and so those men that are fullest of worth, are most humble,
and apprehensive of their own failings.
—**Bishop Edward Reynolds**[3]

Jesus's next rebuke in Matthew 23 warns, "But you are not to be called rabbi, for you have one teacher, and you are all brothers. And call no man your father on earth, for you have one Father, who is in heaven. Neither be called instructors, for you have one instructor, the Christ" (Matthew 23:8–10). Christians have debated how literally they should take Jesus's instructions. Obviously, many denominations have determined they should not be taken literally, since they officially call their pastors "father," or "reverend," which means "revered one." Some Dutch churches even call their pastors *dominie*, which literally means lord or master. I would rather land on the side of caution because Jesus speaks so directly and because of people's natural propensity toward pride, which is likely to be only further puffed up by reverential titles. I prefer the biblical term *pastor*, which simply means shepherd, hardly a position of glory. I use the titled *Reverend* for myself only when it helps gain me access to a prison or hospital— for reasons of utility and service. Conforming to what is expected of leaders in some situations may also be the better part of wisdom and humility. Otherwise, some poor clerk may end up getting an unsolicited discourse on Matthew 23.

After all, Jesus is getting at the attitude of the heart when He rebukes these Jewish leaders. This heart attitude is what matters, not the titles themselves. Jesus says so explicitly in verses 25–28; the problem is on the inside, not the outside. If these leaders had used their titles in a disinterested manner that actually pointed others to the true Rabbi and Father, I doubt Jesus would have rebuked them.

Jesus says the reason leaders are not to be called rabbi is because we are all brothers (Matthew 23:8). For that reason I wonder whether it is wise for pastors with doctorates to wear their academic stripes in the pulpit, or put their title on the church sign out front. After all, they are authorized to preach the Word by the empowerment of the Holy Spirit and the approbation of the church. Their PhDs add nothing to their ability to show Christ. Why are leaders trying to impress the world with credentials when the world will not listen to Moses or the prophets (cf. Luke 16:31)?

In his very helpful lectures, *The Work of the Pastor*, the Scottish minister William Still admonishes pastors that they need to remember, "they are not the spiritual doctor. . . . The Holy Spirit is the Doctor. The work is done through a 'dead man' ministering the living Word in the power of the Spirit."[4] Dead men do not herald their own credentials, but they point their sheep to the only one who can give eternal life, the one Rabbi and Instructor, Jesus Christ.

Of course, it is possible for pastors to wear their academic stripes humbly, and for unlettered people to take a perverse pride in their lack of credentials. As a general rule, I think stripes and titles tend to feed pride and hinder humility, especially when unduly emphasized. My current congregation is blessed to have many men and women with doctorates and amazing accomplishments. Yet, we are even more blessed to have people from all walks of life and educational levels. When we gather to worship, we are brothers and sisters in Christ, period. No distinctions are made at all. The joy and the fellowship of being together as equals all saved by the same grace is tangible. That is the sort of thing a conscious focus on humility can do in the church. For we have one Father who is in heaven, and one teacher, our Lord Jesus. I am blessed to lead a congregation where one has to work to find out whether someone has a doctorate or not. In some cases, it was years before a brother or sister told me, and in every case I remember, it was only because I asked them. That is the kind of humility that binds a congregation together in Christian love. Are pastors not to be as Paul, preaching not with lofty words of wisdom, but rather to know nothing but Christ and Him crucified?

Jesus's real rebuke to the scribes and Pharisees is that they simply did not love the people they were supposed to be leading. Jesus says that they "tie up heavy burdens, hard to bear, and lay them on people's shoulders, but they themselves are not willing to move them with their finger" (Matthew 23:4). They lorded it over their religious subjects by assigning rules and rituals for them to follow, while they sat above, wishing to be served. Today, believers tend to be guarded against such explicit legalism. But Christian leaders have found other ways to lord authority over the sheep. One way they do so is by dominating every conversation and meeting, since after all, they are the ones in charge. William Still has direct words for pastors in this regard.

> When real people come seeking real help, receive them with all grace, patience and forbearance. Let them talk: don't jump to conclusions and turn the interview into another sermon. . . . Let them talk, and you listen. The hardest thing ministers, who are great talkers, find to do is listen. Don't be making up your next speech while the other is talking. Listen! You may hear something you have never heard before. . . . the most you should allow yourself at first, is to ask questions.[5]

Still's advice is simply applying James 1:19 to the work of pastoral ministry: "Be quick to hear, slow to speak, slow to anger." That is one important way Christian leaders can serve their brothers and sisters—by first listening to them, really listening, before pronouncing any solutions. That is part of what it means to lead from below, as Christ did.

But regardless of their title or position, it is critical for all Christian leaders to remember what Jesus teaches several chapters earlier in Matthew.

> At that time the disciples came to Jesus, saying, "Who is the greatest in the kingdom of heaven?" And calling to him a child, he put him in the midst of them and said, "Truly, I say to you, unless you turn and become like children, you will never enter the kingdom of heaven. Whoever humbles himself like this child is the greatest in the kingdom of heaven. Whoever receives one such child in my name receives me, but whoever causes one of these little ones who believe in me to sin, it would be better for him to have a great millstone fastened around his neck and to be drowned in the depth of the sea." (Matthew 18:1–6)

You can learn a great deal about a leader—and a whole church—by the way they treat children. Do leaders treat children as troublemakers who must be tolerated and contained, hoping they will do as little damage as possible? Or do leaders remember that if they are to be great in heaven, they must become like little children themselves? To this end, Pastor Still also tells a story about Karl Barth, the great twentieth-century Swiss theologian, recalling how a colleague came in one day to see Barth rolling on the floor with his two children, "more a child than either of them."[6] According to Jesus, that is a picture of true, heavenly dignity.

One summer, I served as a youth intern at a large, respectable church. As the youth group was preparing to leave for a retreat, all our sleeping bags and camping gear were spread throughout the sanctuary. The senior pastor was a rather regal and dignified man, and I worried about what he might think when he saw the disarray. I gave him a warning of what he would encounter if he looked into the sanctuary, and I will never forget his response, "Don't worry about it; a tidy church is a dead church." Children and their messes were welcome. That is Christian leadership driven by serving the least of these.

Not Showing Favoritism in the Assembly

I did go once [to church] but the people were all shut in,
and the folk in the boxes looked at me as if I had got in without
paying: so after walking up and down several times, like a man
in a station trying to get a seat when the train is full, I went home.
—A man from Monmouthshire, England, 1882[7]

How do Christian leaders treat members and guests? With dignity and equality? Or do they tend toward the creation of cliques and other inner circles? James addresses this directly.

My brothers, show no partiality as you hold the faith in our Lord Jesus Christ, the Lord of glory. For if a man wearing a

gold ring and fine clothing comes into your assembly, and a
poor man in shabby clothing also comes in, and if you pay
attention to the one who wears the fine clothing and say, "You
sit here in a good place," while you say to the poor man, "You
stand over there," or, "Sit down at my feet," have you not
then made distinctions among yourselves and become judges
with evil thoughts? Listen, my beloved brothers, has not God
chosen those who are poor in the world to be rich in faith and
heirs of the kingdom, which he has promised to those who
love him? (James 2:1–5)

It would be rare for a church today to insult a poor visitor like this
by directing them to a different place to sit. Though believers may
no longer discriminate by seating arrangement, churches have learned
other ways of showing favoritism. Facial expressions and body language can communicate welcome or insult. Selective invitations to
church activities can show favoritism. Believers may not purposely
favor the rich; as often as not Christians simply favor the people they
think are most similar to themselves. Indeed, there are times when the
rich may feel unwelcome in church. One man I knew visited a church
and was told by the pastor to leave his tie behind the next time he
came because it made others uncomfortable.

The point is that the scribes and Pharisees of Matthew 23 were
obsessed with their own respectability and so chose their company
carefully. Some of them might have even hung out with those poorer
than themselves just to be looked up to and called "Rabbi." They were
always checking to see how people were greeted in the marketplace and
where people were seated in church. The scribes and Pharisees coveted
the places of honor for themselves. Their worldliness was so severe that
it put their own souls in eternal danger as Jesus warned them, "How
can you believe, when you receive glory from one another and do not
seek the glory that comes from the only God?" (John 5:44).

What about today's church? In my view, the same mind-set Jesus rebuked is prevalent. Some city or national prayer breakfasts are more about awards and speeches than about prayer; they are literally about who is seated where—in direct contradiction to Jesus's rebukes in Matthew 23. At denominational meetings and conferences often the same small circle of men speak each year, despite the abundance of gifted leaders in the church. I often wonder whether it would be better to be slightly bored by a less-gifted speaker than to constantly herald the same few celebrities over and over—for the blessing of humility it would bring the church.

At the congregational level I have seen otherwise wonderful, loving churches make all sorts of distinctions among their membership in terms of whom they regarded as important. I have seen church directories where the size of a staff member's picture is determined by the "importance" of their position—janitors and secretaries get the smallest possible, assistant pastors a bit larger, and the senior pastor a full page. Likewise, one can often look at a church's website to see how well they have thought through the implications of Matthew 23 and James 2 in the way they present their different leaders and members. It is certainly fine and even advisable to give a little more attention to the pastors for various practical reasons if done in moderation and with humility in mind. Do visitors, however, learn more about the pastor's hobbies and interests and favorite things than they learn about the gospel? If so, what kind of needy sinner would want to go to a church like that?

Churches must think upon these things and include humility in their thinking as they put together directories and websites. There is no exact prescription to follow, but they must heed Jesus's warnings in Matthew 23.

And Our Brother, Sosthenes

A truly humble man is inflexible in nothing but in the cause
of his Lord and Master, which is the cause of truth and virtue.
In this he is inflexible, because God and conscience require it.
But in things of lesser moment, and which do not involve
his principles as a follower of Christ, and in things that only concern
his own private interests, he is apt to yield to others.
—Jonathan Edwards[8]

As a principle of humble Christian leadership, the Bible commands a plurality of leaders in the church. The requirement for plurality in Christian leadership should not be surprising, "Where there is no guidance, a people falls, but in an abundance of counselors there is safety" (Proverbs 11:14). Men and women should not trust their own judgment alone, much less if they are in charge of Christ's church, where they lead as His stewards (cf. 1 Corinthians 4:1). No one individual can lead the church alone. A plurality of leaders is often necessary to do the actual work, but also as a check on power and opinions.

One of the ways Moses showed his meekness was by listening to his father-in-law, who advised him to appoint fellow leaders (Exodus 18). Godly prophets, priests, and kings in Israel did not rule by their own authority, but only under God and with an abundance of counselors.

This same pattern of plurality in leadership continues in the New Testament, but heightened, since Jesus is now our sole prophet, priest, and king. When the church needed servants to care for widows, the apostles told them to "pick out from among you seven men of good repute, full of the Spirit and of wisdom, whom we will appoint to this duty" (Acts 6:3). When a controversy arose in the church at Antioch, messengers from all the churches gathered in Jerusalem to deliberate and deliver a decision (Acts 15). No one man made the decision, though some appropriately carried more weight than others due to their experience and scriptural reasoning (Acts 15:6–21). When Paul planted churches, he always left them in the charge of elders, in the plural (cf. Acts 14:23; Acts 20:17; Philippians 1:1). Paul commands the same of Timothy and Titus, his representatives in Ephesus and Crete, respectively (cf. 1 Timothy 3; Titus 1:5).[9] So even the apostolic structure appears designed to work itself out of a job, as churches were established and elders ordained to lead. Paul calls the apostles the "foundation" of the church, with Christ Himself as cornerstone (Ephesians 2:20). Once a foundation is laid, it is done. What goes on top of a foundation is the building, not more foundations.

Even among the temporary, apostolic structure of the early church, there is cordiality and teamwork. The apostles worked together and submitted to one another for correction. Almost all of Paul's epistles are team efforts. In fact, only his personal letters (the pastorals and Philemon) and his systematic treatises (Romans and Ephesians) are not. The others are written to specific churches from Paul and at least one other brother, often Timothy. Galatians stands out even further because the issue in the Galatian church was so serious that Paul wrote to them with "all the brothers" who were with him (Galatians 1:2). The whole church spoke together with Paul.

And then there is Sosthenes, about whom we know almost nothing, but who helped Paul write 1 Corinthians, perhaps the premier epistle on applying humility to congregational life. Why would Paul enlist Sosthenes to help him in such a task? He is almost certainly the same man in Acts 18, the ruler of the synagogue in Corinth who was beaten in front of the Roman tribunal instead of Paul because Paul's Jewish opponents could not get hold of him. Evidently, somewhere along the line, Sosthenes became a follower of Christ and paid the price for it. Paul begins this great epistle on Christian leadership, "Paul, called by the will of God to be an apostle of Christ Jesus, and our brother Sosthenes, to the church of God that is in Corinth" (1 Corinthians 1:1–2). Paul, the great apostle, calls Sosthenes his brother to remind the Corinthians what true leadership looks like. Christian leadership often leads to suffering, and leaders are part of a team that suffers and makes decisions together.

Whatever exact church polity believers embrace from Scripture, it should always involve a plurality of leaders making decisions together. Almost all Christian denominations recognize and honor this biblical principle in the way they are structured. No one individual should have absolute authority; such a structure only tempts and reinforces natural pride. Leaders all need checks and balances, and the humble leader gladly embraces structures that enforce such limits. I cannot count the number of times my fellow elders saved my congregation from some harebrained idea that popped into my head. Of course, my wife has spared my elders from having to even hear all my poor ideas after I bounced them off her first.

But despite this, there are church structures that ignore this principle of plurality and are almost set up for abuse, whether at the denominational or congregational level. Protestants demur against the prelacy of Rome, but some congregations have their own prelates. As J. C. Ryle said, "No pope has ever received such honor as 'Pope Self,'" and such an attitude often manifests itself in church polities.[10] Some pastors consider themselves "the man of God," and their authority must go unquestioned. Others claim to get "a word from God," which must be heeded, even though no one else heard it.

I once knew a young man who was excommunicated from a church simply because he questioned which version of the Bible they ought to read. He was given no notice of the congregational meeting where he was put on trial in absentia, and the membership voted exactly as the pastor told them. Afterward, when the young man told his side of the story to his uncle, his uncle simply stated, "Well, if I had known all that, I guess I would not have voted against you." Having a plurality of leadership is no guarantee against such abuse, but plurality makes abuse a good deal less likely. A humble church enforces a plurality of leaders and insists that its leaders submit to one another.[11]

If a plurality of leaders within a local church is necessary to help maintain humility, it follows that individual churches ought to follow this same principle of plurality. In other words, a humble church sees itself as connected to the larger catholic church, and so ideally belongs to some sort of denomination or structure by which it submits to other, sister churches. This is exactly what Luke portrays after the first Ecumenical Council in Acts 15. The complaint arose from just one congregation in Antioch, but the decision of the Council was delivered to churches in every city, so that all "the churches were strengthened in the faith, and they increased in numbers daily" (Acts 16:4–5). These churches submitted to the joint decision of their representatives in Jerusalem. This principle of mutual submission continues as the gospel spreads across the Mediterranean, when Paul rebukes the Corinthians' unique practices with the simple question, "Was it from you that the word of God came? Or are you the only ones it has reached?" (1 Corinthians 14:36; cf. also 1 Corinthians 7:17; 11:16; 14:33; 16:1). Humble leaders submit to one another within a congregation, and they submit to leaders within other congregations as well, both formally and informally, in both law and spirit.

Nonetheless, such a structure is no guarantee of humility, and there are many exceptions in both directions. I have known denominational churches that have acted all but independent, skirting the rules of their own church and doing the minimal to remain affiliated. There may be reasons of conscience for this in some cases, but often it is just arrogance—a church acting independently despite its official label.

On the other hand, I have seen independent churches that are remarkably catholic in their demeanor and attitude toward the wider body of Christ. Though they are not governmentally connected to other congregations, they nevertheless act as if they were, seeking advice and fellowship. They maintain a confession that is connected to the orthodox, historic Christian tradition. I have even seen such independent churches actively plant churches that go on to join other denominations. I still think it is better for such connections to be formalized, but as in all things, it is even better to actually practice it (cf. Matthew 21:28–32).

Godly Christian leaders distrust their ability to do all the work or to make all the decisions by themselves. They need a team of godly people to provide a check and balance. A plurality of leaders can remind each other that the church is not theirs, but it belongs to Jesus Christ. A church that is serious about humility will have a leadership structure that, by design, hinders pride and celebrates meekness.

I am reminded of this almost every Sunday morning. Our congregation's worship services are structured so that no one individual is up front all of the time. Leadership in liturgy is shared, in part to preserve and communicate the principles discussed in this chapter. There are times when such shared leadership is challenging to my own preferences and agendas. On occasion I have had to change what I had prepared based on the tone set by another leader earlier in the service. Leading humbly and in concert with others requires flexible and dying to one's own agenda.

This great truth was driven home to me a few years ago when I asked a fellow minister to preside over the Lord's Supper, which is a particularly solemn portion of our worship service. This dear brother was well loved and known for his easygoing and sometimes offbeat style, but I knew he would handle communion with the appropriate reverence. After preaching a long sermon, I handed over the service to my colleague. As he got up to introduce the sacrament, he simply said, "What are we doing here?" and then proceeded to stare at the congregation awkwardly. He then, in a very casual and in what I thought was a rather goofy way, explained how the Lord's Supper points to Jesus's sacrifice for sin and feeds us spiritually. I shifted uneasily in my seat, believing his whole tone to be ineffective and inappropriate for the occasion.

Following the service, an unbelieving woman who had attended worship for years, and for whom we had been praying diligently, came to me and said that while my colleague was speaking, she was converted to Christ. Because of his words, she decided, at long last, to trust Jesus with her soul. Now I know that it is God alone who saves.

However, it also pleased Him to use His servant, in all his apparent goofiness, to accomplish what I, in my proper solemnity, could not. Jesus gives a variety of leaders to His church. Not all are Pauls. Some of us are Sosthenes at best and glad for it.

PRAYER

O Jesus! meek and humble of heart, hear me.

From the desire of being esteemed, deliver me, O Jesus.
From the desire of being loved,
From the desire of being extolled,
From the desire of being honored,
From the desire of being praised,
From the desire of being preferred to others,
From the desire of being consulted,
From the desire of being approved,

From the fear of being humiliated, deliver me, O Jesus.
From the fear of being despised,
From the fear of suffering rebukes,
From the fear of being calumniated,
From the fear of being forgotten,
From the fear of being ridiculed,
From the fear of being wronged,
From the fear of being suspected,

That others may be loved more than I,
O Jesus, grant me the grace to desire it.
That others may be esteemed more than I,
That, in the opinion of the world,
others may, increase and I may decrease,
That others may be chosen and I set aside,
That others may be praised and I unnoticed,

That others may be preferred to me in everything,
That others may become holier than I,
provided that I may become as holy as I should,
O Jesus, grant me the grace to desire it.
—adapted from Rafael Cardinal Merry del Val[12]

CHAPTER TWELVE

....

THE ASSEMBLY OF FOOLS: TRUTH, HUMILITY, AND UNITY

I do verily believe that when God shall accomplish unity,
it will be the effect of love, and not the cause of love.
It will proceed from love, before it brings forth love.
—John Owen[1]

So then, my brothers,
when you come together to eat, wait for one another.
—1 Corinthians 11:33

When I was still in seminary, I had the opportunity to preach in an old congregational church near Boston founded in the year 1642. It had a sanctuary that could seat fifteen hundred people and a pulpit so high that its ascent required two sets of stairs. They even broadcast the service on television. All this was heady stuff for a seminarian, or so I thought. The morning I preached, there were approximately thirty people left in the congregation. I remember how they all sat as far apart from one another as possible in that vast sanctuary. It reminded me of C. S. Lewis's vision of hell in *The Great Divorce*; everyone trying to get as far away from other people as possible. After the service, the members asked me why I thought they were not growing as a congregation. Well, can you imagine visiting a church "community" like that and wanting to come back?

Unity among Christians has been a huge theme in church history. The ecumenical movement of the twentieth century is one of most important developments within recent church history, despite setbacks. Large denominations were formed as smaller bodies merged with one another, sincerely seeking to display their unity in Christ in an organizational manner. To give just one example, the United Church of Christ was formed as four different traditions came together. Other denominations can claim similar successes at reunion and structural unity, all in the name of showing the world that Christians are "one," as Jesus prayed in John 17:20–23.

Yet organizational unity rarely leads to a lasting, true spiritual unity. Denominations and congregations continue to split. I remember once driving through a small town and seeing a church sign that read, "Old Fellowship Baptist Church." I thought, *There must be a story there.* Sure enough, thirty seconds down the road, another sign appeared, "New Fellowship Baptist Church."

My own tradition is not much better. Charts of the various Presbyterian denominations through American history look like electrical circuit boards. To counter this human tendency toward schism, other Christian bodies have adopted as their motto the wise sentiment first penned by Rupertus Meldenius around 1627, "In essentials unity, in nonessentials liberty, in all things charity." This is helpful, and a good place to start, I think. Nevertheless, it seems to me to fall a bit short. After all, Christians do not always agree on what belongs in these two main categories of essential and nonessential. What is nonessential for one sister or brother is a nonnegotiable for another. Others consider it uncharitable to discuss the difference at all. Their motto is simply, "doctrine divides."

Something deeper is needed for real unity in Christ besides sharing a common tradition, label, or motto. Shared vision statements and confessions of faith help, but are those enough to sustain unity in Christ? A loving, heartfelt spiritual unity often eludes even those within the same church or ministry. Even when believers share the same denominational label, they often do not sense the joy and beauty of Christian unity that King David wrote about.

> Behold, how good and pleasant it is
>   when brothers dwell in unity!
> It is like the precious oil on the head,
>   running down on the beard,
> on the beard of Aaron,
>   running down on the collar of his robes!
> It is like the dew of Hermon,
>   which falls on the mountains of Zion!
> For there the Lord has commanded the blessing,
>   life forevermore. (Psalm 133)

Instead of oil overflowing down their beards due to their mutual love and unity, Christians often feel fortunate to have just a sprinkling of like-mindedness. It is obvious then that true spiritual unity must be something inward and heartfelt.[2]

Attempts at Unity

Would that the union between all Christ's Churches upon earth were such, that the angels in heaven might join their song of praise.
—John Calvin[3]

Consider these various models that have been tried throughout church history, many of which are commendable, but which are nevertheless insufficient to bring about an abiding, heartfelt spiritual unity:

- an elaborate and highly structured hierarchy (e.g., Roman Catholicism)
- a state-sanctioned church (e.g., most Western European churches)

- uniform prayer books (e.g., liturgical churches, such as Anglicanism)
- comprehensive creeds and polity (e.g., Presbyterianism)
- minimalist creed and polity (e.g., the Restorationist movement)
- common methodology (e.g., monasticism, revivalism, church growth)
- common political causes (e.g., mainline liberal denominations)
- common heroes or culture (e.g., neo-evangelicalism)[4]

This is not to say that these models cannot help achieve some degree of church unity; my own denomination pursues her unity through at least two or three of these. However, none of these models are sufficient in themselves; something deeper is needed for true unity in Christ to be achieved. A unity that is merely outward and organizational will never last long.

Disagreement among Christians will inevitably arise, and that can be good. Otherwise, believers would not be called to sharpen one another (Proverbs 27:17). Biblical truth must always prevail over preference and tradition. When Christians are shown to be wrong by their fellow brothers and sisters, they have a wonderful opportunity to grow in faith and humility, and thus, in unity. On numerous occasions I have been given that opportunity by losing a vote or argument in my denomination—blessed beyond measure.

Peter's example of losing a very public disagreement is recorded in Galatians 2. Peter was first among the apostles, the "rock" of the early church, and yet was clearly wrong about a practical matter that maligned the gospel itself. When Paul, the newest apostle, publicly confronted Peter regarding his sin, Peter could have tried to save face, which would have led to an immediate schism in the young church. Instead, Peter prevents schism by repenting in the face of rebuke. Peter's humility saved the unity of the Christian church. So often someone claims to stand on doctrine or principle, but the real issue at hand is one of power, control, and ego. Not so with Peter.

Even when ego is not in play, sincere brothers and sisters may disagree on how to apply biblical truth. God in His providence allowed Paul and Barnabas to split right after the sweet unity brought about by the First Ecumenical Council of Acts 15. The apostolic era was not a Golden Age of the church where there was no disagreement. The church has always been catholic, but it has never been fully united, even when there was more unity than is enjoyed today. But even when the church enjoyed more outward unity, how much of that existed by threat of force and the suppression of conscience? That is one reason there was a Reformation, followed in time by the blessed separation of church and state. Many today bewail the multitude of denominations that dot the ecclesiastical landscape, but surely, it is better that believers are able to follow their consciences than to be artificially forced into denominational unity by threat of civil law or martial force. Despite its many flaws, denominationalism is a healthy by-product of Christian freedom.

Nonetheless, the impulse toward real, spiritual, and cooperative unity in the gospel is a godly one that stems directly from the prayer of Jesus, "Holy Father, keep them in your name, which you have given me, that they may be one, even as we are one" (John 17:11). Since believers are one in Christ, how are they to maintain unity in the midst of disagreement?

Christian Unity in Ephesians 4

I therefore, a prisoner for the Lord, urge you to walk in a manner worthy of the calling to which you have been called, with all humility and gentleness, with patience, bearing with one another in love, eager to maintain the unity of the Spirit in the bond of peace. There is one body and one Spirit—just as you were called to the one hope that belongs to your call—one Lord, one faith, one baptism, one God and Father of all, who is over all and through all and in all.

—Ephesians 4:1–6

Paul's instructions in Ephesians 4:1–6 have been a useful guide as I have attempted to maintain the tricky balance between truth and unity in my ministry. I have often asked myself which theological hills are worth a fight. Is it ever profitable for Christians to divide? What priority should unity have in Christian ministries, and what should that unity look like?

Ephesians 1–3 is the doctrinal part of Ephesians, what some call the indicatives of the gospel: those things God has already done for believers in Christ.[5] In Ephesians 4–6, Paul then turns to applying those truths: the imperatives that flow from this gospel. The order is important—first the indicative, then the imperative. Paul begins the imperative, practical section of the letter by urging believers to walk in a manner worthy of their calling. And his first application of this is church unity.

Paul first reiterates the gospel. There can be no real unity where there is no agreement on the gospel. By calling us to "walk in a manner worthy of the calling with which we have been called," Paul is simply reviewing the gospel he just outlined in Ephesians 1. If Christians want true spiritual unity, they must begin with the doctrines of grace and hold the line. Any doctrine or habit that undermines this free grace will erode Christian unity.

The word *walk* is also important here. It is the same Greek word Paul uses in Ephesians 2:10, where he tells believers that they are God's "workmanship, created in Christ Jesus for good works, which God prepared beforehand, that we should *walk* in them." The order is critical—good works do not save, but believers will do good works because they have been saved by grace. All believers have to do is discover what these good works are and walk in them.

Then Paul begins his description of the Christian life by commanding believers to eagerly "maintain the unity of the Spirit in the bond of peace" (Ephesians 4:3). Unity comes first. That is why Paul reminds all Christians in Ephesians 4:4–6 that they have one body, Spirit, hope, Lord, faith, baptism, and God the Father of all. Seven times, Paul repeats the word *one*. Seven is the biblical number which symbolizes completion, and Paul may be saying that oneness is already complete in Christ. The only question is whether Christians will live in that reality.

Unity is already accomplished in Christ, but believers must be eager to maintain it. Unity takes hard work, and Christians are to commit themselves to that work. That often means going the extra mile with brothers or sisters one may have substantial differences with, or toward whom one may not naturally gravitate. It also means making an extra effort to overcome cultural and racial differences since Christ has brought peace and made Jew and Gentile into one man (cf. Ephesians 2:14–15). Paul is crystal clear in Ephesians 2 that there are to be no divisions among Christians in terms of race or culture. Christian unity is in Jesus, not in any national or class similarities. That is one reason our congregation does not fly the American flag in its sanctuary or often celebrate our church's Scottish heritage. Rather, when Christian congregations worship, they gather to remember their citizenship in heaven (Philippians 3:20). One of the church's great privileges is to be a counterculture of mixed races and classes in contrast to so much of the world's tribalism. It has been one of my greatest joys in ministry to see our congregation increasingly reflect the cross-cultural reality of Christ's body.

This can be tricky business, but wherever Christian congregations are in this journey, they must each pursue progress toward the heavenly vision John saw in Revelation.

> After this I looked, and behold, a great multitude that no one could number, from every nation, from all tribes and peoples and languages, standing before the throne and before the Lamb, clothed in white robes, with palm branches in their hands, and crying out with a loud voice, "Salvation belongs to our God who sits on the throne, and to the Lamb!" (Revelation 7:9–10)

At the very least, Christians should aim with God's help for their congregations to be as multiracial as their own communities. They can also show unity in Christ among the nations with vigorous support of cross-cultural missions. Such endeavors take great effort and are humbling, but Paul admonishes believers to make the effort. It is well worth it.

Church Creeds and Doctrines in Unity

Now when I meet some brother Christian, any brother Christian,
ignorant of these things and confusing one thing with another,
I can look patiently upon such a man as he utters his opinion . . .
provided he does not hold any belief unworthy of You, O Lord, Creator
of all. Even this weakness in the first beginnings
of a man's faith is borne patiently by Charity, our mother.
—Augustine[6]

Christian unity consists of seven ones—one body, Spirit, hope, Lord, faith, baptism, and Father. In this, Paul is assuming like-mindedness with regard to truth; one body of doctrine bound the church together. Pursuing doctrinal conformity is an important part of unity in Christ, even if believers will never attain perfect agreement this side of heaven. Nevertheless, Paul assumes that Christians will make progress. That is why he writes that the church will

> attain to the unity of the faith and of the knowledge of the Son of God, to mature manhood, to the measure of the stature of the fullness of Christ, so that we may no longer be children, tossed to and fro by the waves and carried about by every wind of doctrine. (Ephesians 4:13–14)

Part of what it means to be humble is willingly conforming to the truth of God's Word, the "pattern of sound words" (cf. 2 Timothy 1:13; 1 Corinthians 11:16; Philippians 2:2). Churches need to develop a self-aware and wise system of determining differing levels of doctrines—figuring out which truths fit where within a biblical system of doctrine. Some doctrines, Christians believe, are *essential* for salvation, and others are not.[7]

This delineation is important because some sincere Christians wish to uphold the integrity of the Bible so meticulously that they give every word in Scripture equal weight. They thus allow very little leeway for disagreement about anything, no matter how small. Many churches are at their most strident regarding matters that occur at the very beginning or the very end of time, the bookends of the Bible. In comparison to the life of Christ, very little information is given about the details of creation or the second coming. Many Christians, however, are the most prone to divide over these issues. Would believers not be better served to moderate their zeal on a matter in direct proportion to the amount of attention that it receives in Scripture? After all, in contrast to these bookends, the gospel of Jesus Christ is central and crystal clear.

I once had the opportunity to sit in a small seminar for pastors with the great Anglican scholar, J. I. Packer, who is especially known for resurrecting an appreciation for Puritan theology. I had not yet attended seminary so it was a great privilege to be included. Attendees were given the opportunity to ask Dr. Packer any question they liked. When it was my turn, I put to him, "What did the Puritans get wrong?" I still remember the gasps from some in the room, but Packer's response was patient and wise. He said that there are three kinds of doctrines, "trunk, branch, and twig doctrines." What the Puritans got wrong is that they considered every doctrine to be a trunk doctrine, even if it was twig-worthy at best. Thus, many Puritans allowed little room for disagreement, even among themselves. Eventually, they splintered. I am a great fan of the Puritans, but surely Packer's analysis of this weakness was correct.

In contrast to such a mind-set, Paul asserts that some choices are matters of Christian freedom, in which believers may sincerely differ. He writes,

> One person esteems one day as better than another, while another esteems all days alike. Each one should be fully convinced in his own mind. . . . Therefore let us not pass judgment on one another any longer, but rather decide never to put a stumbling block or hindrance in the way of a brother. I know and am persuaded in the Lord Jesus that nothing is unclean in itself, but it is unclean for anyone who thinks it unclean. (Romans 14:5, 13–14)

Paul is saying that there is something more important than outward conformity on secondary matters: following one's conscience. In this sense there are gray areas in the Christian life. Not surprisingly, Jesus also teaches that some matters are more essential than others.

> "Woe to you, scribes and Pharisees, hypocrites! For you tithe mint and dill and cumin, and have neglected the weightier matters of the law: justice and mercy and faithfulness. These you ought to have done, without neglecting the others. You blind guides, straining out a gnat and swallowing a camel!" (Matthew 23:23–24)

Jesus does not tell the Jews that they should have ignored small matters of the law, only that they had their priorities topsy-turvy. Jesus makes a distinction between laws, though all were from God Himself. Some doctrines and matters of Christian practice are more important than others.

I am no engineer, but I understand that some of the safest suspension bridges are those with a degree of flexibility built into them in order to withstand earthquakes. It can make for some frightening online videos of bridges swaying in the wind, but otherwise, as I understand it, the whole bridge would collapse if one part came under strain. By analogy, some Christians are so inflexible in all of their thinking that if one small beam or joint is removed, their whole system collapses. In contrast, mature believers have a degree of flexibility built into their doctrine. If some small detail of their thinking is challenged, they may sway a bit or even change their minds, while still holding to the fundamentals of the faith that keep the bridge intact.

Wisdom enables believers to make distinctions between doctrines so that their main beams and towers remain intact and will not budge. They firmly hold to the essentials; however, humble Christians might be persuaded to change their minds on less critical matters. Humble believers are not undone if the earth shakes and if they find themselves swaying a bit, they do not panic as long the bridge itself remains built on Christ and His gospel. Wisdom enables Christians to major on the majors, keeping the main thing the main thing: "Jesus loves me this I know, for the Bible tells me so."[8]

Even so, just because a matter is not essential for salvation does not mean that it is not important. One doctrinal example is whether Christians baptize the children of believers or not. This is a branch doctrine, as J. I. Packer might label it—important but not essential to salvation. How believers answer the question about baptism is still important in their earthly pilgrimage. Among other things, it determines what kind of church many can join. If and when God blesses believers with a child, they have to decide what to do regarding baptism. Does the baby belong to Christ's visible body or not?

Due to matters such as infant baptism, some have suggested that Christians divide doctrines into at least three different categories, not just the two (essential and nonessential). The suggested three categories are similar to Packer's "trunk, branch, and twig" doctrines: the essential, the important, and *adiaphora* (Greek for "things indifferent").[9] Believers who follow this approach are able to accomplish three things as a consequence. First, by delineating those doctrines that are deemed to be essential, Christians may determine as best they can who are their brothers and sisters in Christ. These doctrines include such dogmas affirmed in the Nicene Creed—the Trinity, the full divinity and humanity of Jesus, His bodily resurrection and second coming, salvation that is by grace, and the reality of eternal life. Secondly, on the opposite side of the spectrum, Christians may delineate those doctrines that are merely indifferent—*adiaphora*—and give all Christians freedom in those areas as long as they do no harm to others. These would be the kind of things Paul describes in Romans 14, such as what kind of food to eat or which holy days to observe. There is freedom in these matters.

These two sets of doctrine are critical, but it may be the middle category—the important or branch doctrines—that are the most significant for pursuing Christian unity and humility. These doctrines are those beliefs upon which people of good character and judgment may conscientiously disagree as they each try to understand and follow the Bible the best they can. Christians study the same texts on these doctrines and arrive at different conclusions. Very often, these doctrines concern such things as the sacraments or eschatology or church polity. They are important doctrines, not merely indifferent; however, they are not essential to salvation.

At the same time, believers must humbly confess that the Bible is not always as clear on these matters as they might wish. So what can they do? Keep studying, and in humility, agree to disagree. All believers are wrong about some parts of their doctrine; they just do not know what those errors are yet. Someday Jesus will make all things clear. In the meantime, if I happen to think that you are wrong on one of these important, yet nonessential doctrines, then I will still be sure to profess our unity in Christ; convinced that God will show one of us the truth in His perfect time (cf. Philippians 3:15).[10] Either way, believers stand on Christ and His perfections.

This is why denominations can in fact be lovely structures. They provide a way for believers to love one another across denominational lines despite their differences. In that sense they can actually aid true, spiritual unity in Christ, rather than hinder it. Disagreement gives believers an opportunity to display love and humility toward one another. It is a blessing from God if put in proper perspective.

But if Christians do not have a proper system of doctrine or if they do not pursue a unity of mind as Paul entreats in Ephesians 4:3–6, then this love and humility actually becomes more difficult. Some Christians have decried denominations as unbiblical, opting instead for the hopeful motto, "No creed but Christ, no book but the Bible." It sounds splendid and is a wonderful ideal. Historically, however, these believers found that they could not agree on what Christ required of them or what the Bible teaches in its specifics; they ended up dividing from one another, sometimes even to the point of excommunication. The reasoning was that if someone does not believe the Bible on such and such a point, they must not believe at all. Despite their good intentions, these non-creedal Christians ended up acting on an informal, unwritten creed that can be as divisive as explicit beliefs in denominations.[11]

Those who denied the need for creeds underestimated the insidious remnant of pride that remains within believers. They thought they could ignore two millennia of church history and experience. By not choosing an existing denomination, they soon discovered that they made their own. As Lewis says, it would have been better had they picked one of the existing denominations, even with its flaws.[12] They missed the lesson that creeds—even when they differ from one another—can help believers love one another. Creeds say to other groups of Christians, we may disagree on "x," "y," or "z," but we still call you brothers and sisters in Christ, for together we stand on the same gospel of grace.

In order to have true Christian unity, creeds and loving forbearance are both equally needed. Creeds provide a basis for unity but are insufficient by themselves. Creeds provide the framework for unity, but only the Holy Spirit can work love and unity in any real measure, the kind where oil flows down one's beard in abundance.[13] Likewise, pursuing Christian unity through love alone but with no attention to doctrine is like using Jell-O to try to glue objects together; it may taste good, but it will not bond anything. Christians need glue that is both effectual and sweet to the tongue, an impossible human invention. They need the glue of the gospel.

The Missing Link between Grace and Unity

Of all religions, Christianity is without doubt the one that ought to inspire tolerance most, although up to now the Christians have been the most intolerant of all men.

—Voltaire[14]

So then, how do believers bring both truth and love together as they pursue greater Christian unity? The answer is the key to understanding Ephesians 4:1–6. Before Paul begins his discourse on church unity, he tells the Ephesians to walk worthily of their calls, "with all humility and gentleness, with patience, bearing with one another in love" (4:2). There Paul provides the link between the gospel (verse 1) and church unity (verses 3–6). That link is a character of humility, gentleness, patience, and love. Humility toward one another is the missing link between grace and unity, and it is the glue that holds them together. In order to achieve a true and lasting spiritual unity between believers, it is not enough to believe the gospel, though Christians have to start there. It is not enough to have a common confession of faith, though creeds are helpful. It is not enough to strive to maintain unity.

What is needed in order to bring truth and love, grace and unity together is a deep and growing humility stemming from the gospel. Believers must walk with one another in gentleness and patience. They must bear with one another in love. True unity takes more than good intentions or doctrinal agreement or hard work. It takes gospel-wrought humility. So where unity is lacking, chances are, so is meekness toward one another.

Humility, then, is the key to Christian unity—just as I believe it is the key to the whole of the Christian life. And one of the loveliest fruits that humility bears is sweet unity among sisters and brothers. That is what Paul begins with in the practical section of Ephesians. All other gospel applications flow from there.

Practical Application to the Local Congregation

For no one can lay any foundation
other than the one already laid,
which is Jesus Christ.
—1 Corinthians 3:11 (NIV)

I believe that the order of Paul's logic in Ephesians 4:1–6 can be applied to the three categories of doctrine discussed earlier: the essential, the important, and the indifferent. Remember again Paul's logic: first comes grace (verse 1), then humility (verse 2), and finally, church unity (verse 3). Humility is the link between grace and unity, the glue of the gospel.

Let's consider how this logical order works itself out with each level of doctrine. Start with those "trunk" doctrines that are essential to salvation.

- God's grace brings justification that saves my soul (Ephesians 1:3–14).
- This, in turn, creates a humility which receives the gospel by faith, apart from works, lest anyone boast (Ephesians 2:8–9).
- This humility from my justification then leads to unity through a common confession, treating every believer across all cultures and all denominations as brothers and sisters in Christ (Ephesians 2:11–22).

Grace humbles, which in turn requires and enables believers to be united to all who have been saved by the exact same grace. Christians are all shipwrecked souls in the same lifeboat of the gospel. Indeed, believers are united first in their common predicament and only then in the utter joy of being rescued together. Humility makes Christians so grateful to be saved that they desire for the lifeboat to fill up as much as possible, with all kinds of forgiven sinners.

Here is how this same logic might work with branch doctrines that are not essential but nonetheless still important to following Christ in this life:

- God's grace brings sanctification that renews one's mind (Romans 12:1).
- This, in turn, creates a humility which continues to repent, believe, and study, conforming all beliefs to Scripture (Ephesians 1:17–23; 3:16–19).
- This humility of sanctification then leads to unity through speaking the truth in love, sharpening one another, and bearing with one another's errors (Ephesians 4:7–16; Proverbs 27:17; Philippians 3:15).

Christians are already justified by grace alone, but that same grace continues to sanctify them in all areas of their lives, including their doctrine. As believers' minds are renewed by the gospel each day, they humbly conform to biblical truth more and more. As they grow in doctrinal knowledge, out of love, they will try to sharpen and bring fellow Christians along and receive the same in return. Every believer should change their minds when they are shown positions that are more biblical. When Christians continue to disagree, they give one another space and time to grow as God blesses.

The last level or category of doctrine, those twig issues which are *adiaphora*, matters which are insignificant, might work out this way:

- God's grace brings a wisdom from above that is peaceable, gentle, and impartial (James 3:13–18).

- This, in turn, creates a humility which follows one's own conscience as believers submit to Christ's Lordship as best they can (Romans 14).
- This humility then leads to unity through love for the weaker believers, respect for their Christian freedom, and the avoidance of useless controversy (1 Corinthians 8:1–3; 2 Timothy 2:23).

God's grace in the gospel creates a gospel-wrought humility, which, in turn, leads to a gospel-driven unity. In these indifferent matters of doctrine, God's grace brings wisdom that puts peace and love above the need to be proven right on a minor matter. That helps believers put these twig issues in proper perspective, and they thus dare not disrupt the peace of a brother over a minor matter, as Paul warns, "Who are you to pass judgment on the servant of another? It is before his own master that he stands or falls. And he will be upheld, for the Lord is able to make him stand" (Romans 14:4).

How might God's grace, humility, and unity work itself out practically in Christ's body? Consider my congregation, which is governed by our denomination's polity.[15] Regarding essential doctrines, the call to humility and unity means that my congregation gladly admits to membership anyone who can make a sincere profession of faith in Christ, regardless of whether they agree with us on secondary matters, including some fairly important ones.[16] For instance, we believe in the doctrine of predestination, but we do not require that conviction from all members. It is a difficult doctrine to comprehend, so we happily receive them as full and equal members of our church; they are Christians.

Likewise, we gladly baptize the infants of our church members, but do not require every family who joins our congregation to conform to this practice as they follow their own conscience on the matter. We cannot conceive of denying the parents membership in Christ's church as they sincerely and humbly work these things through before the Lord. These members belong to Jesus, so who are we to deny them membership in His body? Why put God to the test by requiring more for church membership than God requires (cf. Acts 15:10)? It is our conviction that belief in the essential matters of salvation is enough for church membership. Humility receives all who have been saved by grace as full members of Christ's church, regardless of differences on secondary matters.

What about important doctrinal issues? How do God's grace, humility, and unity help guide us regarding these? These are doctrinal issues we do not require members to believe, and yet forthrightly teach and strive to convince every member, in time, with patience and wisdom as God sanctifies them at His perfect pace. When those important issues arise in the sermon text, the preacher will not shy away from them. We do not hide our convictions on those matters, even as we consciously choose to major on the majors and keep our focus on Jesus Christ. Yet it is important that our church knows where we stand on these issues, precisely so that we can stay united. Otherwise we would constantly be debating what we thought about these issues instead of discussing ways that we can advance the gospel by serving our community or helping plant new churches.

Therefore, in our polity, before a man can serve as an officer in the church, he must agree with all these issues (and many more, as spelled out in the Westminster Confession of Faith). Not because we think any of these secondary doctrines save, but because we think they are biblical nonetheless. In order to maintain our unity as a congregation, our leaders ought to be of one mind on such things. At the same time, we cooperate with and enjoy warm fellowship and spiritual unity with a whole host of churches in our community that have different convictions on these important matters. We respect their right to investigate biblical truth and arrive at their own conclusions, following their own consciences. Humility accepts and works with these churches as equals in Christ, even as we agree to disagree on some secondary matters.

Finally, we come to matters insignificant, those things considered *adiaphora*. In these we simply allow for a large range of Christian freedom for every church member. Some members of legal age enjoy alcohol in moderation; others do not drink at all. Some members have strict daily devotions and family worship; others struggle with daily discipline, yet never miss a church activity. Some members love the annual celebration of Easter; others think of every Sunday as resurrection Sunday.

We strive to major on the majors and to preach Christ and Him crucified. Our hope is to disciple people wherever they are in their daily faith and struggles and to lead them in worship with sincerity and truth, whatever style it may be. I desire to have my opinions and express them, but in the end, to let *adiaphora* be *adiaphora*. This is not just a matter of practical wisdom. It is a matter of humility, of dying to self, putting first things first, and, according to Paul in Ephesians 4, being one body with one Lord, one faith, and one baptism.

Humility in Conflict

> *If possible, so far as it depends on you,*
> *live peaceably with all.*
> **—Romans 12:18**

If church unity is to be attained, humility must be right at the center. So often a doctrinal fight is really just a smoke screen for something else, some power struggle between leaders who pretend they are standing on principle.

I once served on a judicial commission in my presbytery that was charged with trying to bring peace to a large, historic church that had more or less divided into two parties. This was an old church, proud of its heritage, and with a statute of a famous nineteenth-century pastor on its lawn. Although both sides claimed to argue from principle, in the end, the conflict was simply about differences in style between a longtime senior pastor and his successor. Some members adored the former pastor's leadership; others preferred the new pastor's style and direction. Given this, I told the feuding parties that they would never resolve their differences until they first tore down the statue on the front lawn. I was met with blank stares. They had no idea what the statue had to do with anything, and they did not tear it down. Having missed the point, soon enough, predictably and sadly, the church divided into two separate congregations. It was a division over style and leadership, not the essentials of the gospel.

Such division must not be so within Christ's church. Division should not occur over differences of style and personal agendas. Believers should submit to one another and be eager to maintain the unity of the Spirit in the bond of peace, with Christ alone as their cornerstone and focus. But the church is not yet perfect. Paul and Barnabas parted for a time. Disagreements are going to arise, but when they do, believers should see them as a great opportunity to display love and humility toward one another, even in conflict, whether over doctrine or something else.

Gene Edwards illustrates this principle well in his unique book about church conflict entitled *A Tale of Three Kings: A Study in Brokenness.* The three kings in the book are Saul, David, and Absalom, whom Edwards uses as a parable to study the dysfunction that leads to power struggles in many churches. The book reflects on David's response to the threats that both Saul and Absalom pose to his leadership. One passage is particularly poignant, based on the episode in 1 Samuel 19 in which King Saul hurls his spear at David in an attempt to kill him.

David had a question: What do you do when someone throws a spear at you?

Does it not seem odd to you that David did not know the answer to this question? After all, everyone else in the world knows what to do when a spear is thrown at them. Why, you pick up the spear and throw it right back!

"When someone throws a spear at you, David, just wrench it right out of the wall and throw it back. Absolutely everyone else does, you can be sure."

And in doing this small feat of returning thrown spears, you will prove many things: You are courageous. You stand for the right. You boldly stand against the wrong. You are tough and can't be pushed around. You will not stand for injustice or unfair treatment. You are the defender of the faith, keeper of the flame, detector of all heresy. You will not be wronged. All of these attributes then combine to prove that you are also, obviously, a candidate for kingship. Yes, perhaps you are the Lord's anointed.

After the order of King Saul.[17]

Believers always have a choice when they face conflict in the church, whatever the issue involved. They can pick up the spear and hurl it back, hoping to win the battle and keep their position, even in the cause of truth and justice. Or they can put church unity at the top of their list, just under the gospel itself. Christians may lose the battle if they refuse to throw the spear back. They may even lose their church and have to move. Then again, the church was never theirs. Humble believers may lose the earthly battle, but they will sow a harvest of righteousness.

Even when Christians think a doctrinal issue is worthy of conflict, they must always lead with humility. Fight for the gospel with humility. Argue for other important truths with humility. Acquiesce in minor matters with humility. Always be prepared to be corrected by anyone who argues God's truth accurately—even as David submitted to Abigail in 1 Samuel 25, in a beautiful display of a superior submitting to his social inferior simply because she was right. That is the kind of "wisdom from above" which is "pure, then peaceable, gentle, open to reason, full of mercy and good fruits, impartial and sincere" (James 3:17). But "where jealousy and selfish ambition exist, there will be disorder and every vile practice" (James 3:16). Conflicts over doctrine can occur over principled differences, or they may be a matter of disorder caused by pride.

I am convinced that if believers pursue humility and love toward their opponents, doing their best to be at peace with all as far as it depends on them, they will experience unity in Christ. The relationship may be one-sided for a while or perhaps for a long while. These believers, however, will do right by Christ and His body. They will do their part to grow the church into the unity of the faith and the stature of the fullness of Christ. They will be part of creating a harvest of righteousness, sown in peace, as one who by God's grace, makes peace. That is not such a bad thing at all.

PRAYER

O God, the Father of our Lord Jesus Christ,
our only Saviour, the Prince of Peace:
give us grace seriously to lay to heart
the great dangers we are in by our unhappy divisions.
Take away all hatred and prejudice,
and whatever else may hinder us
from godly union and concord;
that, as there is but one body and one Spirit,
one hope of our calling,
one Lord, one faith, one baptism,
one God and Father of us all,
so we may henceforth be all of one heart and of one soul,
united in one holy bond of peace, of faith and charity,
and may with one mind and one mouth glorify you;
through Jesus Christ our Lord.
—Anglican Book of Common Prayer[18]

CHAPTER THIRTEEN

. . . .

TURNING WOES INTO BLESSINGS: HUMILITY AND CHURCH IMAGE

*Religion is never a good force per se, but merely the final conflict
between human self-esteem and divine mercy,
and the one is as frequently victorious as the other.*
—**Reinhold Niebuhr**[1]

*The twenty-four Elders . . . cast their crowns
before the throne, saying, "Worthy are you, our Lord and God,
to receive glory and honor and power."*
—**Revelation 4:10b–11a**

The great newspaper columnist and religious skeptic, H. L. Mencken,
once said about America, "Heave an egg out of a Pullman window, and
you will hit a Fundamentalist almost anywhere in the United States
today."[2] He did not say this favorably, having gotten a bad taste of
fundamentalist Christianity from his coverage of the infamous 1925
Scopes Monkey Trial in Dayton, Tennessee. However, one fundamentalist garnered his respect, the Presbyterian theologian J. Gresham
Machen. Upon the latter's untimely death on New Year's Day, 1937,
Mencken wrote the following obituary for Machen:

> He was actually a man of great learning, and, what is more,
> of sharp intelligence. . . . Thus he fell out with the reform-
> ers who have been trying, in late years, to convert the

Presbyterian Church into a kind of literary and social club, devoted vaguely to good works. . . . His one and only purpose was to hold it [the Church] resolutely to what he conceived to be the true faith. . . . He denied absolutely that anyone had a right to revise and sophisticate Holy Writ. . . . In his own position there was never the least shadow of inconsistency.[3]

This commitment to God's Word inspired Machen to write one of his classic works, *Christianity and Liberalism*, in which he describes how the abandonment of orthodoxy was nothing less than a denial of the gospel, replacing grace with a religion of salvation by works. In that vein, Machen concludes the book in this way:

Thus the warfare of the world has entered even into the house of God. And sad indeed is the heart of the man who has come seeking peace. Is there no refuge from strife? . . . Is there no place where two or three can gather in Jesus' name . . . to forget human pride, to forget the passions of war, to forget the puzzling problems of industrial strife, and to unite in overflowing gratitude at the foot of the Cross? If there be such a place, then that is the house of God and that the gate of heaven. And from under the threshold of that house will go forth a river that will revive the weary world.[4]

What would it look like for churches to again become gardens from which this River of Life flows? Not waters of worldly excitement or human cleverness but the water of Christ? The more believers have this River flowing in them, the more Christian churches will become gardens of grace and humility, rather than factories striving to churn out some product.

Having explored what it means to be a humble church together as the body of Christ, what does humility looks like as the church interacts with the fallen world? When unbelievers think of a particular

Christian congregation, what do they see? This chapter returns to Matthew 23 to consider what Jesus has to say about humility and church image, largely by way of rebuke.

Woes Turned to Blessings

> *The humble do not want to be proud;*
> *the proud do not want to be humble.*
> *The humble see their pride and loathe it;*
> *the proud see humbling and loathe it.*
> *The humble do not recognize their humility;*
> *the proud do not recognize their pride.*
> —**Mike Sharrett**[5]

> *He who thinks little of God, thinks much of himself.*
> —**Charles Spurgeon**[6]

What sort of image do believers want their churches to project to the watching world? In a sense, Christians can become too concerned with the question, constantly looking at themselves. A better posture is to be self-forgetful, looking only to Christ, so that those who observe believers cannot help but begin to wonder what has so captured their gaze. By this, perhaps those outside the church will find Him too. That is the goal, after all. At the same time, those who observe believers will see something. What do churches want outsiders to see?

As we observed in chapter 11, Jesus follows up His exhortation to humility in Matthew 23 with the famous seven woes pronounced upon the scribes and Pharisees. They received these maledictions because they were exalting themselves. This passage on humility pronounces God's judgment upon the proud, particularly self-important leaders within the church, who peacock their piety for all to see. Jesus's language indicates that at least some of these leaders were likely unconverted (cf. Matthew 23:13, 27). They were simply incapable of being spiritually humble before God, as they were not born again in the first place and could not see the kingdom of God (cf. John 3:1–8).

But the converted can still take these rebukes to heart and use them as a measure to evaluate themselves. There is much to learn from these woes. As done previously, I will reverse the woes, applying the opposite of their precepts so that churches may receive from Christ not malediction, but benediction—words of blessing. Jesus teaches in verse 12 that when believers humble themselves, He will indeed exalt them. He will bless them. By considering each of these woes, believers may heed their warnings and therefore experience Christ's blessing within their churches.

Humility and Evangelism

"But woe to you, scribes and Pharisees, hypocrites! For you shut the kingdom of heaven in people's faces. For you neither enter yourselves nor allow those who would enter to go in.

"Woe to you, scribes and Pharisees, hypocrites! For you travel across sea and land to make a single proselyte, and when he becomes a proselyte, you make him twice as much a child of hell as yourselves."
—Matthew 23:13, 15[7]

In these first two woes, Jesus addresses the way these Jewish leaders evangelized. They had great zeal for their own religious parties and worked hard to enlarge their own camps. Jesus says plainly, however, that they were not winning people to grace; they were not winning people to eternal life. Rather, the scribes and Pharisees had a religious system that emphasized obedience and merit, so that men and women looked holy and perhaps did all sorts of good deeds, but without hearts of repentance or humility. The scribes' and Pharisees' disciples only ended up fit for hell, where they could continue to worship themselves and their own works, hollowing themselves out with each striving.

What can believers learn from this rebuke as they seek to evangelize? That their focus should be upon grace for needy sinners. Believers do not try to win people to a religious system in which they can look strong but try to win people who are weak to a system of unmerited grace, won for them by Christ on His cross.

In his famous passage on evangelism in 1 Corinthians 9, Paul makes much the same point in a rather different way.

> For though I am free from all, I have made myself a servant to all, that I might win more of them. To the Jews I became as a Jew, in order to win Jews. To those under the law I became as one under the law (though not being myself under the law) that I might win those under the law. To those outside the law I became as one outside the law (not being outside the law of God but under the law of Christ) that I might win those out-side the law. To the weak I became weak, that I might win the weak. I have become all things to all people, that by all means I might save some. I do it all for the sake of the gospel, that I may share with them in its blessings. (1 Corinthians 9:19–23)

This text is well known and well taught today as an apologetic for contextualizing Christian ministry, exhorting believers to major on the majors and not let matters of Christian freedom become an obstacle to the gospel. Paul is answering one of the questions the Corinthians had asked in a letter: whether Christians may eat meat previously used in pagan ceremonies. Across three chapters, Paul famously answers by saying: sometimes yes, sometimes no, depending on one's motive for eating it and what it does to one's neighbor (cf. 1 Corinthians 8:4–13; 10:23–31). The two principles in 1 Corinthians 8:1 and 10:31 frame the debate. First, "Knowledge puffs up, but love builds up" (in chapter 8). Second, "Whether you eat or drink, or whatever you do, do all to the glory of God" (in chapter 10). In other words, the bigger questions when it comes down to matters of Christian freedom are not so much whether to smoke cigars or drink alcohol, but to ask the two questions: Which choice most loves my neighbor? Which choice most glorifies God?

This principle of contextualization is important within its original context. Paul is trying to love both Jew and Greek as best he can to the glory of God and for the advancement of the gospel. It is perhaps even more important to understand 1 Corinthians 9 within the larger context of the whole of Paul's first letter to the Corinthians. Paul wrote this letter to answer a number of questions the Corinthians had, but before he answers, he deals with the *deeper* issues, things he has heard from "Chloe's people" (1 Corinthians 1:11).

Chloe's people reported to Paul that the Corinthians were divided, quarrelsome, and proud. They were the megachurch of their day with many gifts and much wealth, but the Corinthians were dysfunctional in practically every other way. Paul spends the first six chapters reminding the Corinthians of the gospel—going after their pride. Only then does he begin to answer their questions.

So, in 1 Corinthians 9:20–22, Paul describes two pairs of people that he becomes like in order to reach them—except that the second pair is incomplete.

9:20 – Paul becomes as a Jew, to win Jews.

9:21 – Paul becomes as a Gentile (those outside the law), to win Gentiles.

9:22 – Paul becomes as weak, to win the weak.

What is missing? Jews and Gentiles are mentioned over against each other. What about the weak? There is no counterpoint to the weak. Paul never completes the pairing; he never mentions becoming strong to win the strong.

I believe that Paul left out the strong from his list quite on purpose. He writes that believers should make cultural accommodations at times in order for the gospel to go forth. Thus, for instance in

today's culture, few believers worship in Latin or in unheated build-
ings. And Christians can—and should—become weak to those who
are weak. Preachers should follow Paul's example in 1 Corinthians
2:1–5, preaching "in fear and much trembling" of the Savior who was
crucified, something that the weak will begin to understand, but the
strong will not grasp until it is too late.

But evangelism makes no sense if believers try to become strong
to win the strong because the very sin which is keeping them from the
kingdom is their own misguided self-esteem. The strong do not know
that they need a Savior, so why should Christians try to become strong
to win them? How can believers cozy up to the vainglorious with their
own version of vanity and hope in that way to win them to a crucified
Savior? They cannot. Believers might win the strong to their church,
or to a more moral lifestyle, or even as a friend. However, Christians
will never win the strong *to Christ* by pretending to be strong with
them. So churches should not try to win outsiders by the variety and
strength of their programs or by promising health and wealth to converts. They should not try to become strong to the strong, but preach
Christ crucified.

This does not mean that Christians should give up on the proud
and self-righteous. Otherwise, there would be no hope for anyone.
However, if the strong are to come to Christ, it will not be until they
are humbled, until they are weak. Believers must not try to become
strong with them in order to win them, but rather, Christians display
their own weakness and tell of Christ's grace. Such an approach will
do two things at once—it will both repel and attract. It will repel
those who wish to remain strong in themselves, for they see no need
for a Savior on a cross. It will attract those who know they need God's
grace—those who know they are weak.

Churches which offer such a welcome to the weak may begin to
overflow to the point that *members* will be unable to serve all the new
believers—all the more reason for the church to depend on God in its
weakness. If that growth does happen, then a word of warning from

the great preacher Charles Spurgeon is in order. He writes this to ministers, but his words are applicable to all believers:

> In the matter of soul-winning, humility makes you feel that you are nothing and nobody, and that, if God gives you success in the work, you will be driven to ascribe to Him all the glory, for none of the credit of it could properly belong to you.[8]

If churches are reaching the weak, as ones who are weak themselves, saved by grace alone, then they are already well on their way to giving God all the glory. Churches will stand amazed that God might use them to reach a precious soul with the gospel. Believers are but beggars showing other beggars where to find bread.

During my ministry in a previous church as an associate pastor (where I was patiently mentored by a tremendous senior pastor who lives out much of the humility detailed in this book), I was introduced to a woman originally from South Korea who was interested in learning more about Jesus. I met with her over lunch three times, along with the colleague who had introduced us. By the third lunch, she had become a Christian, and she was giving me all sorts of credit regarding her conversion.

She was baptized soon after, and as she gave her testimony before the elders, she also related that she had Christian friends in Korea who had been praying for her for more than twenty years. Surely the work of conversion is entirely in God's hands, so that all the glory belongs to Him (cf. Romans 11:36). But as far as believers had any role to play, who do you think should get more credit for this woman's conversion: a pastor who met with her just three times, or friends who faithfully prayed for her for over twenty years? Of course, it is those who prayed.

It is God who predestines, God who regenerates, and God who redeems. Insofar as He includes believers in the process, that too, is part of God's gracious plan. To Him alone be all the glory in evangelism.

And because it is God who is at work, believers do not try to become strong to the strong, but they become weak to the weak. Evangelism is all about unmerited grace, pure and free.

Humility and Worship

"Woe to you, blind guides, who say, 'If anyone swears by the temple, it is nothing, but if anyone swears by the gold of the temple, he is bound by his oath.' You blind fools! For which is greater, the gold or the temple that has made the gold sacred?. . . And whoever swears by the temple swears by it and by him who dwells in it.

"Woe to you, scribes and Pharisees, hypocrites! For you tithe mint and dill and cumin, and have neglected the weightier matters of the law: justice and mercy and faithfulness. These you ought to have done, without neglecting the others. You blind guides, straining out a gnat and swallowing a camel!"
—Matthew 23:16–17, 21, 23–24

The practice Jesus condemns in this third woe is odd, and scholars are not entirely sure why the Pharisees thought swearing by the gold of the temple was more sacred then swearing by the temple itself. In either case, the ideal is not to swear by anything at all, but to simply reply yes or no (cf. Matthew 5:37; James 5:12). Jesus is pointing out the superstition and hypocrisy of the scribes and Pharisees, who thought one object more sacred than another, as if not holding to an oath is excusable in some circumstances, depending on the ceremony involved. To further demonstrate their hypocrisy, Jesus condemns the scribes and Pharisees in the fourth woe for picking and choosing which parts of the law to observe. Unsurprisingly, they chose to emphasize minor and external precepts over more spiritual "weightier matters of the law: justice and mercy and faithfulness." The scribes and Pharisees always appeared to focus on what others could see, rather than on matters of the heart.

These woes clearly instruct believers in humility. The woes remind disciples to remain spiritually minded, focused on matters closest to God's heart, rather than trivial, external things that can sometimes preoccupy them. Think about the last time you were critical about some aspect of a worship service. What was the criticism? Was it that the gospel was not clear? Was there a discernible lack of warmth and love within the congregation? That your own singing was half-hearted? If so, then, you are thinking spiritually and ought to pray about those matters, while also giving thanks and encouragement where things went well. However, if you are like me, you were bothered because the person in the next pew sang off-key or the preacher gave an anecdote that was a tad too long, or someone messed up a small point in the liturgy. Did I mention the weak coffee or air-conditioning? By focusing on these outward things, believers are effectively saying those things make a fine worship service. At that point, Christians begin to swear by the gold and not the temple. Believers can begin to think that if these details were fixed, the worship would have been more acceptable—at least to them. They are no longer thinking about what God wants.

What does God want when Christians come to worship? What does make their worship acceptable, besides following the basic biblical instructions concerning worship? God tells Christians what He wants at the end of David's famous psalm of confession, written after his great sin with Bathsheba:

> For you will not delight in sacrifice, or I would give it;
> you will not be pleased with a burnt offering.
> The sacrifices of God are a broken spirit;
> a broken and contrite heart, O God, you will not despise.
> (Psalm 51:16–17)

The sacrifice God most wants is a broken and contrite heart, a needy heart that comes to worship, expecting God's grace. That is what makes Christian worship acceptable. Micah the prophet gives the same reminder:

> "With what shall I come before the LORD,
>   and bow myself before God on high?
> Shall I come before him with burnt offerings,
>   with calves a year old?
> Will the LORD be pleased with thousands of rams,
>   with ten thousands of rivers of oil?
> Shall I give my firstborn for my transgression,
>   the fruit of my body for the sin of my soul?"
> He has told you, O man, what is good;
>   and what does the LORD require of you
> but to do justice, and to love kindness,
>   and to walk humbly with your God? (6:6–8)

So even in the ornate sacrificial system of the Old Testament—a shadow pointing to the greater reality of Christ (cf. Colossians 2:17; Hebrews 10:1)—the emphasis was on having a spiritual mind-set, of worshiping with a broken and contrite heart, and of walking humbly with God. Thousands of rams and rivers of oil cannot replace a heart humbled by grace.

In her essay, "Holy the Firm," Annie Dillard explains her pilgrimage through various denominational traditions and then writes the following about worship:

> The higher Christian churches—where, if anywhere, I belong—come at God with an unwarranted air of professionalism, with authority and pomp, as though they knew what they were doing, as though people in themselves were an appropriate set of creatures to have dealings with God. I often think of the set pieces of liturgy as certain words which people have successfully addressed to God without their getting

killed. In the high churches they saunter through the liturgy like Mohawks along a strand of scaffolding who have long since forgotten their danger. If God were to blast such a service to bits, the congregation would be, I believe, genuinely shocked. But in the low churches you expect it any minute. This is the beginning of wisdom.[9]

Dillard makes it clear in the essay that she prefers liturgy. This is no brief for a low worship style. She also rightly points out how easy it is for believers to go through set prayers and hymns by rote, knowing they will not be "blown to bits," and yet also forgetting that is exactly what they deserve. Why else did Uzzah die when he grabbed the ark after the oxen stumbled (2 Samuel 6:7)? Uzzah thought he was holier than mud—literally. He was not. Mud has never rebelled, has had no cause to be redeemed. Christians, in contrast, are those who can come each Sunday and embrace the ark of God's presence on account of Christ's blood. His death rent the veil of the temple, and when God's wrath came pouring out, it landed upon the cross and not on His people. Remembering this each Sunday is also the beginning of wisdom.

Christians may have strong opinions about liturgy, and worship music, and what sort of dress is appropriate for public worship. I certainly do. There is something that can be very humbling about sticking to a set Christ-centered liturgy. On the other hand, such liturgy can be so grandiose that the focus begins to shift to its own beauty, rather than fixating on Christ, who after all was born in a stable. Either way, the real worship war ought always to be in one's own heart, to be most offended by one's own sin. That is the meaning of worshiping with a broken and contrite heart.

Believers who come humbly are still amazed by God's grace, and that off-key singer becomes a delight to their ears. No amount of liturgical excellence or failure can add or subtract from the work of the cross. "It is finished," is still Jesus's effectual cry. The lengthy anecdote in the sermon without a real point only makes the humble laugh because they remember that an illustration has no power to keep Christ in His grave. Jesus is still in their midst, risen and victorious. When believers come to worship with humility, amazed by grace, it never occurs to them to bicker over who did what in the worship service. They do not bother about who swore what by what bit of gold or not. God has sworn His love for them by Christ, and that is all they need.

Humility and Piety

"Woe to you, scribes and Pharisees, hypocrites! For you clean the outside of the cup and the plate, but inside they are full of greed and self-indulgence. You blind Pharisee! First clean the inside of the cup and the plate, that the outside also may be clean.

"Woe to you, scribes and Pharisees, hypocrites! For you are like whitewashed tombs, which outwardly appear beautiful, but within are full of dead people's bones and all uncleanness. So you also outwardly appear righteous to others, but within you are full of hypocrisy and lawlessness."
—Matthew 23:25–28

These two woes are similar to one another as both contrast outward appearances to inward reality. In both, Jesus rebukes the scribes and Pharisees for wishing to appear righteous to others, while neglecting the greed, selfishness, hypocrisy, and lawlessness still in their hearts. Jesus's words are as striking as they are harsh. The scribes and Pharisees are whitewashed tombs, clean and honorable on the outside, while full of the stink of death. Christian leaders worth their salt know exactly what this feels like from time to time as they prepare to teach or lead in worship. They may look resplendent in their dress clothes, but inwardly, they know how their weeks have gone. They know their own unworthiness. Apparently, this was not so with most of the scribes and Pharisees. What mattered most to them was what others saw. They feared man more than God, and the status of their own reputation eclipsed the pursuit of any real holiness.

In the Sermon on the Mount, Jesus expands upon this pursuit of reputation and gives specific instructions about the public display of piety—instructions that are often ignored today.

"Beware of practicing your righteousness before other people in order to be seen by them, for then you will have no reward from your Father who is in heaven. Thus, when you give to the needy, sound no trumpet before you, as the hypocrites do in the synagogues and in the streets, that they may be praised by others. Truly, I say to you, they have received their reward. But when you give to the needy, do not let your left hand know what your right hand is doing, so that your giving may be in secret. And your Father who sees in secret will reward you.

"And when you pray, you must not be like the hypocrites. For they love to stand and pray in the synagogues and at the street corners, that they may be seen by others. Truly, I say to you, they have received their reward. But when you pray, go into your room and shut the door and pray to your Father who is in secret. And your Father who sees in secret will reward you.

"And when you fast, do not look gloomy like the hypocrites, for they disfigure their faces that their fasting may be seen by others. Truly, I say to you, they have received their reward. But when you fast, anoint your head and wash your face, that your fasting may not be seen by others but by your Father who is in secret. And your Father who sees in secret will reward you." (Matthew 6:1–6, 16–18)

Jesus instructs believers in regard to charitable giving, prayer, and fasting. In each case, He teaches them to practice their piety in secret.

Believers are not to herald their generosity, nor to pray on street corners, nor to fast in a way that gains them notoriety. Obviously, how Christians display their piety has everything to do with pride and humility. Often while displaying piety or humility publicly, believers fall exactly into the trap of conceit, illustrated so well by Southey and Coleridge in their famous poem about the devil walking about the earth.

> He passed a cottage with a double coach-house,
> A cottage of gentility;
> And he owned with a grin that his favorite sin
> Is pride that apes humility.[10]

Christians want to give generously, or pray fervently, thinking they are but a simple cottage offering sincere devotion, while hoping all along that people will most notice the size of their coach house and how pious they are, which is pride aping humility.

I cannot count the ways both blatant and subtle that today's church ignores each of these commands from Matthew 6. To name just a few in terms of money, I think of how churches publish the names of their largest givers, sometimes even soliciting and displaying plaques in honor of those who give to a particular cause. I once pastored a church that had plaques scattered throughout the building. I was particularly taken aback one Sunday when I lifted the silver cup to serve Holy Communion and saw that it was dedicated to the beloved memory of Mildred Stamsblach (or some such name). I thought believers were given the cup in remembrance of someone else. Even the ways that some churches solicit newspaper articles regarding their mercy programs in the community make me wonder if they have read this passage. Would it not be better for them to care for the needy in such a way that their left hand does not know what the right hand is doing? Is that not what Jesus says? I am certain that the motives in such cases of publicity are often good, but it still makes me wonder if the church as a whole has considered such self-heralding in light of Matthew 6.

Believers obviously must pray publicly in worship, and Jesus goes on to instruct them specifically in Matthew 6:7–15 by way of the Lord's Prayer. Jesus taught His followers to keep it short and simple. Christians are not heard for their many words. Believers pray according to God's priorities, as outlined in the six petitions of the Lord's Prayer. Public prayer in worship is part of the gathering of God's people, a family affair. But in Matthew 6:5–6, Jesus is addressing prayer in terms of how the world sees Christians—why it is they pray and by whom they are seen. I wonder if the church has thought about this when its leaders are invited to offer prayers at various political and civic events. I was once part of the planning for a small town's National Day of Prayer event where we were literally going to be on a street corner, and some of the other pastors wanted to make sure that reporters would be there and that there would be adequate banners and balloons for the event. I did not last long on that committee. I have since been part of modest National Day of Prayer events, those whose main purpose was fellowship among believers and actual prayer.

Within the church, I have been to meetings and conferences when it seemed like different people were trying to outdo each another by the length and eloquence and number of biblical citations in their prayers. I do not know their hearts, but something seemed amiss. More practically, when I have received email prayer requests sent to multiple email addresses, I have often debated whether to hit "reply all" or not when encouraging the sender that I am indeed praying. If my motive is to display my piety to all the recipients, it is no better than praying loudly on a street corner.

Regarding fasting, Jesus's instructions are as plain as they can be. Do it so that no one knows. As a caution, do not be legalistic about this. For safety's sake, believers should let their immediate family or roommates know they are fasting. Nonetheless, when believers fast sincerely, they do so in order to intensify their prayers, to make their spiritual need before God tangible and felt. Note that fasting does not appear to be a major program of the New Testament church. It is nowhere mentioned in the epistles, and only twice in Acts, both of those incidents at key moments in the advance of the gospel (Acts 13:2–3; 14:23). Regular fasting does not appear to be a part of normal, Christian piety in the New Testament church. Nevertheless, if and when believers fast, Jesus tells them to do it in secret.

A humble faith produces a piety that is sincere, that begins on the inside and works its way outward, displaying itself only when absolutely necessary. There may be times when believers have to declare how much money they have given (say, to the IRS), or when they should pray in public, or when they may let others know they have been fasting. However, believers do not display their piety to impress anyone. After all, they do not need to justify themselves before God or man; the blood of Christ is sufficient. What matters most to believers is first and foremost the state of their own heart, whether they are living in gratitude to such great grace, not what others may think of them.

How do believers implement these religious practices together in such a way that actively promotes giving and prayer and piety, and yet allows their churches to remain humble before the watching world? When it comes to giving, believers should honor and appreciate every member's tithes and offerings, regardless of the size. Jesus taught His followers to do that when He told the story of the widow's mite (Mark 12:41–44). God owns the cattle on a thousand hills and does not need any extra funds. Believers give as part of living lives of sacrifice and worship (cf. Romans 12:2), not to increase their reputation by the size of their gifts. I see no real cause for pledge drives or publications of names or the promises of plaques. I believe that Christians best assist the cause of humility when they take Jesus's words in Matthew 6:1–4 just as they are.

When it comes to giving to the poor, believers should do whatever is necessary to organize sustained help. Practically this may mean advertising their role to some degree. However, once more, they help the poor because it is needed and to encourage others to join them, not because their reputations need polishing.

When it comes to public prayer in worship or at civic events, Christians should pray simply and directly, hopefully with a plurality of believers so that all are reminded there is but One Mediator between God and man (cf. 1 Timothy 2:5). Believers should keep their prayers as brief as is appropriate and fitting to the situation, keeping their language both plain and reverent. In prayer, Christians are approaching a holy God, the King of the universe, but I doubt that He is ever impressed with the breadth of their vocabulary. What Mark Twain reportedly said about writing may well apply to public prayer: never choose a five-dollar word when a fifty-cent word will do. Yes, sometimes five-dollar words are exactly fitting—words such as *justify*, *consecrate*, and *glory*—but when believers pray in public, they do so keenly aware that they pray as part of the larger body, not to stand out as some sort of master prayer guru or to be admired for the passion and eloquence of their piety. God knows the heart; Christians pray to Him.

The real question for churches is what kind of communities they hope to become. What kind of atmosphere are they trying to create? One where their piety is displayed in such a way that visitors and new members can fit in only by imitating exactly the same kind of public holiness? Are those who lead and pray only those whose outward godliness is intense and intimidating? Jesus said, "Those who are well have no need of a physician, but those who are sick. I came not to call the righteous, but sinners" (Mark 2:17). Churches and their leaders choose the sort of public face they wear, the kind of community they are trying to be. They worship a holy God, yes, and so they remain awestruck and reverent before Him. They are also an assembly of sinners saved by grace, no one any better than anyone else in that regard. They should show that in the way they pray together.

Humility and Culture

> *"Woe to you, scribes and Pharisees, hypocrites!*
> *For you build the tombs of the prophets and decorate the monuments*
> *of the righteous, saying, 'If we had lived in the days of our fathers,*
> *we would not have taken part with them in shedding the blood*
> *of the prophets.' Thus you witness against yourselves that you are sons*
> *of those who murdered the prophets. Fill up, then, the measure*
> *of your fathers. You serpents, you brood of vipers, how are you*
> *to escape being sentenced to hell?"*
> **—Matthew 23:29–33**

The final and seventh woe transitions to Jesus's proclamation of the coming judgment upon Israel, even as the gospel went forth to all nations, saving all who cast themselves on Christ, both Jews and Gentiles. This woe is tied to that particular, singular moment in redemptive history. Nevertheless, I believe there is a lesson for believers today. Apparently, the scribes and Pharisees held to a form of chronological snobbery, believing that they would have clearly avoided the sins of generations past, that they were somehow wiser and godlier than their fathers.

A similar mind-set can be found in today's church, both in terms of attitudes toward the past and attitudes toward the wider culture at large. Regarding the past, believers may look with horror upon the sins of slavery and Jim Crow, and rightly condemn both institutions. But do they really think that many believers today would have avoided the cultural pressures that captured so much of the church at that time? Would most of today's white Christians really have been among that small, persecuted minority in the antebellum American South who actively opposed slavery? It is possible, but Matthew 23:30 would suggest caution in that regard. Believers might as well say they would have done a better job than Adam in the garden. The same principle applies to Germany in the 1930s. When today's believers evaluate the sins of past generations, humility and empathy are always in good order, even as they speak the truth and hold to the standards of God's Word. Christians might also consider what future generations will say about today's church when believers look back at our cultural accommodations. All have sinned and fallen short of the glory of God.

A similar caution and humility are in order when believers address the sins and failures of the surrounding culture in their own time. Paul refused to judge those outside the church because his primary concern was with holiness inside the church. He says, "For what have I to do with judging outsiders? Is it not those inside the church whom you are to judge? God judges those outside. 'Purge the evil person from among you'" (1 Corinthians 5:12–13). The church has no jurisdiction over unbelievers.

The church's power is entirely spiritual and declarative. Christians proclaim repentance and faith to all who have ears to hear. People may choose to reject the message, and the church has no further authority over them. In fact, Paul tells believers explicitly in 1 Corinthians 5:10 to continue to live among and interact with the immoral in this world. Otherwise, believers would all have to join monasteries, a concept not found within the pages of the New Testament. Paul tells believers simply not to treat unrepentant people as if they were believers.

How does this apply to the church's attitude toward its larger culture?[11] Paul implies that the culture is full of people sick with sin, and churches are to be a hospital stemming the epidemic as best they can. Ultimately, believers can only help people who admit themselves as patients. Unless patients come to the hospital, believers can do little for an unbeliever's soul. Christians can feed those in their community, house them, warn them of the hell that awaits them, but if they do not respond to the gospel, they are not ultimately the church's responsibility.

This may seem harsh, but ultimately, it is both loving and tolerant. Remember, Christians believe in peaceful coexistence, even as they proclaim the reality of heaven and hell. This approach shows love toward the world because believers tell the world of a Savior. This attitude is tolerant because believers do not expect non-Christians to behave as Christians. Believers do not insist that non-Christians agree about every moral issue of the day. How could they? They do not have a biblical worldview.

In regard to their non-Christian neighbors, the gospel frees Christians to be both bold and humble all at once. They are bold in standing for the truth and for the accuracy of every last verse of the Bible. Christians are humble toward their neighbors, because believers do not expect their non-Christian friends to believe until they have been transformed by grace. Believers play their part, but ultimately, transformation is God's work alone.

I think churches make a grave error when they emphasize and engage in the culture wars of their day.[12] Of course, the church should stand for biblical values when it comes to marriage, divorce, homosexuality, abortion, euthanasia, violence, racism, and a score of other social issues. However, when churches choose to emphasize one or more of these as a major part of their identity and ministry, their main mission of bringing grace to needy sinners is obscured. Instead of being a hospital for sinners, these churches become a citadel standing for selective items of righteousness. The gospel is even more obscured when churches begin de facto siding with particular political parties and advocating particular public policy solutions to societal ills. Has God really commissioned the church to be wise and competent regarding such worldly details? Many congregations today have members who are almost all members of one political party or the other. As a result, the church is seen as one more tribe vying for power and influence, one more special interest to throw in the political mix.

C. S. Lewis made similar observations in his 1940 essay, "The Dangers of National Repentance," when he wrote of the tendency of young Christians to passionately take up the cause of social ills by calling the nation to repent.

The first and fatal charm of national repentance is, therefore, the encouragement it gives us to turn from the bitter task of repenting our own sins to the more congenial one of bewailing—but first, of denouncing—the conduct of others. . . . A group of such young penitents will say, "Let us repent our national sins"; what they mean is, "Let us attribute to our neighbor . . . every abominable motive that Satan can suggest to our fancy."[13]

Lewis's point is that whenever churches address the sins of society, they almost always mean someone else's sins, not their own. That is why churches who actively engage in the culture wars obscure the gospel— they condemn the actions of outsiders rather than focus on their own need for ongoing grace and repentance. Today's culture will often hear only words of judgment and self-righteousness when churches take on the moral issues of the day, even if that is not the church's intent.

Within the midst of the day's culture wars, there must be a place of respite, a place of forgiveness. The church is a place where people of all political persuasions and nationalities can come together and worship the God who saves and redeems this world. Worship is where there can be reconciliation and fellowship between those that would otherwise be enemies. Civil Rights activist and liberal Baptist minister Will D. Campbell was severely criticized for attempting to minister to members of the KKK, to which he responded, "anyone who is not as concerned with the immortal soul of the dispossessor as he is with the suffering of the dispossessed is being something less than Christian."[14] Campbell insisted that Jesus loved bigots as well. Think about the people you disagree with politically. Is your attitude as generous as Campbell's? Do you put the forgiveness of Christ ahead of your political opinions and agendas?

In the 1980s I met a former Iraqi Special Forces soldier who had come to Christ. He spent his days in Turkey trying to bring the gospel to his former enemies, Iranian refugees fleeing the slaughter of the horrific Iran-Iraq war that lasted for eight bloody years. What sort of community can bring rival ethnic groups together like this? It is the community of the gospel, the church.

If an Iraqi can love Iranians for the sake of Christ, even in the midst of a war, is it possible that Republicans and Democrats can worship together? Christians had better hope so, or they have truly lost their way. Of course, believers may not agree on the issues of the day, but there is something greater that unites them, a joint humility that brings them to the foot of the cross. Christians place love, reconciliation, and forgiveness before every other opinion they have.

There is perhaps no contemporary story of forgiveness more powerful than one that comes out of one of the greatest political conflicts and tragedies in recent history, the Vietnam War. One of the most famous photographs from this war was taken by Nick Ut. He captured a group children running from a village that had just been hit by napalm from US bombers. In the middle is a crying, naked, nine-year-old girl named Phan Thi Kim Phuc. In 2008, she told her story to NPR's *All Things Considered*:

> On June 8, 1972, I ran out from Cao Dai temple in my village, Trang Bang, South Vietnam; I saw an airplane getting lower and then four bombs falling down. I saw fire everywhere around me. Then I saw the fire over my body, especially on my left arm. My clothes had been burned off by fire. I was 9 years old but I still remember my thoughts at that moment: I would be ugly and people would treat me in a different way. My picture was taken in that moment on Road No. 1 from Saigon to Phnom Penh. After a soldier gave me some drink and poured water over my body, I lost my consciousness.
>
> Several days after, I realized that I was in the hospital, where I spent 14 months and had 17 operations. It was a very difficult time for me when I went home from the hospital.

Our house was destroyed; we lost everything and we just survived day by day. Although I suffered from pain, itching and headaches all the time, the long hospital stay made me dream to become a doctor. But my studies were cut short by the local government. They wanted me as a symbol of the state. I could not go to school anymore.

The anger inside me was like a hatred as high as a mountain. I hated my life. I hated all people who were normal because I was not normal. I really wanted to die many times. I spent my daytime in the library to read a lot of religious books to find a purpose for my life. One of the books that I read was the Holy Bible.

In Christmas 1982, I accepted Jesus Christ as my personal savior. It was an amazing turning point in my life. God helped me to learn to forgive—the most difficult of all lessons. It didn't happen in a day and it wasn't easy. But I finally got it.

Forgiveness made me free from hatred. I still have many scars on my body and severe pain most days but my heart is cleansed. Napalm is very powerful but faith, forgiveness and love are much more powerful. We would not have war at all if everyone could learn how to live with true love, hope and forgiveness.

If that little girl in the picture can do it, ask yourself: Can you?[15]

That last sentence strikes me. Can believers build communities that extend forgiveness to the watching world? Now, this is a singularly unique and remarkable story, but Phuc's theology of forgiveness is not. That is the province of all Christians. Churches with this sort of humble reconciliation between all kinds of sinners will do far more good than any legislation we could hope to pass.

Refuges of Grace

This poor man cried, and the Lord heard him
and saved him out of all his troubles.
Oh, taste and see that the Lord is good!
Blessed is the man who takes refuge in him!
—Psalm 34:6, 8

When the church turns these woes into blessings, what does the community around it see? It sees Christians who evangelize in such a way that they become weak to the weak. The world sees believers who are utterly unworthy to come into the presence of God, and yet they are bold to do so anyway, covered by the blood of Christ. The community is shown a public piety that accurately reflects the state of believers' hearts. The culture sees a church and a community of love and forgiveness that accepts all kinds of people, rather than standing as one more stockade in the culture wars. Non-Christians see a place from which the River of Life flows freely. Visitors come, and they are pointed to Jesus Christ and His grace by a congregation full of broken but restored sinners. Seekers see a group of people weak in themselves but strong in Christ. They see a place with a great diversity of people, and yet with members who are all united by grace, loving each other as one body. Visitors know that if they are sinners in need of grace, the church will warmly welcome them. This is what humble churches look like—refuges of grace and rest in the midst of a weary world.

PRAYER

We beseech Thee, Lord and Master, to be our help and succour.

Save those among us who are in tribulation;
have mercy on the lowly;
lift up the fallen;
show Thyself to those in need;
heal the sick;

turn again the wanderers of Thy people;
feed the hungry;
ransom our prisoners;
raise up the weak;
comfort the faint-hearted.

Let all nations know that Thou art God alone,
and that Jesus Christ is Thy Son,
and that we are Thy people and the sheep of Thy pasture.
Amen.

—Clement of Rome[16]

CHAPTER FOURTEEN

. . . .

TURNING FACTORIES
INTO GARDENS

The humble Christian is ordinarily the most thriving
and growing Christian. The humble valleys laugh with fatness,
when the high mountains are barren.
—Ebenezer Erskine[1]

Let not the wise man boast in his wisdom,
let not the mighty man boast in his might,
let not the rich man boast in his riches,
but let him who boasts boast in this,
that he understands and knows me, that I am the LORD.
—Jeremiah 9:23–24a

Have you ever visited a busy city and found yourself in need of respite from all of the crowds and noise and pollution? Perhaps you then found a walled garden in the midst of the busyness, a place to rest in the cool of the day that was surrounded by flowers and birds rather than cars and peddlers. There is certainly nothing wrong with the energy and commerce that are part and parcel of city life, but sometimes people just need a break from it all. They need peace and quiet.

Indeed, that is what the Lord's Day is for the Christian, a Sabbath from the worries and labors of this world. A sincere church will be that place of rest and respite for believers as they gather with God's people to worship and remind themselves where their true hope lies. Jesus said to come unto Him, all who are weary and heavy laden, and He will give rest for tired souls. Where else will He do that, if not in His church?

Many of today's churches, however, have become so self-oriented and self-consumed that their constant and only goals are growth and motion and the nonstop advertisement of multiple new programs with the inevitable pressure on everyone to do their part to make the church bigger and busier. Just as in a city, the energy and busyness are not bad in themselves. In fact, energy can be very good, as churches work hard to participate in the Great Commission. However, when churches are self-focused, all about their own growth and branding, then there is no rest there for God's people, no gospel. These churches have become factories, when the world needs a garden—a place to rest in Christ from one's own works, surrounded only by His beauty and grace.

How do churches wish for the world to think of them? Often congregations want to be well regarded in terms of size or growth rate. Because my church is located near a large university, when visitors worship with my congregation during the summer months, I feel obliged to point out that the pews are not as full as usual. Why do I feel that need? After all, what kind of church do I want them to see? William Still recounts how, over the decades, his ministry in Aberdeen, Scotland, had gained enough of a reputation that visitors from North America were often disappointed at how small the congregation was when they came to worship. He explains that in part, their small size was due to the work of the gospel itself, causing many in his congregation to leave for the mission field so that they had a "hard time keeping together a working nucleus."[2] That is the sign of a life-giving church, one that is constantly sending out its people and resources for the sake of the kingdom.[3]

Humility and Church Planting

During the past 16 years, I've been the pastor of [this] church.
We've grown from 32 in attendance to over 5,000 members.
Our budget has gone from $43,000 a year to $4.2 million. . . .
Will you let me help you lead your church to the next level?
—**brochure advertising a conference in Columbus, Georgia**[4]

Too many are worldly enough to think in terms
of numbers and statistics, forgetting that there was only one Christ,
three special disciples, twelve in all—and one of these a devil.
—**William Still**[5]

Francis Schaeffer describes well the American obsession with size in his famous 1974 essay, "No Little People, No Little Places." Schaeffer's insights and conclusions still ring true today.

> If a Christian is consecrated [fully to God's service], does this mean he will be in a big place instead of a little place? As there are no little people in God's sight, so there are no little places. . . . Nowhere more than in America are Christians caught in the twentieth-century syndrome of size. Size will show success. If I am consecrated, there will necessarily be large quantities of people, dollars, etc. This is not so. Not only does God not say that size and spiritual power go together, but He even reverses this (especially in the teaching of Jesus) and tells us to be deliberately careful not to choose a place too big for us. We all tend to emphasize big works and big places, but all such emphasis is of the flesh.[6]

This is not to argue that big churches cannot be places of humility, only that there are more important things to aim for than growth. Humility formed by the gospel ought to be at the top of the list. To that end, active church planting can wonderfully aid the church's attempts to maintain humility. I offer this as a suggestion rather than a rule. When believers allow their local churches to become large and well known, the temptation to pride in their leaders becomes sharper and harder to resist. The challenge is for pastors, and often, this temptation to pride is faced by the two or three most influential families who gave much time and treasure to facilitate growth—they can gain an unhealthy sense of ownership.

The larger the church, the more reasons there may be to cling to and fight over things other than the gospel. The more beautiful the building, the stronger the opinions about how it should be maintained or altered. Often, the larger budget brings the more heated debate about its allocation (though small churches are by no means immune to this). The larger the church, the more it may tend to attract successful men and women from the community with mixed spiritual motives, and who may in time work their way into leadership. Large staffs make infighting and power struggles more likely to arise. Such growth in pride is not inevitable, but it is not uncommon either. Believers must be on guard.

If believers are on guard against such dangers and seek the growth of Christ's kingdom as foremost, then they will be more likely to plant sister congregations, rather than growing their own church larger and larger. This is no guarantee against pride since one may take pride in the planting itself. Scheduling two morning services can also be a humble approach to meeting the needs of a growing congregation; it is a form of sacrificial service by the preacher, musicians, ushers, and so forth. However, if the decision to hold two services is meant only to grow the numbers of one's own congregation, then I am afraid it may take on a Babel-like character, seeking to concentrate fame and power in one place, building one's own little kingdom higher and higher. A modern American preacher's ego can reach just as far into the sky as any medieval cathedral in all its gaudy glory. If believers flattened their own little empires and instead spread God's glory far and wide through planting sister churches, they would better serve the kingdom of God.

The danger of pride is not lessened either by a multi-site model centered upon a celebrity pastor. I know the motives for such a model are often good, but one wonders how it promotes the cause of Christian humility to so elevate one teacher to the point that he is live-streamed into various satellite sites across a city or region. After all, it was Paul who said, "What then is Apollos? What is Paul? Servants through whom you believed, as the Lord assigned to each. I planted, Apollos watered, but God gave the growth. So neither he who plants nor he who waters is anything, but only God who gives the growth" (1 Corinthians 3:5–7).

When done well, church planting decentralizes power by spinning off a portion of one congregation and entrusting it to new leadership. Church planting intentionally sets up a sister competitor of sorts, which visitors may attend instead of the sending church. The sister church may grow at the planting church's expense, in terms of both number and budget. In fact, that is the very goal. Instead of building large staffs in one place under the leadership of one leader, church planting spreads the glory around, remembering the oft-repeated dictum that "Ministers are like manure: pile them up and they begin to stink; spread them around and they do a lot of good."

Church planting also helps ensure that congregations stay small enough to know one another as the family of God. Church planting is one way to prevent churches from turning into factories, by keeping them modest enough to remain gardens of real, authentic community, quirks and all. It is one way to learn continually not to despise days of small things and to trust God to keep laying new plumb lines (cf. Zechariah 4:10).

Church planting takes a good amount of humility, for it involves giving up resources and numbers and control that enable a church plant eventually to become its own congregation. I know how hard this is because my congregation has done it, sending out almost a third of our core members to begin a new work several years back. The two years following this sacrifice were two of the hardest I have endured as a pastor, particularly the toll it took on my self-vaunted humility. I discovered resentments and feelings of entitlement in the recesses of my heart that I did not know existed. Relationships were strained, and it was only by prayer and the patience of others that the congregation was sustained. Despite such a price, I was worried more about the dangers to our congregation if we had not planted; that we would grow to the point that real care and relationships would grow shallow as the pressure to add staff and services increased. We planted for the sake of humility, that the cause of the kingdom would take priority over our own reputation as a growing church. We wanted the gospel to go out more effectively and the means of grace to double, even as our own worldly prestige lessened. In a very real sense, it was our church saying Christ must increase, and we must decrease (cf. John 3:30).

The Church as a Garden

Now the full number of those who believed were of one heart and soul, and no one said that any of the things that belonged to him was his own, but they had everything in common. And with great power the apostles were giving their testimony to the resurrection of the Lord Jesus, and great grace was upon them all.
—Acts 4:32–33

I have been blessed to be part of many wonderful, godly churches, each of which had its own strengths and weaknesses. The little Congregational church my wife and I attended while I was in seminary embodied humility. Located in a small fishing and quarry village north of Boston, it was recommended to us by the reputation of its preacher, who more than lived up to our expectations. My wife and I, however, fell in love with the church itself.

Founded in 1830, the church continued to hold to its original, orthodox statement of faith. It honored its tradition, but rather than being stuck in the past, the church saw the need to reach its own unique, quirky community. The congregation was largely blue-collar, but members were well educated and with a strong thirst to be fed God's Word each week. The worship service was simple and traditional but punctuated by an incongruous drum set in the old sanctuary to remind us that it was no longer 1830. The church was so Christ-focused that it knew it had a great gospel to bring to the world, even in the rocky ground of New England. This little church has an impact far beyond its size in terms of an incredible youth and missions outreach, among many other ministries. In fact, a dear friend of mine has been there in the same position as youth pastor for more than thirty years. Who does that? A man both gifted and humbled by God's grace.

I wish I could describe the overall love and humility of this congregation, but I cannot capture it in words. How could I? The body of Christ is meant to be experienced, not explained. Perhaps one story will suffice.

This little church mentored a number of ministerial students each year. Even though the senior pastor was one of the most outstanding preachers in the region, he kindly shared the Sunday morning pulpit with these students several times a year, to give them a chance to grow in their gifts. One Sunday a classmate of mine was invited to preach, but he had a problem with his printer that morning. My classmate did his best with what notes he had managed to assemble. In the middle of the service, he got terribly lost, and in a flurry of papers, got completely flummoxed and became paralyzed with embarrassment. In the middle of the awkward silence, a well-known professor in the congregation blurted out, "Relax! You are with family!" Everyone sighed, and the student preacher laughed and finished his sermon just fine. We did not need an excellent sermon every Sunday; we just wanted to be together, basking in the gospel of grace.

I once made the mistake of telling the senior pastor that he had a great church, and he gently corrected me, saying no, it was just a normal church. Such a congregation is what can be cultivated when the gospel is preached with sincerity and prayer. I have seen it many times since. A humble church is a place of faith and hope and love, centered on Christ the Lord, feeding constantly on His character and humility.

The Life We Now Live

> *I am crucified with Christ: nevertheless I live;*
> *yet not I, but Christ liveth in me: and the life which I now live*
> *in the flesh I live by the faith of the Son of God,*
> *who loved me, and gave himself for me.*
>
> —**Galatians 2:20** KJV

Coming to the end of this book on humility, my inclination is to aim for some grand finale, some profound and heartrending prose. Instead, I love the way Tolkien concludes his epic *Lord of the Rings* trilogy. Its characters travel to the far reaches of the known world in a quest to save their precious Middle Earth from devastation. Then this great trilogy ends the way it begins—with a simple Hobbit living in his hole in the ground, in his little village in the Shire. After all the drama of this great adventure, this War of the Ring, Tolkien concludes his grand story thus, finishing with Sam the gardener, Sam the servant, returning from his latest journey to his bride:

> Sam turned to Bywater, and so came back up the Hill, as day was ending once more. And he went on, and there was yellow light, and fire within; and the evening meal was ready, and he was expected. And Rose drew him in, and set him in his chair, and put little Elanor upon his lap. He drew a deep breath. "Well, I'm back," he said.[7]

If you have finished this book, chances are that you are in the same place you were when you began it. You look the same, have the same job, the same family, and the same church. Likewise, instead of some grand elfish song or brilliant saying from Gandalf the Wizard, Tolkien closes with Sam simply saying, "I'm back." Tolkien is also clear that the sufferings and triumphs Sam went through on his adventure changed him. He returned nobler and braver—a knight. Outwardly, he was still just Sam, and you are still just you.

But if you approached the subject prayerfully, and as the Holy Spirit worked, I trust you are a little changed, godlier and nobler— a knight. May you end your study knowing the study in humility never ends. You can never grow in humility too much, nor fight pride enough. You are still you, and you still have great adventures ahead of you, even as you dwell in your own modest Hobbit hole wherever that may be. *"I am back,"* you may say. Life continues.

There is no need for some grand quote on my part, some special eloquence. The goal is to grow in humility, not brilliance. I will, however, quote another's eloquence. J. C. Ryle, the prolific nineteenth-century Anglican bishop wrote the following:

> Humility may well be called the queen of the Christian graces. To know our own sinfulness and weakness and to feel our need of Christ is the start of saving religion.
>
> Humility is a grace which has always been a distinguishing feature in the character of the holiest saints in every age. Abraham and Moses and Job and David and Daniel and Paul were all eminently humble men.
>
> Above all, humility is a grace within the reach of every true Christian. All converted people should work to adorn with humility the doctrine they profess. If they can do nothing else, they can strive to be humble.
>
> Do you want to know the root and spring of humility? One word describes it. The root of humility is right knowledge. The person who really knows himself and his own heart, who knows God and his infinite majesty and holiness, who knows Christ and the price at which he was redeemed, that person will never be a proud person.

He will count himself, like Jacob, unworthy of the least of all God's mercies. He will say of himself, like Job, "I am unworthy." He will cry, like Paul, "I am the worst of sinners." He will consider others better than himself (Philippians 2:3). Ignorance—nothing but sheer ignorance, ignorance of self, of God, and of Christ—is the real secret of pride. From that miserable self-ignorance may we daily pray to be delivered. The wise person knows himself and will find nothing within to make him proud.[8]

Ryle calls humility the queen of the Christian graces, and I call it the jester. In many ways, there is no difference. Christ is still the King, and whether he gives believers humility as a queen or as a jester, it is still one of His greatest and most indispensable gifts to them. Apart from humility, believers have no justification, no hope of heaven, no life. For those who exalt themselves will be humbled, and those who humble themselves will be exalted.

Ryle says that humility ought to be sought by all Christians. Believers do not need to be famous, or greatly gifted, or well educated to pursue the greatest of all Christian privileges—holiness through a more steadfast humility. Any and every Christian can seek humility and, in that sense, become great. That is one reason heaven will hold so many surprises, for many who are last will be first. In the end, what will matter is whether believers died to themselves, picked up their cross daily, and followed Christ. Did Christians pursue every endeavor in humble reliance upon God? Did believers put others first, seeking to serve as Christ served them? Did such humility express itself in lives of faith, hope, and love, focusing on that which will last into eternity? Did Christians live crucified lives, living by faith in the Son of God who gave Himself for them? Were their lives about Jesus and His fame and glory and grace, rather than their own glory?

If believers live for Christ and not themselves, then there is no grand or special way to apply all this. They live their lives in the callings and stations that God has laid out for them. Believers love their families, do their jobs, and serve their communities. Christians go to church, worship God, and serve the body. In the end, when God has portioned their time, believers die. They take their last breaths, lay down these earthly frames, and go home. That is it. That is a life of faith, a life of humility. It is nothing special at all, except that it is God who calls and equips believers to walk in these good works. In that sense a humble life is nothing short of remarkable. For God Himself, high and lifted up, who inhabits eternity, comes to dwell with those who are contrite and lowly of spirit. God humbles Himself to come and live in believers who deserve nothing but wrath. This is grace. This is Christ.

PRAYER

Lord, make us instruments of thy peace.
Where there is hatred, let us sow love;
Where there is injury, pardon;
Where there is doubt, faith;
Where there is despair, hope;
Where there is darkness, light;
Where there is sadness, joy.

O divine Master, grant that we may not so much seek
To be consoled as to console,
To be understood as to understand,
To be loved as to love;
For it is in giving that we receive;
It is in pardoning that we are pardoned;
It is in dying to self that we are born to eternal life.
—Adapted from an anonymous French prayer[9]

. . . .

AFTERWORD

At every stage of our Christian development,
and in every sphere of Christian discipleship,
pride is our greatest enemy, and humility our greatest friend.
—**John Stott**[1]

For the LORD *takes pleasure in his people;*
he adorns the humble with salvation.
—**Psalm 149:4**

As I sent this manuscript into potential publishers, I experienced one of the most severe tests of my pastoral career, one that knocked me on my back mentally and physically, compounded by my own pride and misjudgments. The very day I was honored to receive the Foreword by David Wells, I sat in my doctor's office, as he diagnosed me with an acute stress disorder, stemming from my inability to handle certain aspects of the ministry. This is the sort of thing that happens to other pastors, not me. I had grown as David in Jerusalem, lazily peering over the parapets of the ministry I had built, and I was quite pleased with my prescriptions in this manuscript. All was going well, until this great test hit and I was confronted once again with my own arrogance and mortality. Then, I was as Nebuchadnezzar in the grass and all the Psalms became alive to me.

I reread certain portions of this manuscript and realized how I had forgotten the things I had written. I decided that I like humility better in theory than in real flesh and blood. If this is the price for

purporting to know much about humility, then next time I am writing
a book on seven steps to Christian prosperity. This trial had left me in
the dust, wondering if I really knew enough about humility to make
such specific applications to the church. I suppose readers can apply
whichever ones they see fit. In the meantime, I cling to the promise
that all who humble themselves before God will indeed be exalted in
Christ. Believers are those who are born again into a living hope, even
as they bear the cross, a hope that will not disappoint.

If pride is at the root of all sin, and humility through Christ its
only answer, then this modest book has only begun to make a small
dent in the subject. If the gospel's first application is that believers no
longer boast, it will take them a lifetime of learning what that means.
May this book be just one small beginning of the church rediscovering
its primary calling of growth in grace. I do not expect every reader to
agree with all the specific applications I suggest. The point is to spur
thinking in terms of humility—to recover a humble, Christian mind.
Thus, may many more studies issue forth. May whole churches drink
from humility's well together, reminding each other that they owe
everything to God's grace. For not until glory will believers imbibe of
a Christlike humility in all its fullness. In the meantime, may we have
the privilege of counting the ways God is working a greater humility
in each of us through Christ.

PRAYER

O God, of Thy great goodness,
make known to me, and take from my heart,
every kind and form and degree of pride,
whether it be from evil spirits,
or my own corrupt nature; and that Thou
would awaken in me the deepest depth and truth of that humility
which can make me capable
of Thy light and Holy Spirit.
—adapted from Andrew Murray[2]

One Hundred Verses on Humility

Below are one hundred verses and brief passages from the Scriptures that bear on the subject of Christian humility. These may be studied before, during, or after (or in lieu of) reading this book. It may also be helpful to read the surrounding biblical context to discover the full import of each verse or passage. If at first blush, a text does not appear to address humility, perhaps meditate on it, considering that all Scripture points believers to greater humility as they learn to become more God-centered. May God bless His people as they meditate upon His Word, working a greater Christ-wrought humility in them and those they influence by His grace.

Humility toward God
Humility & Conversion ~ John 6:44
Humility & Dependence ~ Mark 10:15
Humility & Discipleship ~ Mark 8:34–35
Humility & Eschatology ~ Hebrews 13:13–14
Humility & Experience ~ Jeremiah 17:9
Humility & Faith ~ Romans 12:3
Humility & Fasting ~ Ezra 8:21–23
Humility & Glory ~ Romans 11:36
Humility & Grace ~ Ephesians 2:8–9
Humility & Gratitude ~ Ephesians 5:20

Humility & Holiness ~ Luke 5:8
Humility & Honor ~ 1 Peter 5:6
Humility & Hope ~ Matthew 5:5
Humility & Immortality ~ Romans 2:7, 10
Humility & Judgment ~ Isaiah 5:15–16
Humility & the Kingdom ~ 1 Corinthians 4:10
Humility & Love ~ 1 Corinthians 13:1–4
Humility & Mystery ~ Romans 11:33–35
Humility & Obedience ~ Micah 6:8
Humility as Paradigm ~ Isaiah 57:15
Humility & Prayer ~ James 4:1–10
Humility & Repentance ~ Luke 18:9–14
Humility & Revival ~ 2 Chronicles 7:14
Humility & Sanctification ~ 1 Peter 1:2
Humility & Simplicity ~ Hebrews 13:9
Humility & Sovereignty ~ Psalm 115:1–3
Humility & Suffering ~ James 1:2–4
Humility & Testing ~ Deuteronomy 8:2–3
Humility & Truth ~ Ephesians 4:4–6
Humility & Warfare ~ Ephesians 6:10
Humility & Worship ~ Psalm 51:17

Humility Regarding Oneself
Humility & Abilities ~ Jeremiah 9:23–24
Humility & Character ~ Mark 2:17
Humility & Christ ~ Matthew 11:29
Humility & Confidence ~ 2 Corinthians 3:4–5
Humility & Education ~ Ecclesiastes 12:11–13
Humility & Energy ~ Isaiah 30:15
Humility & Excellence ~ Philippians 3:7
Humility & Failure ~ Proverbs 18:12
Humility & Goals ~ James 4:13–16
Humility & Health ~ Isaiah 38:9–17

Humility & Heritage ~ Romans 2:28–29
Humility & Intellect ~ Psalm 131
Humility & Knowledge ~ 1 Corinthians 8:1–3
Humility & Legacy ~ Ecclesiastes 2:18–19
Humility & Reputation ~ Matthew 11:19
Humility & Self-Esteem ~ 1 Timothy 1:15
Humility & Self-Estimation ~ Acts 20:19
Humility & Spiritual Gifts ~ Ephesians 4:7
Humility & Status ~ 1 Corinthians 1:26–29
Humility & Success ~ 1 Corinthians 4:7
Humility & Testimony ~ 1 Corinthians 15:10
Humility & Wealth ~ James 1:9–10
Humility & Wisdom ~ Proverbs 11:2; 26:12

Humility toward Others
Humility & Admission ~ Proverbs 6:3
Humility & Ambition ~ Luke 14:7–11
Humility & Apologetics ~ 1 Peter 3:15
Humility & Benevolence ~ Luke 14:12–14
Humility & Boldness ~ Romans 1:16–17
Humility & Comparisons ~ Galatians 6:4–5
Humility & Confession ~ James 5:16
Humility & Conformity ~ Proverbs 3:1–4
Humility & Conversation ~ James 1:19
Humility & Correction ~ Proverbs 13:10; 17:10
Humility & Credit ~ 1 Corinthians 3:7
Humility & Eloquence ~ 1 Corinthians 2:1–5
Humility & Evangelism ~ 1 Corinthians 9:19–23
Humility & Forgiveness ~ Colossians 3:12–13
Humility & Imitation ~ 1 Corinthians 11:1
Humility & Loyalty ~ 1 Peter 2:18
Humility & Needs ~ Ephesians 6:19
Humility & Offense ~ Proverbs 19:11

Humility & Piety ~ Matthew 6:1–8
Humility & Power ~ 2 Corinthians 13:4
Humility & Recognition ~ Proverbs 27:2
Humility & Rights ~ 1 Corinthians 6:7
Humility & Roles ~ Ephesians 5:21–6:9
Humility & Service ~ Philippians 2:3–8

Humility Together
Humility & Church Polity ~ Hebrews 13:17
Humility & Culture ~ Ephesians 2:11–22
Humility & Debate ~ Proverbs 18:2
Humility & Fellowship ~ 1 Corinthians 12:26
Humility & the Gospel ~ Psalm 149:4
Humility & Leadership ~ Mark 10:42–45
Humility & Ministry ~ 1 Corinthians 9:16–17
Humility & Mottos ~ Galatians 6:14
Humility & Numbers ~ Judges 7:2
Humility & Office ~ Matthew 23:5–7
Humility & Peace ~ Romans 14:10, 19
Humility & Purity ~ Philippians 3:15–16
Humility & Rank ~ Romans 12:16
Humility & Restoration ~ Galatians 6:1–3
Humility & Rules ~ Colossians 2:23
Humility & Seating ~ James 1:27–2:5
Humility & Separation ~ 1 John 2:16
Humility & Society ~ Titus 3:1–2
Humility & Support ~ Ecclesiastes 4:9–12
Humility & Titles ~ Matthew 23:8–12
Humility & Tributes ~ 1 Corinthians 3:21
Humility & Unity ~ Ephesians 4:1–3

INDEX
OF SCRIPTURE REFERENCES

....

ENDNOTES

Chapter 1

1. As quoted by John Calvin, *Institutes of the Christian Religion,* vol. 2, ed. John T. McNeil (Louisville, KY: Westminster Press, 1960), 268–69.

2. It may be beneficial to note that "the English word, humility, is derived from the Latin, *humilis,* meaning 'low' and, as often been observed, is related to *humus,* from the soil. . . . An eighteenth-century history of Connecticut . . . speaks of a bird called *humility,* so named because it 'seldom mounts high in the air.'" Jane Foucher, *Reclaiming Humility: Four Studies in the Monastic Tradition* (Collegeville, MN: Liturgical Press, 2015), 1. For an additional scholarly treatment of the subject, see Robert Payne, *Hubris: A Study of Pride* (New York: Harper Torchbooks, 1960).

3. Prince Bee, *The Slave Narrative Collection,* Oklahoma Genealogy & History, accessed at http://www.okgenwebnet/collection/narrative/bee_prince.net.

4. Rick Lints, *The Fabric of Theology* (Grand Rapids, MI: Eerdmans, 1993), 5.

5. I am aware of Murray's connections to the Keswick holiness movement and the errors associated with the Keswick theology, at least in its early manifestations. Nonetheless I find Murray's overall Reformed emphases in *Humility* a welcome corrective to much Christian thinking today. To paraphrase D. L. Moody, I prefer Murray's slightly flawed study on humility compared to failure to study it much at all.

6. Notable exceptions to this trend are excellent chapters on humility in two books: *The Exemplary Husband* by Stuart Scott, and *When Grace Comes Home* by Terry Johnson, both published by Christian Focus Publications (Fearn Tain, UK), 2000.

7. Mark Dever, *Nine Marks of a Healthy Church* (Wheaton, IL: Crossway, 2004), 249–66. It should be noted that many of the 199 listed goals

certainly require Christian humility to be achieved. But the point is that humility itself is not listed by any of the twenty authors.

8. In recent years, two books have come out on humility from traditions not far from my own, one by Wayne Mack, *Humility: The Forgotten Virtue* (Phillipsburg, NJ: P&R Publishing, 2005) and C. J. Mahaney, *Humility: True Greatness* (Colorado Springs, CO: Multnomah, 2005). Both are helpful additions, with Mack's especially insightful and well suited for group study. Other relatively recent additions that I have not reviewed include C. Peter Wagner, *Humility* (Ventura, CA: Regal, 2002); and William P. Farley, *Gospel-Powered Humility* (Phillipsburg, NJ: P&R Publishing, 2011).

9. Billy Sunday, *Face to Face with Satan: A Crystalization of the "Billy" Sunday Revival* (Knoxville, TN: Prudential, 1923), 8.

10. Moreover, I have observed that many church goals and vision statements very often violate the spirit of James 4:14–16 by setting bold objectives without obeying the clear command from James that we ought to say, "If the Lord wills, we will live and do this or that." James says that to set goals without reference to God's sovereign will is boasting in arrogance, and thus evil.

11. Neil Postman, *Amusing Ourselves to Death: Public Discourse in the Age of Entertainment* (London: Penguin Books, 2005).

12. As quoted in *The Baptist Magazine* 35, January 1843: 41.

13. T. S. Eliot, "Ash Wednesday" in *Selected Poems* (New York: Harcourt Brace Jovanovich, 1930), 93.

Chapter 2

1. *Confessions of St. Augustine*, trans, F. J. Sheed (New York: Sheed & Ward, 1943), 33.

2. Thomas Adams, *The Sermons of Thomas Adams: Shakespeare of Puritan Theologians* (Cambridge: Cambridge University Press, 1909), 154.

3. See C. S. Lewis, "Counting the Cost," *Mere Christianity* (New York: Simon & Schuster, 1996), 173–76.

4. As quoted in Henry Fairlie, *The Seven Deadly Sins Today* (Notre Dame, IN: University of Notre Dame Press, 1979), 43.

5. Benjamin Franklin, *Autobiography* (New York: Holt, Rinehart, & Winston, 1959), 78–81.

6. Ibid., 87.

7. Ibid., 88.

8. J. R. R. Tolkien, *The Fellowship of the Ring* (New York: Ballantine Books, 1965), 231.

9. Nathaniel Ward, *The Simple Cobbler of Agawam* (London: Stephen Bowsell, 1647), 94.

10. Lewis, *Mere Christianity*, 109.

11. C. S. Lewis, *The Screwtape Letters* (New York: MacMillan, 1961), 64.

12. John Piper, *Desiring God: Meditations of a Christian Hedonist* (Sisters, OR: Multnomah, 1996), 250.

13. Charles Spurgeon, "The Abiding of the Spirit the Glory of the Church," sermon 1918 in *The Complete Works of C. H. Spurgeon, Volume 32: Sermons 1877-1937*, 2; see https://www.spurgeongems.org/vols31-33/chs1918.pdf. We assume that in this quote, Spurgeon means that the devil uses only false humility because by his very nature he cannot abide true humility in a Christian, which is always more helpful in building God's kingdom than mere productivity. It may be that Spurgeon, as prolific a man as he was, had a small blind spot in this area, placing work ahead of humility in God's economy.

14. Lewis, *Mere Christianity*, 114.

15. John Trapp, *A Commentary Upon All the Books of the New Testament* (London: Nathaniel Ekins, 1656), 4–5.

16. Augustine, *Confessions*, 34.

Chapter 3

1. *Memoir and Remains of the Rev. Robert Murray M'Cheyne*, ed. Andrew Bonar (Edinburgh: Oliphant, Anderson, and Ferrier, 1883), 239.

2. D. A. Carson, *The Cross and Christian Ministry: Leadership Lessons from 1 Corinthians* (Grand Rapids, MI: Baker Books; 2004), 37–38.

3. Ibid., 26.

4. *Homilies of St. John Chrysostom* (Oxford: John Henry Parker, 1852), 423.

5. Arthur Bennett, *The Valley of Vision* (Edinburgh: Banner of Truth, 1975), 1.

Chapter 4

1. John Owen, *The Works of John Owen*, vol. 6, ed. William Goold (Edinburgh: Banner of Truth, 1965), 200.

2. John Calvin, *Institutes of the Christian Religion,* vol. 1, ed. John T. McNeill (Louisville, KY: Westminster Press, 1960), 242.

3. Richard Baxter, *The Reformed Pastor*, abridged by Daniel Wilson (Glasgow: William Whyte & Co., 1829), 86.

4. David Wells, *God in the Whirlwind* (Wheaton, IL: Crossway, 2014), 84.

5. Martin Luther, "The Freedom of a Christian," *Martin Luther: Selections from His Writings*, ed. John Dillenberger (New York: Doubleday, 1961), 58.

6. While this is not the place for it, I believe the application to humility can provide an important key to reconciling the alleged discrepancy between Paul and James when James famously says, "You see that a person is justified by works and not by faith alone" (James 2:24). But when one sees that the main thrust of James is a faith proven by wise humility (cf. James 1:5, 9, 19, 26; 2:1–13; 3:13–18; 4:1–10, 13–17; 5:1–6, 14–16), then the works of James 2—treating fellow sinners with the same grace we have received by faith alone—resolve the supposed conflict with Paul. For Paul says the same thing (cf. Ephesians 4:32; Colossians 3:13); giving the same warning that an ungracious, prideful "faith" is no real faith at all, cf. Romans 2:1ff; James 2:17 (and Jesus Himself in Matthew 6:14–15). But this humility, wisdom, and graciousness all stem from first resting in Christ alone, by faith alone. That is what saves believers; the works of humble graciousness follow as a result, cf. Ephesians 2:8–10. How can they not? In agreement, the church father Peter of Damascus comments, "At the Last Judgment the righteous will be recognized only by their humility and their considering themselves worthless, and not by good deeds, even if they have done them. This is the true attitude," (http://www.orthodox.net/gleanings/the_judgment.html).

7. "Ah, Holy Jesus," by Johann Heerman, *Devoti Musica Cordis*, 1630; trans. Robert S. Bridges, 1899.

8. Andrew Murray, *Humility* (Springdale, PA: Whitaker House, 1982), 64–65.

9. John Piper, *Desiring God, 10th anniversary edition* (Colorado Springs: Multnomah, 1996), 249.

10. Jonathan Edwards, "God Glorified in Man's Dependence," *The Works of Jonathan Edwards*, Vol. 2, ed. Edward Hickman (Carlisle, PA: Banner of Truth Trust, 1974), 2:6.

11. *Westminster Shorter Catechism*, Question 1.

Chapter 5

1. As quoted in Fairlie, *The Seven Deadly Sins Today*, 57–58.

2. Such thinking is not new, of course. As Augustine wrote, "The notion began to grow in me that the philosophers whom they call Academics were wiser than the rest, because they held that everything should be

treated as a matter of doubt and affirmed that no truth can be understood by men," in *Confessions of St. Augustine*, 96.

3. See for instance, David Wells, *No Place for Truth: Or Whatever Happened to Evangelical Theology?* (Grand Rapids, MI: Eerdmans, 1993), for a study of how postmodern relativism has infiltrated and watered down the concept of truth within American evangelicalism.

4. John Geoffrey Saxe, "The Blind Men and the Elephant" in William James Linton, *Poetry of America, selections from one hundred American poets from 1776 to 1876* (London: George Bell & Sons, 1878), 150–51.

5. G. K. Chesterton, *Orthodoxy* (New York: Doubleday, 1990), 129. (Original published 1908.)

6. David Wells, *The Courage to Be Protestant: Truth-lovers, Marketers, and Emergents in the Postmodern World* (Grand Rapids, MI: Eerdmans, 2008), 77–78.

7. Augustine, *Confessions*, 255, altered slightly.

8. Ralph Waldo Emerson, "Self-Reliance," in Warfel, *The American Mind* (New York: American Book Co., 1937), 1:559.

9. Blaise Pascal, *Pensées*, trans, W. F. Trotter (Grand Rapids, MO: Christian Classics Ethereal Library, 1660), 46.

10. "Thus there is a difference between having an *opinion* that God is holy and gracious and having a *sense* of the loveliness and beauty of that holiness and grace. There is a difference between having a rational judgment that honey is sweet, and having a sense of its sweetness." Edwards, "A Divine and Supernatural Light," *Works*, 2:14.

11. T. S. Eliot, "Preludes," *Selected Poems* (New York: Harcourt Brace Jovanovich, 1934), 24.

12. William Cowper, "The Task," in *The Complete Poetical Works of William Cowper*, ed. H.S. Milford (London: Oxford University Press, 1913), 221.

13. Consider this example from Augustine's journey to faith in his *Confessions*, 100: "So I came to Milan, to the bishop and devout servant of God, Ambrose. . . . All unknowing I was brought by God to him, that knowing I should be brought by him to God. That man of God received me as a father, and as a bishop welcomed my coming. I came to love him, not at first as a teacher of the truth, which I had utterly despaired of finding in Your church, but for his kindness towards me."

14. See also this often misquoted example from Augustine: "I come now to answer the man who says: 'What was God doing before He made Heaven and earth?' I do not give the jesting answer—said to have been

given by one who sought to evade the force of the question—'He was getting Hell ready for people who pry too deep.' To poke fun at a questioner is not to see the answer. My reply will be different. I would much rather say, 'I don't know,' than hold one up to ridicule who had asked a profound question and win applause for a worthless answer." *Confessions*, 269.

15. Corydon Ireland, "Seal of Approval," *Harvard Gazette*, May 14, 2015, accessed at: https://news.harvard.edu/gazette/story/2015/05/seal-of-approval/. The official cause for turning the third book over has not to my knowledge been definitively determined, but given the optimism in human reason and progress arising out of the Enlightenment, the idea of eliminating mystery is a reasonable conclusion.

16. *The Book of Church Order of the Presbyterian Church in America*, 6th ed. (Lawrenceville, GA: Office of the Stated Clerk of the PCA, 2015), 10–11.

17. Large segments of the so-called Emergent Church have believed that there are no correct answers—with disastrous consequences. See Wells, *The Courage to Be Protestant: Truth-lovers, Marketers, and Emergents in the Postmodern World*.

18. See Richard Hofstader, *Anti-Intellectualism in American Life* (New York: Knopf, 1963).

19. "In the days of the great evangelist, George Whitefield, the Countess of Huntington used to say that she was saved by an *m*: God's word declares, 'not many noble,' not 'not any noble.'" D. A. Carson, *The Cross and Christian Ministry*, 28.

Chapter 6

1. Dietrich Bonhoeffer, *The Cost of Discipleship*, 2nd ed. (New York: MacMillan, 1959), 7.

2. This passage is one reason children are seen as such valued members of Christ's church and why most denominations indicate this by some kind of ceremony, usually water baptism. This story is an example of Jesus welcoming those who had nothing to offer Him, thus indicating how the church is to be a community marked by humility, not utility.

3. Murray, *Humility*, 68.

4. Derek Thomas,"Not in Regal Robes of Grandeur," unpublished hymn, Jackson, MI, 2005. Used by permission.

5. As pointed out by Gordon Watt, *The Meaning of the Cross* (Rushden, UK: Stanley L. Hunt, 1922), 85–121. If possible, read each passage in its context to get the full meaning.

6. Frank Houghton, "Thou Who Was Rich Beyond All Splendor," in *The Trinity Hymnal*, rev. ed. (Atlanta: Great Commission Publications, 1990), 230. The hymn is based on 2 Corinthians 8:9.

7. St. Augustine, in *Nicene and Post Nicene Fathers*, vol. 7, ed. Philip Schaff, (Edinburgh: T&T Clark, 1888), Tractate XV, Section 6; accessed at the Christian Classics Ethereal Library: www.ccel.org/ccel/schaff/npnf107.iii.xxvi.html.

8. For instance, I cannot delve into the loving relationship between the Son and the Spirit. The Spirit "proceeds" from the Son, supporting His work. And yet, Christians confess that Jesus was "conceived by the power of the Holy Ghost," and was raised from the dead by the Spirit's power, thus showing the Son's submission to His "supporting cast" within the Trinity as well, if I can write that without too much error.

9. Murray, *Humility*, 22. All Scripture used by Murray is from the KJV.

10. From a list compiled by Jeffrey D. Hutchinson, adapted from Alfred J. Poirier, "The Cross and Criticism," *Journal of Biblical Counseling*, 17.3 (Spring 1999): 16–20.

11. William Bridge, *The Works of the Rev. William Bridge*, vol. 2 (London: Thomas Tegg, 1843), 186.

12. John Calvin, "I Greet Thee Who My Sure Redeemer Art," in *The Trinity Hymnal*, rev. ed. (Atlanta: Great Commission Publications, 1990), 168.

Chapter 7

1. Thomas Kelly, *A Testament of Devotion* (New York: Harper & Brothers, 1941), 62.

2. *The Andy Griffith Show*, as quoted in *IPC Messenger*, April 2015 (Savannah, GA: The Independent Presbyterian Church), 4.

3. C. S. Lewis, "The Inner Ring," in *The Weight of Glory and Other Addresses* (New York: MacMillan, 1965), 93–105. I think this essay should be required reading for all young adults.

4. John Pollock, *Wilberforce* (London: Constable and Company, 1977), 236.

5. As Pascal wrote, "Do small things as if they were great, because of the majesty of Christ, who does them in us and lives our life, and great things as if they were small and easy, because of his almighty power." Blaise Pascal, *Pensees* (London: Penguin, 2003 edition), 553.

6. C. S. Lewis in a letter to his friend Arthur, from Alan Jacobs, *The Narnian* (New York: Harper One, 2008), 133.

7. Michael C. Sharrett, "Constantly Clashing Powers: The Relentless Battle of Humility and Pride" (unpublished manuscript, 2016), 59. I have edited the list slightly.

8. Murray, *Humility*, 69.

9. Ebenezer Erskine, *The Whole Works of the Rev. Ebenezer Erskine*, vol. 1 (Philadelphia: Wm. S. & A. Young, 1836), 167.

10. Richard Sibbes, *The Bruised Reed*, rev. ed. (Edinburgh: Banner of Truth Trust, 1998), 95. Sibbes's work was first published in 1630.

11. Thomas Watson, *Select Discourses on Important and Interesting Subjects* (Glasgow: Blackie, Fullarton & Co., 1829), 129.

12. Isaac Watts, "When I Survey the Wondrous Cross," in *The Trinity Hymnal*, rev. ed. (Atlanta: Great Commission Publications, 1990), 252.

Chapter 8

1. John Flavel, *The Whole Works of Rev. John Flavel*, vol. 5 (London: J. Matthews, 1799), 112.

2. I will not much discuss the difference between the heavenly reward which awaits all believers (by virtue of faith in Christ alone) and the differentiated rewards based upon believers' works that are fruit of this saving faith (cf. Matthew 25; 1 Corinthians 3).

3. Such patience extended into the early church. As Christopher Dawson writes about Augustine as the Roman Empire was besieged, "To the materialist nothing could be more futile than the spectacle of Augustine busying himself with the reunion of the African Church and the refutation of the Pelagians, while civilization was falling about his ears. It would seem like the activity of an ant which works on while its nest is being destroyed. But St. Augustine saw things otherwise. To him the ruin of civilization and the destruction of the Empire were not very important things. He looked beyond the aimless and bloody chaos of history to the world of eternal realities," quoted in *Confessions*, vi. On a similar theme, see also C. S. Lewis's sermon, "Learning in War Time," in *The Weight of Glory*, Rev. Ed. (New York: MacMillan, 1980), 20.

4. An Excerpt from *Reliquiae Baxterianae*, ed. Francis John, Bishop of Chester (London: Longmans, Green & Co., 1910), 37–38; as quoted by Alan Simpson, *Puritanism in Old and New England* (Chicago: University of Chicago Press, 1955), 98.

5. "Trouble Don't Last," Unpublished song, personally witnessed and documented by the author at a worship service at Bulloch County Correctional Institute, Statesboro, GA, 2001. Sung on several occasions.

6. Samuel Rutherford, *Quaint Sermons of Samuel Rutherford Hitherto Unpublished* (London: Hodder & Stoughton, 1885), 86.

7. Annie Dillard, "An Expedition to the Pole," in *Teaching a Stone to Talk* (New York: Harper & Row, 1982), 31.

8. Paul Gerhardt, "Why Should Cross and Trial Grieve Me?" 1653; translated composite, based on John Kelly, 1867. I am partial to the full hymn, and the tune, *Warum Sollt' Ich Mich Denn Grämen*, by Johann Ebeling, 1666.

9. For a wonderful treatment of our heavenly hope, see Paul D. Wolfe, *Setting Our Sights on Heaven: Why It Is Hard and Why It's Worth It* (Carlisle, PA: Banner of Truth Trust, 2011).

10. Sibbes, *The Bruised Reed*, 3.

11. For an excellent exposition of this text, see J. I. Packer, *Weakness Is the Way: Life with Christ Our Strength* (Wheaton, IL: Crossway, 2013), to which this section is largely indebted.

12. John Updike, *Rabbit, Run* (New York: Fawcett Crest, 1960), 158–59.

13. Henry Smith, *The Sermons of Mr. Henry Smith Gathered into One Volume* (London: T. Nabb, 1657), 214–15.

Chapter 9

1. As paraphrased by Roland H. Bainton, *Here I Stand: A Life of Martin Luther* (New York: New American Library, 1950), 181.

2. Murray, *Humility*, 44.

3. Sibbes, *The Bruised Reed*, 23.

4. Ironically, this verse also shows how Christianity raised the status of women in the early church in contrast to the surrounding culture. If Euodia and Syntyche were merely on the fringe of the church, their conflict would not merit his attention.

5. Will Peters, *Leadership Lessons: Dwight Eisenhower* (e-book) (New Word City Inc., 2014), 1. This saying was not original with Marshall, but likely lifted from C. E. Montague, *Disenchantment* (New York: Bretano's, 1922), 260.

6. As Tim Keller remarks, "Another mark of the moral-performance narrative is a constant need to find fault, win arguments, and prove that all opponents are not just mistaken but dishonest sellouts. However, when the gospel is deeply grasped, our need to win arguments is removed, and our language becomes gracious. We don't have to ridicule our opponents, but instead we can engage them respectfully. . . . We find a lot to laugh at,

starting with our own weaknesses. They don't threaten us anymore because our ultimate worth is not based on our record or performance." Tim Keller, "The Advent of Humility," *Christianity Today*, 52, no. 12 (Dec. 22, 2008), www.christianitytoday.com/ct/2008/december/20.51.html.

7. Further meditation on James 1:19 can produce a good deal of fruit as believers prayerfully think through how to apply it to their relationships. Here are ten suggestions:

1. Be quick to hear about others but slow to speak about oneself (Proverbs 27:2).

2. Be quick to learn but slow to show your learning (1 Corinthians 8:1).

3. Be quick to hear questions but slow to answer them (Proverbs 15:28; 18:13).

4. Be quick to consider commitments but slow to make them (James 5:12).

5. Be quick to think well of others but slow to flatter them (Proverbs 28:23).

6. Be quick to receive advice but slow to give it (Proverbs 26:12; 29:20).

7. Be quick to hear criticism but slow to offer it (Proverbs 11:2; 19:11).

8. Be quick to hear an opponent but slow to argue back (Romans 12:17–21).

9. Be quick to witness with deeds but slow with words (1 Peter 3:1–2, 15; in light of Romans 10:14).

10. Be quick to listen to God's Word but slow to talk back (James 1:21).

8. John L. Girardeau, "The Diaconate," *The Southern Presbyterian Review*, 31.1 (January 1880), 120, pcahistory.org.

9. So the early church took care of the poor in their body, cf. Acts 2:42–47; 4:32–36; 6:1–7. As John Newton wrote, "One would almost think that Luke 14:12–14 was not considered part of God's word. . . . I do not think it is unlawful to entertain our friends; but if these words do not teach us that it is in some respects our duty to give a *preference* to the poor, I am at a loss to understand them," *The Works of John Newton*, vol. 1 (Carlisle, PA: Banner of Truth Trust, 1985), 136. For a balanced approach to mercy ministries, see Tim Keller, "The Gospel and the Poor," in *Themelios*, 33.3 (2008), 8–22.

10. Mary Ann Jeffreys, "Colorful Sayings of Colorful Luther," *Christian History*, 34 (Carol Stream, IL: Christianity Today, Inc., 1992), 27.

11. Note how Paul sandwiches the duties of civil, secular government between his admonitions to Christian love in Romans 12 and 13, perhaps in a chiastic structure as seen below. The church and the government live side by side with different ethics; one of love and mercy, the other of order and justice. In this manner is social order preserved so that the gospel can spread until Christ comes again to triumphantly consummate a true theocracy in the New Heavens and the New Earth.

A. 12:9 - Heading: "Love must be sincere. Hate what is evil; cling to what is good" (NIV).

B. 12:10–16 - Love fellow believers with spiritual zeal, fervor, joy, and patience.

C. 12:17–21 - Love our enemies, personally showing mercy not justice (since we are not of this world).

C.13:1–7 - Obey the civil government, which shows justice not mercy (since we are still in this world).

B.13:8–9 - Love all men, owning no one anything except love.

A.13:10 - Closing: "Love does no harm to a neighbor. Love is the fulfillment of the law."

12. For a thoughtful and important discourse on this subject, see John Winthrop's famous 1630 sermon, "A Model of Christian Charity," given aboard the *Arbella* just before these non-separatist Puritans disembarked to attempt to establish a just and merciful "Bible Commonwealth," that would be a "city on a hill," for England and the rest of the world to emulate. One does not have to agree with New England Puritan theology to appreciate the logic, sincerity, and biblical reasoning that went into Winthrop's attempt to lay out this vision for a just, Christian-led society that maintained strict social structures even as they preached God's grace.

13. Jonathan Edwards, *Charity and Its Fruits* (New York: Robert Carter and Brothers, 1852), 206.

14. Alphonsus de Liguori, *Uniformity with God's Will* (Charlotte, NC: St. Benedict Press, 2013), 18.

15. John Newton, "Indwelling Sin in the Believer," in *The Letters of John Newton*, April 1772, public domain.

Chapter 10

1. John Donne, *The Works of John Donne*, vol. 3 (London: John W. Parker, 1839), 288.

2. Dietrich Bonhoeffer, *Life Together* (New York: Harper & Row, 1954), 60.

3. Fairlie, *The Seven Deadly Sins Today*, 40 (emphasis original).

4. Augustine, *Confessions*, 159–61.

5. For an excellent treatment of applying humility to daily devotions, see Greg Johnson, *Freedom from Quiet Time Guilt: The Rare Beauty of Weakness Christianity* from: https://sites.google.com/site/dthatcher7/freedom-from-quiet-time-guilt. Publication date unknown.

6. Note that almost all the pieces of armor that Paul names in Ephesians 6 are direct quotations from Isaiah, describing the armor borne by the Messiah (Isaiah 11:5; 52:7; 59:17). Paul's point is that we "fight" by putting on Christ and His righteousness, not our own armor, which is why he concludes that text by an admonition to pray (6:18–20).

7. Donne, *Works*, 575.

8. As my own tradition's confession puts it: "The grace of faith, whereby the elect are enabled to believe to the saving of their souls, is the work of the Spirit of Christ in their hearts, and is ordinarily wrought by the ministry of the Word, by which also, and by the administration of the sacraments, and prayer, it is increased and strengthened" (Westminster Confession of Faith, 14.1).

9. Marilynne Robinson, *Gilead* (New York: Farrar, Straus & Giroux, 2004), 158.

10. John Fawcett, "Blest Be the Tie That Binds," *The Trinity Hymnal*, rev. ed. (Atlanta: Great Commission Publications, 1990), 359.

Chapter 11

1. Augustine, *Sermons on Selected Lessons of the New Testament*, vol. 1 (Oxford: John Henry Parker, 1844), 160. Quote altered slightly for ease of translation.

2. One small, symbolic way that our church tries to communicate this priority is how we list leaders in our bulletin. Missionaries are listed first, then deacons, then the ruling elders, and only after that, the pastors and campus minister at the bottom. We do not have a full-time custodian or music minister, but I am always impressed with churches that list these right alongside their pastors as those deserving equal honor as members of the body of Christ.

3. Edward Reynolds, *The Whole Works of the Right Rev. Edward Reynolds*, vol. 5 (London, S. & R. Bentley, 1826), 47.

4. William Still, *The Work of the Pastor* (Fearn Tain, UK: Christian Focus, 2010; first published in 1984), 58, given as lectures in the United Kingdom in 1964 and 1965.

5. Ibid., 47.

6. Ibid., 71.

7. Christopher Howse, "Sacred Mysteries: Renting the Best Seats in the House," *The Telegraph* (May 7, 2010), www.telegraph.co.uk/news/religion/7693232.

8. Edwards, *Charity and Its Fruits*, 205.

9. I acknowledge the argument for a continuing episcopal structure (rule by bishops) based on the examples of Timothy and Titus. At the same time, however, I must note that the Greek words for elders (*presbyters*) and bishops (*episcopos*) appear to be used of the same office in Acts 20:17, 28 and Titus 1:5, 7. In other words, to be an elder in the New Testament church was to be a bishop or overseer. I also note that Paul calls Timothy an "evangelist," a word used only three times in the New Testament, so its original meaning may be lost (Acts 21:8; Ephesians 4:11; 2 Timothy 4:5). Some have, therefore, speculated that it signifies a temporary, sub-apostolic office that has since passed away. Having said all that, I for one, would rather serve under a humble, godly bishop than within a prideful presbytery. Some things are more important than getting one's polity just right. As many have pointed out, proper polity relates to the well-being (*bene esse*), not the existence (*esse*) of the church. For this, and for a contemporary, accessible defense of Presbyterian polity, see Guy Prentiss Waters, *How Jesus Runs the Church* (Phillipsburg, NJ: P&R Publishing, 2011). Waters includes an annotated bibliography that lists many excellent older resources too numerous to elaborate here. The point is for believers to think through how their formal polities either reinforce or hinder humility.

10. J. C. Ryle, *The Gospel of Luke* (Wheaton, IL: Crossway, 1997), 131.

11. Most denominations, including my own, reserve the right of the congregation to vote on such matters as the selection of new pastors and officers, as well as major property decisions, since it is their tithes and offerings that pay for it. It is a simple matter of justice and recognizing that, ultimately, Christ entrusts His power to the whole body, not just the leaders (cf. *Book of Church Order*, 3.1).

12. Rafael Cardinal Merry del Val, "A Litany of Humility," as found in James Sodias, *Handbook of Prayers,* Student Ed. (Downers Grove, IL; Midwest Theological Forum, no date), 67–68. It appears that Merry del Val adapted his litany from an early nineteenth-century version.

Chapter 12

1. John Owen, *The Golden Book of John Owen*, ed. James Moffat (London: Hodder & Stoughton, 1904), 167.

2. Other texts that teach the beauty and importance of church unity are John 17:20–23; Acts 2:1–11; Romans 12:3–10; 1 Corinthians 3:1–11; 11:17–34; 12:1–26; Ephesians 2:11–22; 4:1–16.

3. As quoted in T. H. L. Parker, *Portrait of Calvin* (Minneapolis, MN: Desiring God, 2008), 124. PDF from: https://www.desiringgod.org/books/portrait-of-calvin.

4. For further thought on the inadequacy of these models to ensure true unity, see Francis Schaeffer's evaluation of "False Notions of Unity," in his famous essay, "The Mark of the Christian," in *The Great Evangelical Disaster* (Westchester, IL: Crossway, 1984), 166–68.

5. Because of some textual clues, most scholars are convinced that Ephesians was meant to be a "circular" letter, written to several churches, not just the church at Ephesus. This is important because Ephesians thus acts as a small, systematic theology rather than an "occasional" letter written to correct specific, local errors. Therefore it serves as a wonderfully succinct summary of the essentials of the gospel and the Christian life.

6. Augustine, *Confessions*, 88.

7. John M. Frame makes the astonishing assertion that "to (his) knowledge, no one has ever studied the question (of doctrinal tolerance in the church) in a truly systematic way." In *Evangelical Reunion: Denominations and the One Body of Christ* (Grand Rapids: Baker, 1991), 90.

8. Illustrated by the famous anecdote about Karl Barth, that took place on his US tour in 1962, either at the University of Chicago or Union Seminary in Richmond, Virginia (and possibly both). A student asked Barth if he could summarize his whole life's work in theology in a sentence. Barth replied, "Yes, I can. In the words of a song I learned at my mother's knee: 'Jesus loves me, this I know, for the Bible tells me so.'" See Roger Olson, *Patheos* (January 24, 2013); http://www.patheos.com/blogs/rogereolson/2013/01/did-karl-barth-really-say-jesus-loves-me-this-i-know/.

9. Much of the following is indebted to David Anderson Bowen, "John Calvin's Ecclesiological Adiaphorism: Distinguishing the 'Indifferent,' the 'Essential,' and the 'Important' in His Thought and Practice, 1547-1559," doctoral dissertation, Vanderbilt University, 1985 (Ann Arbor, MI, University Microfilms International, 1994).

10. So Augustine on the length of the creation days: "But there are those, not enemies of the book of Genesis but admirers, who say: 'The Spirit of God, which wrote these words by his servant Moses, did not mean by them what you say, but some other thing which we say.' Thus I answer them, O God of us all: do Thou judge between us," *Confessions*, 298. It is

also important to note that Augustine goes on to argue for his position and denies the possibility that two contradicting claims can both be true, cf. *Confessions*, 309, 315.

11. See Robert Lewis Dabney, "The System of Alexander Campbell: An Examination of Its Leading Points" in *Dabney's Discussions*, vol. 1 (Sprinkle Publications, 1992). This was first published in the *Southern Presbyterian Review*, July 1880.

12. Lewis, *Mere Christianity*, 11.

13. One might also ponder the parallel to the roles within the economic Trinity to redeem us: God the Son, who is the Word who brings Truth; and God the Spirit, who softens believers hearts and causes them to love Christ. As Christians need both persons to work upon them, in church unity believers need both head and heart, truth and love. See Edwards, "A Divine and Supernatural Light," *Works*, 2:12–17.

14. Voltaire, "Tolerance," *The Philosophical Dictionary*, trans. H. I. Woolf (New York: Knopf, 1924), https://history.hanover.edu/texts/voltaire/voltoler.html.

15. See *The Book of Church Order of the Presbyterian Church in America*, 6th ed. (Atlanta, GA: Office of the Stated Clerk, 2016).

16. Here are the five membership vows every communing member of the Presbyterian Church of America must take (*Book of Church Order*, 57-5):

1. Do you acknowledge yourselves to be sinners in the sight of God, justly deserving His displeasure, and without hope save in His sovereign mercy?

2. Do you believe in the Lord Jesus Christ as the Son of God, and Savior of sinners, and do you receive and rest upon Him alone for salvation as He is offered in the Gospel?

3. Do you now resolve and promise, in humble reliance upon the grace of the Holy Spirit, that you will endeavor to live as becomes the followers of Christ?

4. Do you promise to support the Church in its worship and work to the best of your ability?

5. Do you submit yourselves to the government and discipline of the Church, and promise to study its purity and peace?

17. Gene Edwards, *A Tale of Three Kings: A Study in Brokenness* (Wheaton, IL: Tyndale House, 1980), 15–16.

18. "A Prayer for Unity," *Prayer Book Parallels*, vol. 2, ed. Paul V. Marshall (New York: The Church Hymnal Corporation, 1990), 537.

Chapter 13

1. Reinhold Niebuhr, "Religion as a Source of Values," chapter 17 in David Van Tassel, *American Thought in the Twentieth Century* (Austin: University of Texas, 1967), 177.

2. As quoted in George Marsden, *Reforming Fundamentalism: Fuller Seminary and the New Evangelicalism* (Grand Rapids, MI: Eerdmans, 1987), preface.

3. H. L. Mencken, "Dr. Fundamentalis," *Baltimore Evening Sun* (January 18, 1937), sec. 2, 15.

4. J. Gresham Machen, *Christianity and Liberalism* (Grand Rapids, MI: Eerdmans, reprinted 1998; first published 1923), 179–80.

5. Sharrett, "Constantly Clashing Powers," 6.

6. Spurgeon, "The Planter of the Ear Must Hear," sermon 2118 in *The Complete Works of C. H. Spurgeon, Volume 35: Sermons 1877-1937*, (https://www.spurgeongems.org/vols34-36/chs2118.pdf), 1.

7. Some manuscripts add here (or after verse 12) verse 14 (NASB): "Woe to you, scribes and Pharisees, hypocrites! For you devour widows' houses and for a pretense you make long prayers; therefore you will receive the greater condemnation."

8. Charles Spurgeon, *The Soul-Winner* (New York: Fleming H. Revell, 1895), 47.

9. Annie Dillard, *Holy the Firm* (New York: Harper & Row, 1984), 59.

10. Robert Southey and Samuel Taylor Coleridge, "The Devil's Walk," in *The Poetical Works of Robert Southey* (Boston: Little Brown, 1860), 3:75–91.

11. For a classic study of this general question, see H. Richard Niebuhr's helpful *Christ and Culture* (New York: Harper & Row, 1951). Niebuhr outlines five different approaches various traditions have tended to take in regard to the gospel's relationship to the world at large. This chapter comes closest to the position Niebuhr describes in "Christ and Culture in Paradox" (chapter 6, 149–89).

12. For an excellent critique of this common approach, particularly among evangelicals, see James Davison Hunter, *To Change the World: The Irony, Tragedy, & Possibility of Christianity in the Late Modern World* (New York: Oxford University Press, 2010).

13. C. S. Lewis, *God in the Dock* (Grand Rapids, MI: Eerdmans, 1970), 189.

14. Will D. Campbell, *Brother to a Dragonfly* (New York: Continuum Books, 1980), 201.

15. Phan Thi Kim Phuc, "The Long Road to Forgiveness," June 30, 2008, on *All Things Considered*, from the This I Believe series, originally produced by Anne Penman for the Canadian Broadcasting Corp.

16. Clement of Rome, *The First Epistle of Clement to the Corinthians*, trans. J. B. Lightfoot (Philadelphia: Athena Data Publications, 1990), I Clem. 59:4, ccat.sas.upenn.edu/gopher/text/religion/churchwriters/ApostolicFathers/1Clement. `

Chapter 14

1. Erskine, *Works*, 167.

2. Still, *The Work of the Pastor*, 85, 98.

3. Many of the same principles of humility discussed below in regard to church planting should be applied when it comes to the support of overseas missions. The humble church is one that seeks to see the kingdom grow across the world, even at great personal expense and sacrifice. I think most churches should seek to give away at least a tithe of their own income to the cause of missions, if at all possible—and hopefully much more. Moreover, any objective observer notes that the gospel is exploding in many parts of the world, notably China and Africa, while losing its influence in the West. In fact, the American church is holding its own almost entirely as a result of these international Christians immigrating to the US, a fact that alone should keep believers humbly grateful to God for the worldwide expansion of the gospel. Thus, one other mark of a humble church is great support for overseas missions, while avoiding the pitfalls of boasting in their missions program.

4. Received in the mail by the author, 1999. Names withheld intentionally.

5. Still, *The Work of the Pastor*, 98.

6. Francis A. Schaeffer, *No Little People* (Wheaton, IL: Crossway, 2003; original 1974), 25–26.

7. J. R. R. Tolkien, *The Return of the King* (New York: Ballatine Books, 1965), 385.

8. J. C. Ryle, *The Gospel of Luke* (Wheaton, IL: Crossway, 1997; first published 1858), 196–97.

9. This prayer is commonly attributed to St. Francis of Assisi, though it was most likely written by an unknown French priest for the magazine *La Clochette* around 1912. See franciscan-archive.org/franciscana/peace.html.

Afterword

1. John Stott, "Pride, Humility, and God," in *Alive to God: Studies in Spirituality*, ed. J. I. Packer and Loren Wilkinson (Downers Grove, IL: InterVarsity Press, 1992), 119.

2. Murray, *Humility*, 105. Murray precedes this prayer with the suggested instructions: "Retire from the world and all conversation, only for one month. Neither write, nor read, nor debate anything with yourself. Stop all the former workings of your heart and mind. And with all the strength of your heart, stand all this month, as continually as you can, in the following form of prayer to God. Offer it frequently on your knees. But whether sitting, walking, or standing, be always inwardly longing and earnestly praying this one prayer to God."